HOW TO GET A GOOD JOB AFTER 50

Rupert French has 20 years' experience in career development with a special interest in developing effective job search strategies. He has developed and run successful training programs for mature-age job seekers, many of them long-term unemployed, and his job search strategies have been featured on national television.

HOW TO GET
A GOOD JOB
AFTER 50

A step-by-step guide
to job search success

RUPERT FRENCH
A JOB WINNERS® GUIDE

EXISLE
PUBLISHING

'At last, a practical, comprehensive and engagingly written job hunting guide targeted at the over 50s. Rupert French is an expert in Career Development who provides motivating and practical step-by-step support to help overcome the prejudices and barriers that often confront the older job seeker. I highly recommend this book to any job hunter wanting to improve their chances of getting a job that meets their needs, skills and interests.'

— *Dr Jim Bright, Professor of Career Education and Development, School of Education, Australian Catholic University; career development consultant; speaker and author*

'*How to Get a Good Job After 50* goes beyond the typical overview of what is needed in an effective work search. Rather than leaving people wondering how to actually do what they are told to do, Rupert French gives detailed advice, tools, examples, and resources that enable people to navigate the practical how-tos of key work-search practices such as using social media, résumés, cover letters, informational interviews, and job interviews.

— *Gray Poehnell, author of* Hope-Filled Engagement: New Possibilities in Life/Career Counselling and Guiding Circles.

'This is a compelling read for anyone in job search mode. Rupert effortlessly weaves together his sage counsel with tried-and-tested pragmatic strategies that deliver results.'

Dr Edwin Trevor-Roberts, PhD, career expert and CEO

'A former journalist turned highly experienced career practitioner, Rupert has created a wonderful read outlining all the steps we need to take to be an outstanding job applicant. Readers will find loads of practical advice including lots of sample résumés and an all-important chapter on using social media. Rupert has also provided lots of activities readers can do to help us connect with our unique selling points and maintain a positive outlook during the job search. Job hunting can be daunting but is far less so with the right support — and here it is.'

Kate Southam, career blogger, speaker and coach

'These days, individuals are increasingly expected to look after themselves, to be responsible for the decisions in their lives as they navigate the world of work, and to develop the "adaptive capacity and skills" required to be able to respond to industry restructure and new technology impacts, as well as find a niche that best suits their needs. Rupert's book responds to these issues as it explores the strategies to take that next step, equips the reader to review the key elements of their life, and provides the tools to equip them to adapt to the challenge of the knowledge economy. I endorse this book not only for the individual reader seeking personal guidance but also to those charged with the responsibility to assist, direct, counsel and place those who require assistance. Read and be enlightened.

— Andrew Rimington, National President, Career Development Association of Australia

First published 2015

Exisle Publishing Pty Ltd
'Moonrising', Narone Creek Road, Wollombi,
NSW 2325, Australia
P.O. Box 60–490, Titirangi, Auckland 0642, New Zealand
www.exislepublishing.com

A CiP record for this book is available from the National
Library of Australia.

ISBN 978-1-921966-64-4

Designed by Mark Thacker of Big Cat Design
Typeset in Sabon 11/17pt
Printed in Shenzhen, China, by Ink Asia

This book uses paper sourced under ISO 14001 guidelines
from well-managed forests and other controlled sources.

10 9 8 7 6 5 4 3 2 1

This book is dedicated to Anne whose presence, continuous support and encouragement, good advice and editorial sense has helped make this book possible.

Contents

Introduction

It's not news that people aged 50 and over often find it difficult to get a job. However, if they approach the job search the right way, they can and will get the sort of job that they are seeking and usually within a fairly short period of time. This book describes an approach to job seeking that has been proved successful over several years. It contains strategies that will help older job seekers get the sort of employment they are looking for.

Job seekers who carefully follow all the strategies described in the book will be a lot more competitive than other job seekers. As a result, they can almost guarantee getting a good job, no matter what disadvantages they face. This is because the book uses sound marketing practices — practices that effectively market them for the job that they want, a job that will bring them satisfaction and success.

Some job seekers may not feel disadvantaged at all, not even by the age factor, and so they may not need to use all the strategies described in this book. In this case, they should be selective and use the ones that they believe will be of most use. If they find as the job search progresses that they need to implement a few more of the strategies, they can do so. The important thing is to get that good job in as short a time as possible.

The book is organised in the order that job seekers would use it: identifying the right job, developing a résumé and written application, carrying out research and networking, attending interviews and transitioning into the new job. It starts with how job seekers can adopt the right approach — having the right approach from the beginning is an important key to winning a good job. Part of this approach involves focusing on a small range of jobs rather than applying for all that seem possible. This allows more time and energy for each application. It is the candidate who puts the most effort into the whole application process, and in so doing demonstrates the greatest motivation for the job, who is the most likely to be successful.

Chapter 2 contains a series of activities to help the job seeker identify the best career direction or their 'niche market'. This is important if they are not sure of which direction to take.

Chapters 3 and 4 take readers through writing their résumé, their 'brochure' to show how they would perform in the job. As they launch into their 'marketing campaign', they may not know exactly what prospective employers are looking for. The résumé they first produce from these chapters is a draft based on what they know up to this point. This is the résumé to use for networking and one that can be developed as they gain more information about the occupation they are seeking. Once they have carried out research and networking, and they have found a specific job to apply for, they can come back to these chapters to complete a tailored résumé.

Chapters 5 and 6 explain how they can describe skills in a convincing way without sounding boastful. Achievement statements are the basic ingredients in effective résumés and written applications and they are also an essential element of every answer to interview questions. The last part of Chapter 6 explains how to develop a Key Skills Spiel, a valuable tool for networking.

Chapter 7 is the final chapter on written applications. It explains how to write effective cover letters, expressions of interest, and statements addressing the selection criteria. As a result, readers will probably want to return to this chapter once they have identified a specific position, which may well be after networking and information interviews.

Chapter 8 discusses the advantages of establishing an online presence using social media to support the claims in a written application. Employers are increasingly likely to Google job applicants and, if they can find positive information on social media, it can only help the applicant's chances of being selected for a job interview.

Chapters 9, 10, 11 and 12 cover two sorts of interview: information (or network) interviews and job (or employment) interviews. The topics here include:

- **how to prepare for each interview**

- **how to set up an information interview**

- **how to build an effective network**

- **practical strategies to maintain positive self-esteem and self-confidence**

- **how to prepare questions to ask in a job interview**

- **how to prepare answers to possible interview questions.**

Chapter 13 looks at assessment centre activities (which may be encountered by people responding to a mass recruitment program), and explains how to focus on demonstrating essential skills such as teamwork and communication.

The final chapter discusses making a smooth transition into the new job; evaluating job offers, negotiating the right conditions, accepting and declining offers, letters of resignation and then succeeding in the new job.

Age is not the issue; it is the perception of being too old that creates the barrier and, too often, that perception is greater in the mind of the job seeker than it is in the mind of an employer. Be confident that you could do the job and do it well. Then, using the strategies described in this book, go out and persuade employers that you are the right person for the position. Be proactive, use your initiative, take risks and seize opportunities while all the time holding a clear vision of where you want to be — and you'll get there!

CHAPTER 1

The Right Approach

So, you are over 50 and you're looking for a job. Perhaps your job search isn't as easy as you would like it to be and you are beginning to think that no one wants you because you're too old.

Well, think again. You can, and almost certainly will, get a good job within a reasonably short period of time if you follow the strategies described in this book. By 'good job' I mean one that will give you job satisfaction — one that matches your interests, your values and personality; and one that is a job of your choosing. It may not be the same as your last job. That sort of job may no longer be available due to changes in technology or economic circumstances. But it will be a job that will give you fulfilment and, as a result, a feeling of success.

Many of my clients, older and younger, have used this methodology over the past ten years and in doing so have proved its effectiveness by winning the sort of job they were seeking. The strategies do require a bit of effort but the tasks are not complex and, importantly, they do get results.

The strategies are equally effective whatever sort of role you may be seeking. You may be aiming for promotion or the next job along in a career progression. Or perhaps you are considering a different career direction, a winding-down-towards-retirement type of job, or you may be striving to get back into the workforce after finding retirement a bit empty. Whatever your situation, you are likely to face hurdles in your job search. However high the hurdles may appear to you, this book will show you proven ways to overcome them.

One of the first steps to take towards job search success is to adopt the right attitude. This will make a huge difference to the likelihood of your success and is key to your job search. The right approach is based on two fundamental truths and four fundamental principles. Keep these in the front of your mind at all times.

The two fundamental truths are:

1. **Employers do value older applicants.**

2. **Employers are looking for three things in every applicant for every position:**

   I.   **The *skills* to do the job.**

   II. **The *motivation* to do the job well.**

   III. **The *ability* to fit well into their team.**

The four fundamental strategies you need to keep in mind are:

1. **Be positive and in control, the CEO of Yourself Pty Ltd.**

2. **Focus on just two, or a maximum of three, job leads at**

any one time and pursue each with as much determination as you can. (Sometimes you may need to follow three job leads at the same time, but this should be the absolute maximum. Concentrating on just two job leads is more effective in that it allows you to put 50 per cent more effort into each one.)

3. **Find jobs before they are advertised through structured networking.**

4. **Treat the job search as a full-time job.**

If you accept and adopt these truths and strategies, you will be seen by employers as someone worth employing and you will have the greatest likelihood of being offered the sort of work that you want.

The first fundamental truth: Employers do value older applicants

Let's start by tackling the first fundamental truth. Certainly, there are some employers who prefer younger candidates but there is convincing evidence that there are more employers who value older workers and welcome applicants in their 50s and 60s than those who don't. These are employers who know the benefits of hiring mature applicants, people who have handled difficult situations in the past and who will confidently do so again, people who are not continually looking for 'greener pastures'.

There are a number of major benefits for hiring older workers. Those who have been in the workforce for a long time tend to be more responsible. Susan Adams writing in *Forbes* magazine in 2012 quoted a survey of 1500 hiring managers conducted by the multi-national human resources consulting firm Adecco. She states that given the choice of hiring a millennial (someone born between 1980 and 2000; also known as Generation Y) or someone aged 50 or over, 60 per cent of those surveyed said that they would hire the mature worker.[1] Ninety-one per cent of those surveyed associated mature workers (defined as age 50 or above) as being reliable and 75 per cent said that they had a good work ethic.

According to a report in the London *Daily Mail*, a survey conducted by British building society Nationwide reported that younger staff like having older workers around because they act as mentors.[2] The report also showed that older workers had fewer sick days than younger ones and were better at arriving at work on time; in fact, the report stated that most people over the age of 55 'usually arrived early to work'. The survey reported that almost half of Nationwide's workers in this age group had not taken a sick day in the past year.

Mature workers tend to be more loyal to their employer and they are not as likely as younger people to be continually looking for better jobs in other companies. According to the US Bureau of Labor Statistics in 2012, 'more than half of all workers age 55 and over were employed for at least 10 years with their current employer in January 2012, compared with 13 percent of workers age 30 to 34'.[3] The average tenure of workers aged 25–34 was reported to be just 3.2 years. The situation is similar in Australia and New Zealand. A Queensland government publication *Valuing Older Workers* states: '... people over the age of 45 tend to stay with an employer 2.4 times as long as do younger employees. Older people can bring reliability and loyalty to an organisation'.[4] Employers value employees who will stay with the organisation, be good members of the team, and be a steadying influence.

In high-tech fields such as software development, mature-age employees are sought after. The technology entrepreneur and academic Vivek Wadhwa writes:

> *What the tech industry often forgets is that with age comes wisdom. Older workers are usually better at following direction, mentoring, and leading. They tend to be more pragmatic and loyal, and to know the importance of being team players. And ego and arrogance usually fade with age.*
>
> *During my tech days, I hired several programmers who were over 50. They were the steadiest performers and stayed with me through the most difficult times.*[5]

Employers value people who have experienced crises and who can act calmly in difficult situations. One employer, seeking a night-time console operator for an all-night petrol station, told me that he would not employ anyone under the age of 45. 'I want someone who can face an armed hold-up one night and still turn up to work the next day.' Hopefully you won't have to face an armed hold-up but crises often arise at work and generally older people handle them more effectively than those who are younger and less experienced.

Some people have a perception that older applicants are 'set in their ways', resistant to change and not innovative. Perhaps this is true for some but that doesn't mean it is the case for all older applicants. In fact, research by Thomas Ng at the University of Hong Kong, and Daniel Feldman at the University of Georgia showed conclusively that older workers are no less innovative or creative than younger workers and that, under the right circumstances, they can be much more so.[6]

If you feel that you might be seen as a bit resistant to change, deliberately bring some change into your life. Take some training in a new area in which you would like to develop your knowledge or ability. If your computer skills are not as good as you think they should be, make this a priority. Not only will this sort of training develop and demonstrate your ability to accept change, it will also boost your confidence.

It is important to be aware that age gives you a competitive advantage and to be confident that the qualities you have developed over the years will be valued by the sort of employers you want to work for.

The second fundamental truth: Employers are looking for three things

As we said earlier, there are three things that every employer is looking for in every applicant for every position. The first, and least important quality (not unimportant, but least important), is the *skills* to do the job. The second and far more important quality is the *motivation* to do the job well. The third, and equally far more important quality, is the *ability to fit well* into their team. Skills, Motivation and Team; it is worth remembering the acronym SMT. I refer to it regularly throughout this book because it is so important to your job search success.

While skills may be essential for the job, it is likely that your motivation for the position will be given more weight in the selection process as will the employer's perception of how well you would fit into their team. Therefore, don't apply for jobs that have little appeal for you; focus on those that you would really enjoy and organisations that you would love to be part of and your motivation is likely to get you across the line.

Sir Richard Branson, the founder of the Virgin Group, was quoted as saying:

> **The first thing to look for when searching for a great employee is somebody with a personality that fits with your company culture. Most skills can be learned, but it is difficult to train people on their personality.**[7]

Your attitude or personality, like your suitability for the position, will be judged more by the *motivation* you will bring to the job and by your *ability to fit well* into the team rather than by your *skills*. This truth is emphasised by the number of recent books and other publications stressing the importance of 'fit' with the company culture.

Now let's discuss the four fundamental strategies.

STRATEGY 1:
Be positive and in control

Employers want positive people with a can-do attitude. Positive people are those who have confidence in themselves, people who show that they feel in control of their lives and careers. Employers value this sort of person because they see them as able to help the organisation achieve its objectives. Therefore, it is important to use the strategies suggested in this book to ensure that you develop or retain a positive self-image and a can-do attitude no matter how difficult the job search may be.

The sort of applicants that employers don't want are those who appear to be desperate to get a job, sometimes described as a 'job beggar'. Even if you are currently finding it difficult to get a job, do not show yourself to be a job beggar. You are someone with knowledge, skills and experience that would benefit an employer and you need to have confidence in yourself to be able to convince the employer that you have these qualities. A beggar is passive, someone who lacks confidence in his own ability and is pleading for a job, someone who can't do it on his own, someone who needs help; in other words, a loser. Employers want winners. Show yourself to be a winner by being positive. Take deliberate steps to be in full control of your life and career.

If you are out of work, don't think of yourself as unemployed; think of yourself as self-employed, the CEO of Yourself Pty Ltd, a micro-business currently without 'clients'. As CEO of Yourself Pty Ltd, you will be proactive and totally in control of your job search campaign unlike the many job seekers who are more passive, looking through the job ads and applying for any that they think they could do. This latter approach does not work as you may already have found out.

On the other hand, if you see yourself as the CEO of Yourself Pty Ltd, you would want your chief sales rep to be out there, Monday to Friday, 9.00 a.m. to 5.00 p.m., looking for those 'clients' or prospective employers. Small businesses don't wait for someone to advertise that they need their services; they proactively market themselves, they send out their sales reps to talk to prospective clients. As CEO, that's what you want your chief sales rep to be doing. And you are the chief sales rep. To be successful, you need to be out there talking to people who are working in the field you want to work in, asking them about their needs or difficulties, considering ways you could alleviate their problems and saying, 'I might be able to help you there.' Be seen as someone who wants to help, not as someone who wants a job.

You might even be considering starting a small business or buying a franchise. If so, you will need to use the strategies described in this book to convince financial institutions and franchisors that you have the skills, the tenacity and the commitment to customer service to make a good business out of it before they will lend you the capital or sell you the franchise. This is because, in effect, you would in some respects be working for the financial institution or the franchisor and they will be assessing you in the same way that an employer would.

If you believe that your last job was taken away from you unjustly, and perhaps it was, try to forget it. It is water under the bridge; it has happened and there is nothing that you can do to retrieve the situation. Don't look back at what life was like before it happened or you may fail to see the windows of opportunity opening up in front of you.

When small businesses lose a client, they go out and find new clients and that's just what you have to do.

Do a bit of 'business planning': look ahead to what you want your life to be like in six months' time and keep this vision in the front of your mind. Make a timeline: 'I will start the new job on ...' and set a date somewhere between six weeks and three months ahead. And then work out the best way to get there. By focusing on the solution rather than on the problem, you will spend your energy and efforts in a positive way. You will see the future you want more clearly every day; you will gain confidence in your ability to achieve it; you will start once again to feel good about yourself; and you will come across to employers as someone they would like to have on their team.

If you take a positive, proactive approach to the job search, working at it as if it were a full-time job, and using the strategies described in this book, you will have the greatest likelihood of finding and winning a good new job in the shortest possible time.

STRATEGY 2:
Focus on just two job leads at any one time

Successful small businesses identify a market niche and then concentrate on developing a relationship with that niche. They don't try to sell to everyone because they know that this doesn't work. There is a business cliché that says: 'If you're marketing to everyone, you are marketing to no one.'

This is equally true in job search. If you send out résumés to every possible advertised position, you will almost certainly end up with nothing.

As CEO of Yourself Pty Ltd, you need to decide on the sort of work that you would most like to do, the product or service your micro-business wants to deliver, and the niche employers who could best use your skill set. Then you will be able to concentrate all your time and energy on finding and winning a job in that one occupation and to find out what employers are looking for in applicants for that sort of position. And once you have identified the occupation or field you want to work in, focus on researching and applying for just two positions.

Spending all your time trawling through the online job ads and sending applications for all the positions that seem possible is not effective. This doesn't mean that you shouldn't look at these online 'job boards'; it means that you should very carefully select only those jobs that would really suit you well and then put a lot of effort into each application. Looking at job ads can easily become 'busy work' that keeps you from the real task of finding jobs in the hidden job market, of getting out there and undertaking that structured networking.

If you are receiving unemployment benefits and you are required to apply for a certain number of jobs each fortnight, it is important that you do so. However, it is very unlikely that you will have the necessary time and energy to put the sort of effort into each of those applications that would get you an interview. Therefore, do the necessary applications as quickly as possible and spend most of your time on the two leads which you are really keen on and which are, therefore, the ones most likely to bring you success.

It is not necessarily the best-qualified applicant who wins the job. It is the person who puts in the best job application performance. By job application performance I mean performance across the whole job application process: written application, interview, research and networking. A candidate who has researched the organisation thoroughly, made herself known and liked by people in the organisation, who has tailored her résumé and her answers to interview questions to the detailed knowledge that she has of the position, is the candidate who will be seen as the one most likely to 'hit the ground running' and therefore offered the job. In spite of what many books try to tell you, job search is not a numbers game. It's the quality of the application that will bring you the results you want, not the quantity of applications you send out.

Job search is a bit like competing in the Olympic Games, only there are usually no silver or bronze medals. You've got to go for gold! And athletes who win gold can only do so if they have put in the hours, weeks and years of hard training beforehand. And they can only do this if they put all their efforts into training for the one sport. Likewise, you are most likely to 'win gold' if you put all your efforts into applying for a maximum of two jobs at a time.

Effective job search requires hard work but most of it is not difficult work. And, overall, it requires less total effort to complete two applications really well and get a result than to send off 50 not-so-good applications and still have no job.

This is why people who say 'I just want a job, any job' usually end up with nothing, but those who say that they want to market left-handed widgets just seem to go out and get a job marketing left-handed widgets. Job seekers in the second group focus on that specific job and put all their time and energy into getting it. By concentrating on just two job leads at any one time, you can put in a much better application performance than can those who want 'any job' or who send off applications to as many jobs as they can find. (In the early stage of your job search, the term 'job lead' may refer to an occupation that you have selected. As your job search progresses, the meaning of 'job lead' will change as you get closer to your ideal job. Towards the end, your job leads will be the specific positions that you are chasing.)

STRATEGY 3:
Find the job through structured networking

Suppose you were applying for an advertised position and you find a position vacant for marketing widgets. You have experience in marketing and you have good product knowledge of widgets but because it's a good job with an attractive salary and good prospects, you believe that it will attract a lot of applicants. You fear rightly or wrongly that the employer may tend to shortlist younger applicants and you wonder how you could win the job without having to face all the competition.

The answer is by finding and winning that job before the competition knows that it exists — before the job is even advertised.

This is not an improbable idea. In fact, research in many countries, including Australia and New Zealand, has shown that knowing and being known by the right people in the right places is the best way to get a job. It's not what you know, it's not even who you know; it's who knows you. According to the University of Sydney careers website, 80 per cent of jobs are found through word of mouth.[8] Many variables impact the ways people find jobs and I sometimes wonder at the accuracy of such statistics, but research all over the Western world suggests that more jobs are gained through knowing the right people than through applying for an advertised position. Avoid competition with other applicants by carrying out a structured networking process (see Chapter 9) and finding jobs before they are advertised. I know that this puts many people outside their comfort zone. For this reason, I have taken care to break the process down into manageable tasks and to coach readers through the process. The strategies described will ensure that you do know the right people and that the right people know you and that you know about job opportunities before they are advertised. Although you'll have to put tremendous effort into each application, you only have to apply for a small number of jobs before achieving success.

Networking is not easy for everyone. It requires courage to get outside your comfort zone, to set up meetings or network interviews with people you don't know. And job search can be a lonely, dispiriting process especially after knockbacks or rejections — and they are, unfortunately, more likely than not to be part of your job search. To help you overcome any reluctance to getting out there and networking and to keep you feeling positive and upbeat in the job search, ask a small group of people you know and trust to be your support group. Perhaps you might like to make them honorary directors of your micro-business, Yourself Pty Ltd. Keep them up-to-date with your progress and share with them the challenges you face. You will find it much easier to confront these challenges knowing that you have people behind you, encouraging you and coaching you through the whole job search process. This, and other strategies for maintaining self-confidence and self-esteem in the job search are fully discussed in Chapter 10. However, this is a strategy that you might want to consider right at the beginning of your campaign, which is why I mention it now.

STRATEGY 4:
Treat your job search as a full-time job

Effective job search is a full-time job. At least, it is as full-time as you can afford to make it. Some job seekers have part-time or casual positions that put food on the table while they look for the right job. Don't give up the work you have but do use the rest of the working week as fully and effectively as possible in proactive job search. As CEO of Yourself Pty Ltd, what time on Monday morning do you want your sales rep to be out there looking for clients?

If one candidate puts an application together in a couple of hours and another candidate spends two days on research and talking to people in the organisation, finding out exactly what the job is about and then specifically addressing the needs of the position in the application, which of those two candidates is the more likely to be short-listed? The more time and effort that you put into each application, the better the application is likely to be and therefore more likely to get you called to an interview.

And if you are going to set up, prepare for and carry out a series of information interviews as part of a structured networking program, you are going to need to make your job search as full time as possible.

Putting these fundamental strategies into action

The best way to start your job search is to select your target occupation — the sort of job you want to apply for and the career path that you want to follow. Carefully planning your career path means that you channel all your efforts into seeking employment in a fairly narrow field of employment. Chapter 2 will help you do this.

WRAP-UP

- Older workers are valued by employers. While you may face some age discrimination, you can and will get a good job if you undertake the job search the right way. Consider yourself to be self-employed, the CEO of Yourself Pty Ltd, and approach the job search as if you were a sales rep and employer organisations were prospective clients. Identify your 'market niche' (your chosen occupation) and focus on that rather than going for every opening that seems possible.

- In fact, concentrate on just two or three job leads at any one time. This will give you the time to put in the effort necessary to create a better application than other candidates. Be enthusiastic in your approach and aim to get all those you meet to like you, remembering that employers consider motivation and the ability to fit well into their team more important than skills. To minimise competition, find positions before they are advertised through structured networking.

CHAPTER 2

Choosing the right career path

The aim of this chapter is to help you choose the career direction that motivates you most, the one that will give you the greatest satisfaction, the greatest enjoyment. To put it another way, this chapter is to help you identify your niche market, the sort of employer you want to work for and the sort of service that you would like to provide. If you put all your efforts into getting a job that is exactly right for you, there is every likelihood that you will get it — and sooner rather than later.

Perhaps you already know exactly what sort of job it is that you are seeking. You may want to continue in the field that you have been working in. If this is the case, skip this chapter and go straight to Chapter 3 to write a résumé tailored for the sort of position or occupation you are seeking.

If you are unsure of the career direction which would suit you best in your current circumstances, the activities in this chapter can help. However, you need to understand that undertaking these activities does not equate to using the services of a qualified careers adviser. If, after completing these activities, you are still not confident that you have identified the right path, see a professional careers adviser (see 'Careers advisers' in the Useful resources section on page 327).

STEP 1:
Possible career options

These activities may be all that you need to find that right career direction. The first step is to list the various career options you believe would best suit you. List them all and leave room for more options that may come to you later. It could well be that you want to pursue your current career direction, to continue in marketing or administration for example, but with another organisation and perhaps in a more senior position. As an example, Tom Matlock (see his specimen résumé in the Appendix, page 283) has considerable experience in occupational health and safety in the RAAF and is now seeking an OH&S position in civilian life. If your situation is similar to this, list the possible positions that you might go for.

On the other hand, you may want to change direction completely. Richard Parker (see specimen résumés, page 271) is beginning to feel that he is getting too old to be on the road all the time selling roofing materials and is seeking work in a hardware store. Katharina Hochstein (see specimen résumés, page 313) is leaving teaching for an administrative position at Museum Victoria because an ankle injury is making it difficult to sustain the significant standing and walking required for teaching.

List all the occupations that you would like to consider below:

While it is worthwhile having a long list of options to consider, you now need to shortlist those so that you focus only on positions that are going to give you the most satisfaction — and, therefore, the greatest likelihood of job success.

The self-employment option: small business start-up and franchises

Many people making a career transition in their 50s or 60s start their own business or buy a franchise and this might be an option for you to consider. When, in Chapter 1, I refer to considering yourself to be self-employed, I am describing an approach that many of my clients have used to find salaried employment, not to start up a small business or buy a franchise. However, self-employment of this sort could be an option, but it's not an easy one.

Starting your own business requires a lot of work and often a significant amount of capital, and it may not start giving you an income for some time. If you want to follow this path, tread carefully and undertake very thorough research. If you are thinking of a franchise, talk to other franchisees to find out exactly what the up-front costs are and what might be the likely returns before signing up.

You are also likely to have to go through a process similar to applying for a job when establishing your business. Unless you already have sufficient capital, you will, in effect, be working for those who have put up the finance and they will want to be just as convinced of your credentials as would any employer. If you are considering a franchise, the franchisor has a huge investment in the name of the business and will want to ensure that any new franchisees will uphold that name.

If you think that self-employment, starting or buying a small business or taking on a franchise are options that you would like to consider, add them to your list of occupations.

STEP 2:
Job satisfiers

The next step is to start shortlisting the occupations that you have listed. First, let's look at the factors that you need for maximum job satisfaction.[1]

To maximise the likelihood of your winning a job, you need to show your motivation for the position. That motivation will be significantly greater if you can be confident that the position will offer you the conditions you need for job satisfaction.

The list below describes many of the conditions that bring job satisfaction. It does not claim to be exhaustive but as you go through the conditions, you may think of others that you want — add them to the blank list at the end of this activity.

ACTIVITY

Work that allows or encourages you to:

Social

1. Meet and interact with a lot of different people.

2. Establish and maintain supportive personal relationships with a close group of colleagues.

3. Work with people whom you respect, people who are stimulating, efficient, collaborative and resourceful.

4. Work in an environment free from interpersonal conflicts.

5. Work alone or with a small group of people whom you know and trust.

Creativity

6. Be part of a creative team, working together to develop innovative products, processes or services.

7. Establish your own systems rather than insisting that you follow established protocols.

8. Use a creative approach to problem-solving.

Stability and organisation

9. Follow clearly set down procedures.

10. Undertake clearly expressed assignments with well-defined boundaries and expectations.

11. Work in an organisation that is well organised, so that you can be confident that everything will happen according to plan.

Leadership and autonomy

12. Organise material, processes and people to make efficient use of time and resources.

13. Take responsibility for handling crises and solving problems in your own way.

14. Let members of your team grow and reach their full potential.

Freedom

15. Work independently, to make decisions and take responsibility for them.

16. Concentrate on one project or task at a time.

17. Personalise your workplace so that it shows your individuality.

Practical, hands-on

18. Roll up your sleeves and get involved directly in the action.

19. See the practical results of your labours.

20. Undertake technical work that relies on your ability to understand technical issues and to work to accurate specifications.

Benefit to others

21. Undertake work that produces practical benefits for people, the community or the environment.

Rewarded and acknowledged

22. Work to precise and exacting standards where your skill is respected and acknowledged.

23. Work with affirmative colleagues.

24. Be confident that your performance is evaluated by fair standards and to established criteria.

Variety, fast-pace and spontaneity

25. Take risks to find the best solution.

Quiet workplace

26. Concentrate on developing ideas and theories rather than tangible product.

27. Work in a quiet workplace where you are not likely to be continually interrupted.

On-going learning and development

28. Undertake work that is intellectually stimulating, challenging and continually developing your skills.

29. Continually learning new things, developing new skills and undertaking relevant training.

The next step is to list the conditions that are most important to you. List as many or as few as you wish. You are encouraged to re-word the conditions so that they can more accurately reflect what you need for job satisfaction.

Remember to add others that you may have thought of but were not included in the list.

<table>
<tr><td></td></tr>
<tr><td></td></tr>
</table>

STEP 3:
Values

Your values are an important factor when choosing your career path. You can have a job that matches your interests perfectly but if it clashes with your values, you are likely to suffer stress and therefore be less productive and less successful and certainly a lot less happy. Once again, this list is not exhaustive; there may be other values that you hold dear that are not mentioned. Include them in the spaces provided at the end of the list in the activity below.

ACTIVITY

Your task is to select just THREE values from this list, ones that are really important to you, and rank them in order of importance. To do this, first rate each value according to its importance to you: 5 being 'very important' to 0 being 'unimportant'. Put the score in the Rating column. Second, using the Ranking column, rank the three most important to you in order of their importance, where the most important is ranked 1. You may have two or three rated equal first but you must restrict yourself to the THREE values that really are important to you. Use a highlighter to identify your top three values.

Value	Rating	Ranking
Autonomy Working unsupervised; being able to make decisions.		
Challenges Having the opportunity to solve challenging problems.		
Change and variety Having a job that requires you to perform a range of different tasks.		
Health Knowing that your work is helping to keep you fit and healthy.		
Helping others Being able to help others when they need help; customers, co-workers or the community.		
Integrity/moral fulfilment Knowing that your work is morally right and is not harming other people.		
Location Work that allows you to live where you want.		
Security Knowing that you are unlikely to lose your job as long as you do it properly.		

Status/Being well paid Having enough money to maintain the lifestyle that you would like. Being respected by your workmates and by the community for the work that you do.		
Teamwork; being a valued member of a team Having good workmates. Working on a productive and successful team.		
Using your skills Feeling pleased or proud of your work. Doing work that you know you are good at.		
Work and life balance Having a good balance between work and personal/family life.		

STEP 4:
Other factors

This activity is for you to list other factors that might impact your decision as to the best career path to follow. These factors could include further education or training, a sporting commitment such as membership of a bowls team, or the need to live close to an elderly or infirm friend or relative. Some factors have already been listed which may or may not be relevant to you. Delete any factors that are not relevant to your situation. Space has been left for you to add other factors that you believe are relevant to making the right decision.

ACTIVITY

List factors in the left-hand column, and in the right give them a weighting indicating their importance. Take the factor 'The need to relocate': if it is extremely important that you relocate, mark it +5; if it is unimportant, mark it -5. If it's not really important either way but you would probably prefer not to, you could mark it -1.

Factor	Weighting
The need to relocate	
Need to live near another person (e.g. elderly relative)	
Long commute required	
Requirement for frequent travel away from home	
Long hours/weekend work expected	
Requirement to undertake further education or training	
Effect on further education/training already being undertaken	
The working environment/the people you would be working with	
Corporate culture	
Pay and conditions	
Effect on social/family/personal life	
Potential to help you achieve your personal and career goals	

STEP 5:
Setting personal goals

Setting goals is fundamental to success. People from all walks of life use goal setting to help them to achieve. Goal setting helps you organise each day by focusing on the things that are most important to your ultimate success and your overall satisfaction with life.

Personal goals are an important part of selecting the right career path. People go to work primarily to achieve their personal goals and it is therefore essential that their career planning is in line with these goals.

One way to start setting your personal goals is to create a vision of what you want your life to be like at the end of a specified period. This period might be ten years, or it might be when you want to retire. For which year do you want to create your vision? _____

With that in mind, you can then start working out how best to achieve your goals in the activity below.

ACTIVITY

Write down what you want to have achieved by that date under the following headings:

Annual income of _____

Savings/superannuation of _____

Paid off the mortgage/reduced it to _____

Physical shape: for example, reduce my weight to ___ kg; play three sets of tennis each week _____

_____

_____

Personal development/learning/educational: for example, learn a language; study Asian cookery _____

_____

_____

_____

_____

Recreational: for example, take up woodwork or quilting; go on 'grey nomad' trips_____

_____

_____

_____

_____

_____

Social: for example, join the local film society or a service club _____

_____

_____

_____

_____

_____

Are there any other things that you would like to be part of your life at the end of this period? _____

_____

_____

_____

_____

STEP 6:
Career Planning Matrix

The Career Planning Matrix, shown overleaf, is designed to help you shortlist the career options that you identified at the beginning of this chapter. Write these options down in the left-hand column of the matrix.

In the next column, 'Satisfiers', decide how well you believe each of your career options would match with the satisfiers that you have identified. If it is a good match, put an A in the relevant space; if the match is reasonable, mark it B; if it's a case of 'yes, I think so', perhaps you should mark it C; and if the match is decidedly doubtful, then definitely mark it D.

Then do the same for 'Values', 'Other factors' and 'Personal goals' and you will find that you have a simple but rather mechanical way to shortlist your options. However, if you use your intuition in the process, this can be a very useful way to make your career decisions.

CAREER PLANNING MATRIX

Career options	How does it match with			
Occupations that interest you (from page 23)	Satisfiers (p 25)	Values (p 30)	Other factors (p 32)	Personal goals (p 33)

Continue	Comments	Rank
Yes/No		

STEP 7:
The pros and cons

The Career Planning Matrix helped you to determine which career options would be most likely to bring you job satisfaction and success. However, the career planning process that you have undertaken in this program is not as thorough as if you had been through a program with a qualified careers adviser. You may now have three or more career options that interest you and you may need help to rank them in order of priority. For this reason, it may be worthwhile to undertake the following activity to confirm whether or not you have identified the right career path for you.

ACTIVITY

This activity is designed to help you rank your career options by having a closer look at the advantages and disadvantages of each of them. Think about all the factors that make each option good for you — and all the factors that detract from it. List the factors in the Pros and Cons columns in the tables below. Think of such things as:

- the tasks and responsibilities of the job
- the working environment; the people you will be working with
- pay and conditions, the hours you would be working
- the commute; parking
- effect on social/family/personal life
- further study/training required
- its potential to help you achieve your long-term goals
- associated costs (e.g. clothing, dry cleaning).

In the Impact column, indicate how seriously you believe each factor would impact your quality of life by using a number where 5 means very seriously and 0 signifies hardly at all. Then add up the figures in both columns, subtract the Cons total from the Pros and you will get a score for each option. Be aware that this, once again, is a mechanical process, so engage your intuition to help you choose a career option that really suits you.

Option 1_____

Pros	Impact	Cons	Impact
Total pros		Total cons	

Total score: pros minus cons _____

Option 2_____

Pros	Impact	Cons	Impact
Total pros		Total cons	

Total score: pros minus cons _____

Option 3_____

Pros	Impact	Cons	Impact
Total pros		Total cons	

Total score: pros minus cons _____

Option 4_____

Pros	Impact	Cons	Impact
Total pros		Total cons	

Total score: pros minus cons _____

Option 5_____

Pros	Impact	Cons	Impact
Total pros		Total cons	

Total score: pros minus cons _____

Should the activity result in you having two or more options with more or less the same totals, you might want to consider modular work, following one option on certain days of the week and another option on other days. However, if you want to follow just one option, you are still going to have to decide which you prefer.

STEP 8:
Preferred career options

The purpose of this activity is to help you confirm in your own mind your choice of occupation or career direction. As you write down the reasons behind your decision, your choice becomes clearer in your mind and you become more committed to achieving it.

However, it is still necessary to leave the door open for other options or to have a fall-back position. Your first choice may not turn out to be as good as you hoped it would be, or it might not be feasible for some reason. Another reason for having more than one option is the possibility that you might want to share your time between two or more occupations.

If you are seeking a single occupation, focus all your efforts on your preferred option until it becomes evident that you need to move to your second choice. If, on the other hand, you would like to spend some time in one sort of work and some time in another, you should concentrate equally on the two options. Consider yourself to be self-employed and work on the products or services that you would like to provide.

ACTIVITY

My preferred career option is: _____

_____

The reasons behind my choice are:

_____

_____

_____

This is the occupation I will tailor my résumé for.

My second choice is: _____

_____

The reasons behind my choice are: _____

_____

_____

_____

Other options that interest me are:

_____

_____

_____

_____

Sometimes you may find that there is little likelihood of winning a position in your preferred option. This is why it is important to have contingency plans. However, concentrate on the preferred option until you are convinced that such a position is unobtainable.

The first step is to start drafting a résumé specifically for your chosen occupation. That is what the next chapter is all about.

WRAP-UP

- Being successful in the job search, like being successful in running a small business, means identifying your 'market niche'. For a job seeker, your 'market niche' means your chosen occupation and the sort of organisation you want to work for. This sort of career plan allows you to focus on the areas where you are most likely to be successful and where you will gain the most satisfaction and, therefore, the greatest likelihood of success.

- Your chances of a successful job search without this clear picture of your career future in mind are severely limited. Make sure of your future career direction before leaving this chapter — list the various career options you believe will suit you, outline the conditions that will bring job satisfaction, and rate whether the job will clash with your values or personal goals. And, if you have doubts at a later stage, come back to the chapter to revise your plan.

CHAPTER 3

Your résumé

An essential part of a written application is your résumé or curriculum vitae (CV). The terms 'résumé' and 'curriculum vitae' (or CV) refer to the same sort of document. In Australia, New Zealand and North America, the French word *résumé* (which means 'in brief') is more commonly used. In the UK and, ironically, in France the Latin term *curriculum vitae* (meaning 'course of life') or CV is more frequent. But basically the terms are synonymous. I will use the term 'résumé' throughout because the literal meaning of the word more accurately reflects the sort of document that is required — a brief description of why you are right for the position.

An effective résumé is a brochure that sells an applicant for a specific job. It needs to grab the employer's interest within the first few lines and then hold that interest through to the end. It can only achieve this if every line helps the employer envisage how the applicant would perform in the role.

That principle is worth repeating: *an effective résumé is one that grabs the employer's interest with the first few lines and retains that interest all the way through, showing how well the applicant would do the job.*

A tall order, but by no means impossible. This chapter and the next explain how to do it.

A different résumé for each application

To enlarge on the statement 'an effective résumé is a brochure that sells an applicant for a specific job', each résumé must be tailored to one specific job. A so-called generic résumé is junk mail and usually gets the round-bin treatment.

Yes, a different résumé for each job means more work for you in the short term but, in the long run, it will actually mean less work. If you tailor a résumé to each specific position you apply for, you will almost certainly get a good job a lot sooner than you otherwise would. And the sooner you get the job, the fewer résumés you will need to send out. As I said in Chapter 1, 'job search is not a numbers game. It's the quality of the application that will bring you the results you want, not the quantity of applications you send out'. Five really well-written résumés are more likely to get you a good job than 50 more generic résumés.

Please believe and adopt this maxim from the start. It is much more likely to get you the results you want than is the more generally accepted view of sending off applications to every possible opening in the hope that you might score one of them.

Put yourself in the shoes of the employer; you want to employ someone and you advertise a position. There are lots of applications, many of which are more or less generic. However, there are a few which carefully address the requirements of the position. Which résumés are more likely to interest you?

However, in order to start your job search, it is a good idea to develop a draft résumé. You can adapt this as you find out further information about a specific job.

Developing your draft résumé

A draft résumé is not tailored to any specific position. It forms the basis of the résumés you will use when you start applying for jobs. When you identify a specific position, you will need to undertake more detailed research in order to tailor your résumé exactly to that particular job. Chapter 9 explains how to do this research in some detail.

To help you start, go to an online job board and find an ad for a position in the field you are interested in (see 'Career websites' under Useful resources on page 327). It does not matter where the advertised position is located because you are not applying for it. Use the ad or position description to identify and list the qualifications, skills, experience and personal qualities that employers are looking for.

Once you have a reasonable understanding of the qualifications, skills, experience and personal qualities needed for the sort of position you are seeking, you are ready to start drafting the résumé. Select the résumé that you most like the look of from the specimen résumés in the Appendix. It doesn't matter what sort of job the specimen résumé is targeting, nor what the section headings are. What matters is what the résumé looks like because that's what you want your résumé to look like too. Then go to the Job Winners™ website at www.jobwinnersguides.com and under the heading Specimen Résumés and Applications, download the MS Word version of the résumé you have chosen to use as a template. Save it as a new document on your hard drive.

The masthead

'Masthead' is a newspaper term; it refers to the bit at the top of the first page that gives the name of the paper, the date and possibly contact details. The masthead of your résumé is the bit at the top of page 1 that gives your name and contact details.

Highlight the name at the top of the résumé and type your own name in its place. Use the name you want to be known by. Don Bradley didn't write Donald James Bradley. The name he uses at work is Don Bradley, so that's what he wrote in the masthead of his résumé.

Don Bradley

Bridlington, SA 5678
08 3462 1792 (h)   08 3460 8879 (w)   0434 220 187 (m)
bradleyd@wellington.sa.gov.au
au.linkedin.com/don_bradley

Next replace the contact details with your own. It is essential that an employer can contact you easily. They will normally try by telephone or email and, once you start applying for positions, you need to monitor phone calls, messages and emails regularly.

There has been some discussion among professional careers advisers recently on whether or not to put in your full residential address. The argument against is that (1) employers are unlikely to contact you by letter, and (2) you don't know who else will see those details at the top of your résumé. However, many employers do want to know whether you live locally. With those considerations in mind, you may just want to write the town or suburb you live in as Don Bradley has done. However, your phone number is essential and your email address is highly desirable.

You will note that some of the specimen résumés, including Don's (see specimen résumés in the Appendix), also give details of how to look up the applicant on LinkedIn or other social media platforms. This can be a big plus, especially for mature-age job seekers because it shows that they are computer literate. Not only does this dispel the fear that some employers have regarding the computer literacy of older applicants, a LinkedIn profile provides supporting evidence for the claims made in the résumé. There is more about this topic in Chapter 8.

The body of the résumé

Don't delete all the text in the specimen résumé. Once you have changed the details in the masthead, leave the rest of the text in the résumé so that (1) it retains its formatting ready for your text, and (2) continues to look like the sort of document you want your résumé to look like.

The body of your résumé is likely to contain seven or more sections. The most frequently used sections are:

1. **Career Objective or Career Summary**

2. **Skills and Achievements (functional résumés — see page 52)**

3. **Employment History**

4. **Education and Training**

5. **Personal Details**

6. **Referees**

7. **Key Personal Attributes.**

Other sections may include:

- **Professional Memberships or Affiliations**
- **Publications and/or Presentations**
- **Foreign Language Skills**
- **Community and/or Sporting Involvement.**

Your next step is to decide on the headings you want for each section of your résumé. At this stage you do not need to put any text under the headings. The headings may be taken from the lists on the next few pages or could just as well be composed by you if you believe that this would serve your purposes better. In this case, just use the lists to give you ideas. Once you have decided on the heading you want to use for a particular section, insert the wording that you have chosen onto the template résumé. Remember, none of the headings is set in concrete; any one of them can be changed whenever you find a better way of wording it.

The various sections are set out in the order that will usually hold the employer's interest. The aim is to give employers the information that they want in the order that they want it. That means putting the sections that are of greater relevance to the position first and then moving on to those sections which, while important, are of lesser interest to the employer. Change the order around if you believe that a section that I have put later would actually interest the employer more than one I have put earlier. The aim is to hold the employer's interest and that means giving the most important, the most relevant, information first.

SECTION HEADING:

Career Objective/Career Summary

Generally speaking, start with either a Career Objective or a Career Summary section. A Career Summary section is usually the better choice if the skills that you used in your current or most recent employment are similar to those required for the position you are applying for. A Career Objective section is more effective when you are seeking employment that is different to your current or recent employment history. In a Career Objective section, you show that you have the skills and qualities that the employer needs without stating where they were developed. You will be providing evidence that you have the necessary skills in the Skills and Achievements section, which frequently follows a Career Objective section, or in a statement addressing the selection criteria, which is a separate document and explained in Chapter 7.

Be aware that the purpose of a Career Objective section is not to state what benefits you want to get out of the job but to demonstrate the benefits that you want to bring to the organisation.

Suggested headings for the Career Objective or Career Summary section include:

Career Objective

> Career Goal
> Goal
> Objective
> Employment Goal
> Employment Objective
> Position Sought

Career Summary
    Summary
    Career Outline
    Career Synopsis
    Profile
    Career Profile

Some careers advisers, mostly in the United States, are starting to say that a Career Objective should not be included. This, I believe, is because in the US, Career Objectives have often been used to state what the job seeker wants for him- or herself rather than what the job seeker wants to do for the employer. The key to an effective Career Objective is to show the employer that you have both the skills and the motivation to fill the position and perform well in it. That sort of Career Objective will always be well received because it tells the employer what the employer wants to hear.

SECTION HEADING:

Skills and Achievements

If you selected to write a Career Objective rather than a Career Summary, you may well now want to support the claims made in it with a Skills and Achievements section. This section becomes a miniature statement addressing the selection criteria and demonstrates why you are right for the position you are applying for even though it is significantly different to your current or recent employment (Chapter 7 covers in more detail statements addressing the selection criteria set by the employer for the position). Some suggested headings for this section are:

Skills and Achievements

Summary of Skills and Achievements

Relevant Skills and Achievements

Key Skills and Achievements

Summary of Capabilities

Record of Achievements

Breadth of Experience

Professional Achievement Record

When you include a Skills and Achievements section, your résumé could be described as a functional résumé. (Strictly speaking, if the résumé also includes an Employment History section, it should be called a hybrid. However, résumés without an employment history are rare, especially for older job seekers. Therefore, in this book, a functional résumé is one with a Skills and Achievements section and a chronological résumé is one without.)

You may well want to choose a functional résumé when:

■ **The job that you're applying for is distinctly different to your current or recent employment; or**

■ **You want to emphasise skills gained in roles other than current or recent employment; or**

■ **You want to demonstrate skills gained from voluntary work or community involvement; and**

■ **You are not addressing selection criteria in a separate statement or cover letter.**

If you do not include a Skills and Achievements section, your résumé is known as a chronological one. Generally speaking, a chronological résumé is the better format when:

- The job you are applying for is similar to your current or recent employment; or

- You want to emphasise skills developed and demonstrated in your current or recent employment; or

- You will be addressing the selection criteria in a separate document or, more briefly, in a cover letter (see Chapter 7).

SECTION HEADING:
Employment History

Next is the Employment History section. As with the rest of the résumé, your objective is to grab and hold the employer's interest. Therefore, you should not go back more than about ten years unless a position you held further back demonstrated skills that are very relevant to the position you are applying for. Some suggested headings are:

Career History

Career Record

Career Path Record

Professional Experience

Employment History

Employment Record

Some job seekers may find it useful to include voluntary positions if these have helped to develop the skills and experience needed for the chosen occupation. This will be discussed in detail later in the chapter (see page 64).

SECTION HEADING:

Education and Training

Educational qualifications and training is usually the next section and can be especially important for older job seekers. Employers want to be reassured that you are not 'set in your ways', not resistant to change, and that you are keen to keep learning new skills. If, as you write this section, you realise that you have not updated your skills for a while, it might be worthwhile finding and enrolling into a relevant training program.

If your education and professional development include one or two major qualifications and a number of short courses, you may decide to break the section into two smaller ones: the first section could list major study programs, university or trade qualifications, and the second might contain the relevant professional development courses that you have attended. See which format works better in your particular situation. Suggested headings for this section are:

Education and Training

Training and Education

Relevant Education and Training

If you decide to separate the major courses from recent training, you might want to consider the following headings for the major courses:

Qualifications

Formal Qualifications

Trade Qualifications

University Qualifications

Graduate (or Postgraduate) Qualifications

And for more recent or more relevant training programs:

Professional Development

Recent Courses

Relevant Training

Recent Seminars

Recent Training Programs

Recent Training Undertaken

Skill Up-Dating Programs

Short Courses

SECTION HEADING:
Professional Memberships and Publications
If you belong to a professional association such as the Australian Human Resources Institute, the Master Builders Association, the Chartered Institute of Management Accountants or the City and Guilds of London Institute, a body that is relevant for the position that you want to apply for, you may want to include a section under one of these headings:

Professional Associations

Professional Memberships

If you have any relevant publications or have made presentations that you believe could help you win the job, they could be listed under a heading such as:

Publications and Presentations

Relevant Publications

Recent Presentations

SECTION HEADING:

Community or Sporting Involvement

Another section that you may find useful is one in which you describe your community or sporting involvement. Involvement in the community or in sport is highly regarded by employers and its inclusion in your résumé is well worth considering. This is discussed more fully later in the chapter when the text of the section is covered. However, you may find it better to express these activities under the Skills and Achievements section earlier in the résumé. Suggested headings for the section on community and/or sporting involvement are:

Community Involvement

Involvement in Community Organisations

Membership of Community Groups

Involvement in Local Government

Involvement in Service Clubs

Sporting Involvement

Church Activities

Involvement in Sport

Sporting Achievements

SECTION HEADING:

Personal Details

The next section is usually Personal Details. The employer has by now had the chance to recognise your match for the job prerequisites. Now is the time to help him envisage you in the position with a few personal details. I encourage you to include your date of birth in this section even though you are over 50. It's not something that employers should ask but it is something that they will probably — perhaps unconsciously — take into consideration. However, hopefully your résumé will already have shown them that you are not set in your ways, that you do embrace and perhaps even stimulate change with innovative and lateral thinking and that you have the energy to make things happen and be productive. Most employers would, therefore, be willing to give you a go and invite you to attend an interview. If, on the other hand, you fail to disclose your date of birth or age and appear at the interview looking older than they had imagined, they may think that you are too old (more about this later in the chapter). Possible headings for this section are:

Personal Information

Personal Details

Personal Data

More Information about Me

Biographical Details

SECTION HEADING:

Referees

The next section is the Referees section. Some résumé specialists suggest putting 'referees available on request'; others recommend leaving this section out altogether. However, the section is valid as long as you have your referees' permission to give their names and contact details to your prospective employer. You will, as a matter of course, send a copy of your application to your referees so that they will know what to expect if they are contacted by the employer. Suggested headings for this section are:

People Who Know Me Well

People Who Can Vouch For Me

People Who Can Vouch For My Work

or, very simply,

Referees

SECTION HEADING:

Key Personal Attributes

The last section is a reiteration of the reasons why you are right for the job. As Richard Lathrop says in his book *Who's Hiring Who?*, the résumé is getting a bit dry and boring at this stage of facts and figures, so he suggests that you light up the employer's face with 'the sky-rocket in the tail', a reiteration of the key personal qualities that you will bring to the job.[1] Strategic repetition is sound marketing practice and your résumé is a marketing document. Some possible headings for this section are:

Key Personal Qualities

Key Personal Strengths

Key Personal Attributes

Special Strengths

Personal Qualities

This completes the skeleton of your résumé. Now it's time to start putting flesh on the bones.

Writing the text

I have found it best to start with the sections that are easier to write. In this way, you will have two-thirds of the résumé completed before you get to the more challenging bits.

Employment History

The first of the 'easy bits' is your Employment History. This is a list of the positions that you have held over the past ten years or so. Because employers want to read the most relevant and most important information first, put your current or most recent position at the top of the list. Then proceed in reverse chronological order to the one that you held ten years ago. If there are any positions that are relevant to the position that you are applying for but which you held more than ten years ago, it could well be worthwhile including those as well.

What you did, the position that you filled, is more important than the organisation that you did it for or when you did it. Therefore, write the position in bold in the first line. Immediately underneath it, write the organisation you worked for and, at the end of the line, the dates that you held the position. Sarah Vaughan is applying for the position of Health Promotion Coordinator, a position requiring teaching and training skills. This is how she wrote her first entry:

Teacher, science and maths

Seymour College, Seymour, Vic, 2005–2014

When you have completed your list, check to see if there are any that would have absolutely no relevance to the position you are applying for and that would not interest the employer in the least. If so, you might consider taking them out. But, you may say, it leaves a gap in my employment history. And if you were in that position for some time, it probably would. There are two possible solutions: (1) change the heading by adding the word 'relevant' (Relevant Employment History or Relevant Career Record), or (2) decide to include that position after all.

In some of your positions, you may have achieved some outcomes that you are really proud of, achievements that make you stand out from the crowd. If this is the case, under the relevant position, put in an achievement statement. Achievement statements and how to write them is fully covered in chapters 5 and 6 but to give you an idea of the effect this can have, let's look at some of the entries in Sarah's Career Record:

Teacher, science and maths

Seymour College, Seymour, Vic, 2005–2014

- Taught human biology to senior classes, 2010–2014.
- Got students engaged and motivated resulting in high end-of-year marks.

Pharmaceutical sales representative

Omicron Pharmaceuticals (Aust) Pty Ltd, Townsville, QLD, 2002–2005

- My territory included Ingham, Charters Towers and Mackay. Established a strong working rapport with pharmacies throughout the territory and was meeting sales targets within three months. In my final year, I exceeded my original sales target by 85%, almost doubling total sales.

- Quickly learnt the benefits/characteristics of the pharmaceuticals that I was marketing and able to be an effective sales rep within two weeks.

Teacher, science, maths and computer studies

Nightcliff High School, Darwin, 1996–2002

Sarah included 'Taught human biology ...' because that is relevant to the health education position she is applying for. What she didn't do is to describe the position by giving a list of the tasks and responsibilities she had as a teacher because such a list is usually not relevant and, therefore, boring.

David Campbell, applying for the CEO position in a youth service organisation, described his positions and achievements very fully and in a way that would interest a prospective employer:

Professional Experience

Residential Care Worker/Supervisor and Group Manager
Widdicombe Downs Residential Care, Sudbury, since 2007 (Supervisor since 2009, Group Manager since 2011)

Widdicombe Downs has three houses in the Sudbury area,

providing accommodation for up to ten young people, aged between 13 and 17. These young people have challenging and complex needs. They have often suffered great distress and significant harm growing up with violence, neglect, abuse, trauma and poverty.

Widdicombe Downs is a not-for-profit, non-government organisation overseen by a Community Board of Management.

- Through involving staff and volunteers, and where appropriate the young people themselves, in the day-to-day management of the homes, we have built a close-knit team and a harmonious environment in all three houses.

Joint Owner/Manager
Sudbury General Store, 1998–2010

This is the only grocery business within 15 km of Sudbury and the main source of groceries for local residents.

- When a major supermarket chain planned to open a store in Bright, we developed strategies with our permanent and casual staff to retain our local customer base through enhanced customer service.

- Established a service of free home delivery to make it easier for rural customers to get their groceries.

Compliance Manager
Cornwallis Bank, Wodonga, 1995–1998

Other positions in banking back to 1978

- Identified emerging and changing regulations that could affect the business and informed internal stakeholders, providing them with sound and practical advice on corporate risk and compliance issues.

Achievement statements can be particularly effective if they were achieved in recent positions, as Sarah's were. David also has concentrated on achievements from his last two positions, achievements which demonstrate the skills he would need in the position he is applying for.

Don Bradley, applying for the position of Technical Services Manager for a rural municipal council, went back 30 years in his Career Record because he wanted to show that he not only had 20 years' experience in local government but that he also had more than ten years' experience in the private sector:

Assistant Manager, Engineering Services
Wellington Shire Council, 2008–present

- Initiated self-directed work teams. This approach has improved productivity by up to 20%, particularly in outlying areas of the shire.
- Designed and implemented, with the approval of the Manager, waste transfer and recycling system and infrastructure. This undertaking won the Premier's Environmental Projects Award in 2010.

Design Engineer
Wellington Shire Council, 2003–2008

Site Supervisor
Wellington Shire Council, 1996–2003

Site Engineer
Bolton Constructions, Curriedale, NSW, 1991–1996

Assistant Contract Engineer
Cambridge, Danderfield & Associates, Consulting Engineers
Pembroke, NSW, 1985–1991

Sometimes it is useful to include voluntary work in this section. Jenny Barnes had been a stay-at-home mum for more than 30 years when she decided to apply for a part-time position with Kidsafe. She saw that her role as an active committee member of a soccer club was relevant to the position and so this is how she presented her Career History:

Career History
Teacher
Calderwell East Primary School, 1983–1989

- Taught grades 3, 4 and 5.
- Planned and implemented the 'Adopt a Grandparent' program, 1986.

Committee member, currently Secretary/Treasurer (voluntary)
Waterloo Soccer Club, 1998–present

- Part of the sub-committee that planned the Girls' Soccer promotion, 2003. This resulted in the formation of the first two girls' soccer teams in the club.
- Lobbied Belltrees Council to change the layout of Waterloo Park to allow the creation of an extra soccer pitch for junior players.
- Organised the itinerary, travel arrangements, accommodation and matches for the Under-19 team's tour of southern NSW, September 2005.

Notice how she has strengthened the section by the use of achievement statements. An employer working for the Australian organisation Kidsafe, who read this fictitious application, said that he would definitely want to interview Jenny despite the fact that she had been out of the paid workforce for more than 30 years. He said, 'The best applications are those which concentrate on providing evidence of competence without going overboard. The key priority is to ensure that the reader will want to read the full application and not skim because of waffling and inconsequential information.'

The best way to judge the right length to make this section is to think like the employer. 'How much information would I want if I were assessing these applications?' If you think the information would help, put it in; if you think that the employer might think it irrelevant, leave it out.

Education and Training

The next 'easy bit' is the Education and Training section. As with the Employment History section, your qualifications should be listed in order of greatest interest to the employer. This, however, may not necessarily be reverse chronological order.

In this section, it is the qualification (the subject studied) that is the most important. The organisation that delivered the training and the dates are of secondary relevance and so, as with the Employment History section, they are expressed on the second line.

Narendra Chaudhry, applying for an electrical engineering position, listed his Education and Training like this:

Tertiary Electrical Engineering Qualifications

Bachelor of Engineering (Electrical)
Maharashtra Sayajirao University of Baroda, India, 1985

- 65% (Credit) average
- This degree is recognised by IPENZ

Member, Institution of Professional Engineers New Zealand (IPENZ)

Postgraduate Diploma in Management (Information Technology)
Nirma Institute of Management, India, 2001

PMI Certificate
PMINZ, Christchurch, 2013

Currently completing **Graduate Certificate in Business Administration**
via Distance Learning through Massey University

Rather than reverse chronological order, Narendra's study record is listed with the earliest first and the most recent last. This is because his electrical engineering degree is essential for the position that he is applying for; the other qualifications are highly desirable but not mandatory.

Notice, too, how he has used bullet-pointed achievement statements to highlight important aspects of his degree.

Some courses, such as those for a university degree, take years to complete. Other training programs may be completed within a day. You might decide that you would like to separate major courses from the shorter training seminars or workshops in two distinct sections under different headings. University or Tertiary Qualifications (tertiary includes TAFE) could be one heading and Professional Development might be another.

For instance, an applicant for a midwife position might make this section look like this:

QUALIFICATIONS AND TRAINING

Diploma of Midwifery
City University/St Bartholomew's Hospital, London, 1991–1993

Registered with the United Kingdom Central Council for Nursing, Midwifery and Health (UKCC)

Registered Nurse
The Townsville Hospital, 1981–1984

Critical Care Endorsement, 1988

PROFESSIONAL SELF-DEVELOPMENT

2013   Documentation, delegation and dilemmas (ANF)
Mechanical compression training for VTE, prophylaxis

2012   Lifting and handling, fire and safety, neo-natal resuscitation, basic life support, infection control and drug calculation.

2011   Foetal Surveillance Education,
Domiciliary midwife experience, Alice Springs Hospital.

2010   Diabetic Educator to pregnant women in Alice Springs and remote communities.
Glucometer training, Alice Springs Hospital.

For certain jobs in the mining, engineering and construction industries certain 'tickets' are required. The fact that you have a white card and certificates of training for hazardous work must be prominently shown if you are seeking a position requiring them. Again, a separate section could well be the right choice.

The important thing is to realise what is important to the employer and to then demonstrate clearly that you have the qualifications that the employer wants.

There is no need to list every training program you have done or qualification you have obtained. Only include the training and qualifications that are relevant to the position you are applying for.

Richard Parker, for instance, applying for a sales position in hardware, just put down the essential qualifications for the position and left out all the short courses that he had undertaken during his career simply because he did not see that including them would improve the strength of his application for an internal sales role in a hardware business:

Relevant Training

Certificate IV in Business Sales
TAFE WA, 2005

Certificate IV in Building and Construction (Estimating)
OTEN (Open Training and Education Network), 1998

Building Certificate
Perth Technical College, 1978

James Schofield, applying for the supervisor position in an engineering workshop, lumped all his short courses together in a single sentence. This is how he wrote this section:

Training and Development

National Certificate in Joinery, qualifying in Cabinetry, from the Joinery Industry Training Organisation, 1982.

- Won award for best third-year apprentice.

Currently enrolled in the NZIM Certificate in Management (part-time) through Wellington Institute of Technology.

Numerous short courses in OSH, communication and customer service.

Notice how he has slipped in an achievement statement under his National Certificate in Joinery training. We have already seen the use of achievement statements in the Employment History section. They can be slipped in almost anywhere in your résumé. This one shows that James was a motivated and conscientious student and implies that he probably still has the same attitude to his work.

Publications, Presentations and Professional Memberships

If relevant, there are two sections that can follow Education and Training. These are:

- **Publications and/or Presentations**
- **Professional Memberships or Affiliations.**

If both are relevant to you, you will need to decide which section would be of greater interest to your prospective employer and put that section first.

Presentations are well considered by employers. If you have not written any articles or publications, you may have presented talks or workshops on topics relevant to the employer and you might decide to head the section Professional Presentations or something similar.

If you have written articles for professional journals, you might head the section Publications or Peer-Reviewed Publications.

There are different ways to compile these sections but it is best to keep the sections as simple as possible. Firstly, only include those publications or presentations that are relevant to the job you are seeking. No one wants to read pages of publications or presentations that are not relevant to the position unless, of course, making presentations or authoring articles is an important part of the role.

A presentation that I made to the Career and Transition Education Association might be shown like this:

Developing an effective job search training program
Career and Transition Education Conference, Rotorua, 2011

In this way, you would be following a similar format to the ones you used for both your Employment History and Education and Training sections. A journal article or book would be described in the same way. Title in bold on the top line, then the journal it was published in or, for a book, the publisher and town, followed by the date on the second. If you were a co-author, it is important to say so; put the publication details on a third line and on the second put: 'Authored by ...' and list the authors in the order they are listed for the publication, lead author first.

Handle professional memberships in a similar way. The way I describe my memberships is like this:

Fellow member
Career Development Association of Australia

Affiliate member
Australian Society of Authors

Community and/or Sporting Involvement

If you have voluntary roles in community organisations or service clubs, or if you are involved in sport, whether as a player, coach or administrator, this can provide convincing evidence of your communication and interpersonal skills as well as your can-do attitude. Show them in the same way that you showed your employment record; put the role first in bold type and the organisation on the second line in normal type. Here is how David Campbell did it:

Community Involvement

Member
Sudbury Lions Club since 1999

- Member of the finance committee organising and managing budgets for the annual music hall and mountain bike championships.

Note once again how he has slipped in an achievement statement. Achievement statements bring your résumé to life and clearly demonstrate motivation. Employers like them, so use them wherever you believe they will be useful.

If you have included voluntary roles in your Employment History section, as Jenny Barnes did, don't repeat them in this section. Unless you have other sporting or community involvement that is relevant to your new position, it may be best to leave this section out.

Personal Information

The next section is one that causes quite a lot of controversy. It is the Personal Information section. Understanding that we don't know who is going to read our résumé, how much personal information do we want to give? As I said earlier in the chapter, this information gives the employers a chance to develop a more accurate picture of you. They have already been convinced that you have the aptitude and attitude to perform in the role and now they want to be better able to envisage you as a member of their team. Therefore, I do suggest that you state your date of birth and also your place of birth. This may show that you're a local through and through or it may show that you were born in some far away location that might make a topic of conversation at the start of the interview. If you were born overseas, it is important to give your citizenship status. Then, to allay any fears that you may be starting to suffer health problems due to ageing, I suggest that you state what your health is. If it is excellent, say so. Unless you have already described your sporting involvement in the preceding section, your claim of good health will be a lot more convincing if you can back it up by describing your regular exercise. It is also worth telling employers that you are a non-smoker if that is the case. David Campbell wrote this:

Personal information

Born   Geelong, 23 November 1956

Health   Excellent, non-smoker, regular fitness program

Happily married 32 years, 3 adult children

Did he need to mention that he had been happily married for 32 years? Possibly not, but the fact does help to give a picture of someone who has built a successful family life and that could be a plus in the role he is applying for.

Katharina Hochstein has suffered a health problem and this is how she composed this section:

Personal Information

Born   Bremerhaven, Germany, 17 September 1955

Nationality   Australian citizen since 1976

Health   Excellent except for an ankle injury which restricts
              the amount of walking or standing that I can do

She tackles the health issue by stating that her health is excellent except for an ankle injury that prevents her doing too much walking or standing — prerequisites in her former profession of teacher.

Referees

The last of the easy bits to write is the Referees section. Referees are the people who will provide supporting evidence for the claims that you make in your résumé and other documents in your written application. This means that you must make sure that you give your referees copies of every application that you send out, plus the ads and position descriptions for those jobs. Even more effective is to discuss your applications with your referees, asking them for advice on how to improve what you have said. Sometimes they will remember occasions when you performed well, occasions that you have forgotten. This would be a bonus but the main advantage of discussing your résumé with your referees is to ensure that they have thoroughly read it and agree with it. A united voice is very convincing.

Who do you choose to be your referees? The best referees are people who can vouch for your work. These may be supervisors, managers, colleagues, customers, suppliers and also subordinates. It is usually expected that you provide your current or most recent supervisor but don't do so if you do not want your current boss to know that you are job hunting. Referees do not have to be 'big names'; in fact, unless they know you extremely well, it is usually better not to use a big name.

What information about them are you going to give, bearing in mind issues of privacy? The answer is none unless you have their permission to do so. When you do have their permission, you would normally just give their contact phone number and/or email address.

Ask them and they will tell you what details to put in.

You will also need to give their names, their relationship with you and their current roles. Let's see how Don Bradley did it when applying for Manager, Technical Services in local government:

Referees

Colin Hammersley	08 3460 8851 (w)
Manager, Engineering Services	0418 353 869 (m)
Wellington Shire Council	hammers@wellington.sa.gov.au

Brendan Huxworth	08 3461 4341 (w)
Immediate Past President	brendanh@tolpuddle.com.au

Bridlington Lions Club and co-organiser with me of Bridlington Wheel Cycling Carnival

Colin Hammersley is Don's boss at Wellington Shire Council, so the relationship is clear. With his permission, Don has given Colin's office landline and mobile phone numbers and his work email address.

Don's other referee, Brendan, is a fellow member of the local Lions Club and the relationship is further explained through their joint involvement in the organisation of the annual cycling carnival. Brendan has suggested that Don give his office landline and work email address as contact details.

Some people advocate writing simply 'Referees available on request' to avoid privacy issues, but this means nothing. If the employer is interested in the application and wants to confirm details, having contact details for referees in the résumé rather than her having to go through the rigmarole of requesting their contact details is going to make life easier and help retain her interest in you as a candidate.

WRAP-UP

- A résumé is a marketing document, a 'brochure' for Yourself Pty Ltd, showing how you would perform in a particular job.

- When you start the marketing process, it is possible that you won't be fully aware of the skills and qualities required by your prospective 'clients' or employers. At this stage, you produce a draft résumé.

- As you gather further information, revisit this chapter and the next one to help you tailor your résumé to the new information. Keep doing this until you have a document that effectively demonstrates the relevant qualities and skills that you would bring to a specific position — an effective marketing document!

CHAPTER 4

Writing the challenging bits of your résumé

While the sections of your résumé that are covered in this chapter are more challenging to write, they are also the bits that will provide you with the most satisfaction and do the most for your self-esteem — and a healthy self-esteem is essential to winning that good job.

Career Objective/Career Summary

The first section of your résumé should be either a Career Objective or a Career Summary. You may have chosen different words for this section heading when you were reading Chapter 3. Whatever heading you have chosen, the purpose of this section is to state why you are the right person for the job and to demonstrate your motivation for doing the job well. This needs to be achieved in one or two short paragraphs.

The difference between a Career Objective and a Career Summary is that a summary presents the skills and motivation developed over recent employment, whereas an objective lists the skills and motivation that you would bring to the job from a different field of work. A summary is normally the better option if the job that you are applying for is similar to the work you have been doing.

The Career Objective section

A Career Objective is usually the better choice if the job you are applying for is significantly different to your most recent position. The reason for this is that you need to show the employer up-front that (1) you have the skills to do the job in spite of its being different to your last one, (2) that you have the motivation to do the job well, and (3) you know what is required to achieve the Key Performance Indicators or KPIs — the factors by which your work in the role will be assessed.

For an objective section there is a formula that you can use which helps to get things started. David Campbell followed this formula when he wrote his Career Objective for the position of CEO for a youth organisation (see his full résumé under the specimen résumés in the Appendix).

Career Objective

Chief Executive Officer where my passion for helping young people coupled with my business background and ability to build and lead happy teams will help Star Futures remain financially secure and continue to provide much needed support for Wangaratta's youth.

First, David wrote the job title exactly as written in the advertisement. Then he put the word 'where'. After this, he wrote why he was right for the position, his motivation for the job, and the personal qualities, skills and knowledge that he would bring to the position. He then completed the statement with the benefits that the employer would enjoy from bringing him into the team.

The last bit is important because the employer can see from it that the applicant acknowledges what is required and what needs to be achieved. This gives the employer confidence in the applicant.

Narendra Chaudhry used the same formula in his Career Objective and then added another paragraph which is virtually a career summary:

Career Objective

Project Manager, Electrical Operations, where extensive graduate electrical engineering experience in an industrial environment (including design, energy management and project management) will help ensure well-designed and implemented electrical and communication systems across all campuses of the school.

I bring more than 20 years' graduate experience in electrical design, project management, electrical generation, installation, maintenance and fault-finding in electrical distribution systems in heavy industry.

Richard Parker, in his résumé for a sales position in hardware, changed the formula slightly in that he didn't start with the position but with the skills and personal qualities that he would bring to the position, which he identifies in lines three and four. He described in a second sentence the benefits that the employer would accrue from hiring him.

Career Objective

To use the skills developed over 25 years' successful experience in building and a further 10 in sales and marketing of roofing products and services to the building trade with the aim of providing excellent service to inbound customers at Barnard's Building Supplies and Hardware. This will result in strengthening and growing the existing loyal customer base and thus increase sales, market share and profitability.

These examples demonstrate that there is no need to closely follow the formula. Use it to get started and then make whatever changes you need to for it to read more effectively. However, never let yourself be tempted to write about what you personally want to get out of the job. A Career Objective is all about what you are *offering to the employer*.

The Career Summary section

As already stated, a Career Summary section is often the better choice if the job that you are applying for is similar to your current or most recent role. There is no clear-cut formula to writing a Career Summary; the aim is to demonstrate very briefly your career record and show how you have developed the necessary skills to do the job and that you have the motivation to do it well.

Job seekers are sometimes tempted to use clichés like 'motivated self-starter' in their Career Summary. Resist this temptation. Clichés like this mean nothing and the employer is likely to get the impression that the job seeker really can't think of anything worthwhile to say. Instead, write content that is specific to you and that is relevant to the position. The following two examples are filled with specific and relevant information and, as a result, give a much more convincing picture of the candidate's motivation for the job.

Let's examine how James Schofield wrote his Career Summary for a position of Engineering Workshop Supervisor:

Summary

A cabinetmaker by trade, I have nearly 20 years' experience as Foreman at Wildwood Furniture, a high-quality furniture manufacturing plant. I have participated in OSH training courses, taken part in skills audits, assisted the factory manager with job procedures, shut-downs and maintenance, and upheld close contact with all the workers on the shop floor.

To ensure that all orders are delivered in full, on time and in spec (IFOTIS), I have been active in all management meetings, including sales budgeting and reviewing performance measures in all areas of the factory — machine shop, assembly area and spray line. I participate in stocktakes and liaise with the Purchasing Officer re inventory control.

Although James is moving from working in wood to an enterprise working in sheet metal fabrication, most of the skills required for a supervisory position are the same and he demonstrates this through talking about his responsibilities at the furniture factory. You will notice that through using words like 'high quality' and 'active', and mentioning that he assists the factory manager and maintains close contact with the workers, he demonstrates a keen motivation, something that employers value highly.

So, how did he write this section? He started with his formal qualification and trade background. He then listed all the tasks and responsibilities that he had taken on in the supervisor role. Benefits to the employer are implied through that first sentence in the second paragraph: 'To ensure that all orders are delivered in full, on time and in spec ...'

Marama Tuatini wrote her Career Profile for the position of Artist Development Manager with Chamber Music New Zealand like this:

Career Profile

A career centred around music with a special passion for chamber music. Since graduating 30 years ago, I have played the cello in chamber music ensembles in New Zealand, Australia and Canada. Currently librarian at Orchestra Wellington and a regular performer in the Wellington Chamber Orchestra (WCO).

In the early 1990s I studied part-time for a degree in journalism and since then I have become a by-line music correspondent for Fairfax New Zealand with credits in *The Dominion Post* and *The Press* as well as articles in several other newspapers and magazines.

Notice how she talks about her motivation, her 'passion', in that first short sentence. In her first paragraph, she describes her career as a performer and librarian. In the second paragraph, she talks about her career as a journalist and music critic. In this way, she demonstrates three abilities of great value to the position of Artist Development Manager.

Key Personal Attributes section

We now move to the end of the résumé to write the Key Personal Attributes section. This section is for a reiteration of the key qualities and qualifications that make you absolutely right for the job you are applying for. It's a very quick sales pitch. As you may have noticed towards the end of the last chapter, this part of the résumé is getting a bit dry with biographical facts and contact details for your referees.

We don't want to finish the résumé on a flat note; we want the employer to think, 'This is the person I want!' To achieve this, we need to liven up the end of the résumé by repeating the greatest qualities that you would bring to the job.[1]

This section normally comprises three bullet-pointed lines. Three is about the right number: any more and it gets too long and the employer stops reading; less, and it's hardly worth reading. However, each line may include two or three related qualities.

Tom Matlock, applying for an OH&S management position, wrote the section as follows:

Key Personal Attributes

- Clear thinking, good problem-solver.
- Effective team leader with good communication and people skills.
- Hard-working, responsible and efficient.

Jenny Barnes, applying for a part-time position with Kidsafe Australia, wrote:

Key Personal Attributes

- Passionate about promoting the safety and development of children.
- Excellent organisational skills.
- Good people skills, hard-working and efficient.

Both are short and to the point. Both are quick sales pitches to encourage the employer to want to discuss the position further with the two candidates. Katharina Hochstein's is similar:

Key Personal Qualities

- Highly organised and efficient

- Reliable, responsible and dependable

- Open and friendly, a good team member and enjoy helping others

The lines in Richard Parker's are a bit longer but there are still just three dot points:

Key Personal Strengths

- Strong communication and interpersonal skills.

- Committed to providing excellent service to customers — understanding client needs and ensuring that they are fully met.

- Well organised, efficient, reliable and hard-working — I like to get the job done to the best possible standards within the right timeframe.

Skills and Achievements section

If you decided to write a chronological résumé (see Chapter 3 for the definitions of chronological and functional résumés), you have now completed it. However, if you decided that a functional résumé would be more effective, we have now reached what is arguably the most important section of your résumé — the Skills and Achievements section. This is the one in which you show how your skills match the requirements of the job. It is, in fact, a miniature statement addressing the selection criteria set inside your résumé.

You may have read suggestions from recruiters, mainly those in North America, that a functional résumé is not well regarded today because it can 'hide a lot of gaps'. These suggestions refer to functional résumés that do not include an Employment History section and so can hide the fact that an applicant has large gaps in his or her employment. I strongly recommend that you do include an Employment History section even if there are gaps. It's your story and it backs up where you developed and demonstrated your skills. By this, I mean functional résumés will be well regarded by employers and the comments from employers about the specimen résumés in this book support this viewpoint.

The first step in writing the Skills and Achievements section is to identify the selection criteria for the job. Even if there are no written selection criteria, there will be skills and qualities that an employer will be looking for in applicants for any job. These can be discovered easily by finding an advertisement for a similar job on one of the online job boards or by talking to others who are working in roles similar to the one that you are seeking.

List these selection criteria or desired skills and qualities in an MS Word document and then, under each one, identify instances when you demonstrated the skills that the employers are asking for. This is not always an easy task and it may be worthwhile turning to the next chapter to identify and describe your achievements. But, before you do that, let's have a look at a few examples.

Linda Heatherton, applying for a position as Tour Guide to the *Lord of the Rings* film locations in New Zealand, wrote:

Relevant qualifications for the role
Knowledge of *The Lord of the Rings* and *The Hobbit*

- Have read *The Lord of the Rings (LOTR)* at least five times and *The Hobbit* three times just for my own pleasure.

- Have regularly used *LOTR* as a major text for years 9 and 10 English and Drama since filming began in late 1999.

Commitment to excellence in customer service

- Customer service in the teaching profession means providing excellent teaching service to students and advice to their parents. I have an absolute commitment to both and my success in this area is demonstrated by the rapport I have with both students and their parents.

- Frequently help by booking lessons and classes for my husband's ski school with potential and existing clients. My effectiveness in encouraging people to sign up for his training is in part due to the way I treat these clients.

Cheery, can-do attitude and effective problem-solving

- Directed the school musical for the past 7 years. This involves motivating and directing the efforts of 20 or more students and continually thinking on my feet to solve the many problems that arise.

Interpersonal and communication skills

- Teaching is all about establishing a good rapport with students and communicating with them.

- I have made several presentations to parents on the benefits of Drama to the development of self-confidence and good communication skills.

- Working knowledge of Mandarin; have travelled to China.

Ability to work autonomously and as part of a team

- As a teacher, I work autonomously but I am always aware that I am part of the team at Wakatipu High. The relationship that I have developed with my colleagues is testimony to my success in this area.

Driving licence and ability to get P endorsement

- Manual licence and clean driving record since 1982. Have enquired about P endorsement and willing and able to undertake the full licence test and the vetting for 'fit and proper person'.

What Linda has done is simply write one or more achievement statements under each criterion to demonstrate that she has the skills and personal qualities that the employer is looking for.

Matteo Buonopane goes a little further through inserting a brief introductory sentence for each criterion before giving his achievement statements:

Relevant skills and achievements

Previous hotel experience

Twenty years in the hospitality industry as Owner/Manager of a motel and of an award-winning heritage B&B.

- With my wife, built the Welcome Nugget B&B in Ballarat from a three-room establishment to a 20-room luxury accommodation enterprise.

- Over the past three years, achieved a 77% occupancy rate through providing exceptional customer service and off-season special events.

- A large percentage of our customers became regulars, staying with us whenever they were in town or just enjoying a weekend break.

Availability to work shifts and weekends

Able and willing to work shifts and weekends. With 20 years in hospitality, I am well accustomed to the 24/7 nature of the industry.

Well developed problem-solving and analytical skills

Twenty years in accommodation management have given me excellent problem-solving and analytical skills.

- The wild storm in December last year caused the roof to leak in two suites when we were fully booked. One leak was in the ensuite but the other was over a bed.

  The occupants of both rooms were regular and valued customers. For those whose suite had the leak over the bed, I immediately phoned other suitable accommodation venues, booked and paid for a room and then provided a taxi at no cost to our clients.

  For those whose suite had the leak over the bathroom, I provided extra bathmats to minimise the risk of slipping and waived payment for the room.

  As a result, both clients have since stayed at Welcome Nugget and both attended my farewell in April.

Previous experience in a reservation system

Used RMS at both the Mountain View Motel and the Welcome Nugget. Confident that I could learn other systems reasonably quickly.

Ability to work autonomously and as part of a team

- As joint Owner/Manager, I worked autonomously much of the time but always in collaboration with my wife and business partner. I always saw us as a team.

- As a member of the Rotary Club of Ballarat South, I have been part of the team organising our stand at the Sunday market for the past five years.

Exceptional customer service skills

Commitment to excellence in customer service has been the hallmark of my more than 30 years in customer service industries, both retail and hospitality.

- A regular customer at the Welcome Nugget wrote: 'We have really enjoyed staying at your B&B because of the outstanding customer service you and your wife always provide.'

A strong work ethic and the ability to lead

Without a strong work ethic and without the ability to lead, we would not have been able to run such a successful, award-winning B&B over the past 15 years.

James Schofield has taken a slightly different approach in that he has written one or more paragraphs under each criterion:

Relevant Skills and Achievements

Interpersonal, communication and team leadership skills

Since being appointed Foreman, I have supervised the work of a team of six full-time employees. My former co-workers were quick to accept my leadership and have worked well under my direction. During this time we have improved quality control as well as increasing production.

I initiate team meetings to talk through issues as they arise. This has led to a good team spirit and a commitment to working together to achieve our team goals. It has also led to specific improvements to both products and processes.

Occupational Safety and Health (OSH)

Have just renewed my first aid qualification which I have held since I was appointed Leading Hand in 1994.

Have undertaken training in harassment and government regulations regarding reporting levels of injury.

Further enhanced housekeeping procedures, ensuring all tools and materials are put away, trolleys moved in an orderly manner and floors swept. This has resulted in keeping both product loss and minor injuries to an absolute minimum.

Knowledge of operations and maintenance

Made sure that I know the proper procedures for stopping, starting and operating each machine (but not including programming).

Performed fault-finding procedures on various machines to correct boring and cutting tolerance inaccuracies.

In conjunction with the operators, I have ensured scheduled maintenance is properly performed on each machine, records kept and any problems reported for immediate rectification.

Understanding of IFOTIS

During my time at Wildwood, we have created a reputation as a reliable producer of high-quality furniture. In May 2009, when Perrimans first listed the Royale bedroom suite for their catalogue sale for all stores in both North and South Islands, I worked with the Purchasing Officer to make sure that we had the inventory, and briefed machine operators so as to ensure proper flow through the shop, in preparation for expected orders. When these came, we were able to produce 62 suites within the stipulated four-week timeframe, with not one unit requiring repair or touch-up.

During the first three years of my being Foreman, the production team reduced callouts for repairs from 4% to less than 1%.

Understanding of design drawings and lateral thinking.

Over the past eight years, have been involved in the design of new furniture lines from the productivity point of view so as to make sure that the job flows smoothly through the workshop. Have developed good skills in visualising products and processes.

Proposed two modifications to the Royale bedhead to simplify assembly. These modifications were adopted and resulted in reducing average assembly time by 34 minutes — a considerable saving when working on the 62 suites ordered for Perrimans.

Saw a way of modifying four of the old jigs to suit the new Impériale dining suite, resulting in considerable cost saving in the set-up phase.

Inventory control

Suggested modifications to the job cards issued for each job. These now give not only a description of each job, the number to be cut and the next location, but also record the number completed and the number, if any, to be reworked or discarded.

Continue to work in close cooperation with the Purchasing Officer to decide on stock levels, the quality of hardware etc.

In the nineteen years I have been Foreman, we have been able to reduce inventory levels by almost 20% without impacting on production or quality.

It does not matter which approach you take as long as you believe that the section will convince the employer that you have the right skills and attitude to perform well in the position.

The last two examples have been fairly long, especially James Schofield's. If you believe that the section is getting too long to include in the résumé, you might want to consider taking it out and making it a separate document, a statement addressing the selection criteria. How to write statements addressing the selection criteria are discussed in Chapter 6.

How to tell if your résumé will be a winner

Résumés need to be dynamic documents showing clearly how you will perform in the new job. They need to express your motivation to do the job well and to communicate this in the top half of page one!

To grab and keep the employer's interest, résumés need to be talking more about the job you are applying for and how well you will perform in it rather than about you and your background.

Put each section in a logical order, the order that will appeal most to the employer.

Use achievement statements to demonstrate skills and motivation without sounding off-puttingly boastful.

Make the document attractive. Use an easy-to-read font and leave plenty of white space.

Most of all, be enthusiastic about the job and let that enthusiasm show through the résumé. Express your motivation to do the job well right from the beginning.

Once you have completed your résumé, check whether it outlines the following:

- **Does the résumé sell you for this specific position?**
- **Will it grab the employer's interest from the first few lines and does it keep this interest through to the end?**
- **Does it talk about your motivation in the top half of page one?**
- **Can the employer envisage you performing well in the position from reading the résumé?**

WRAP-UP

- The Career Objective/Career Summary and the Key Personal Attributes sections, plus the Skills and Achievements section if you are writing a functional résumé, are the most important sections of your résumé because they show how you meet the specific needs of the employer.

- The best way to present these sections is to outline the skills and motivation you have developed over recent or relevant employment, reiterate the key qualities and qualifications that make you right for the job, and describe how your skills match the requirements of the job. Do these sections well and the likelihood of winning the job you are seeking is strong.

- These sections are the most difficult parts of the résumé to write and they are the bits that will require the most changing as you apply for different positions but they are also the bits that are most likely to convince the employer to take you on.

CHAPTER 5

Identifying achievements

If I were applying to you for a position that required someone who was physically fit and I told you that I was a very fast runner, I would need to give you some evidence or you probably wouldn't believe me. And if I told you that I was very good at this and very good at that, you would think that I was 'full of myself' and you wouldn't like me. Then it wouldn't matter how skilful I was, you wouldn't employ me.

So, how do we convince employers that we have the skills they require without sounding boastful? We use achievement statements, statements like: 'Ran the mile in 4 minutes 16, Caribbean Games, Barbados, 2008.' That is a much more effective way of demonstrating physical fitness. It also demonstrates the motivation that employers are looking for because competitive running requires hours of arduous training. At the same time, it sounds interesting rather than boastful because it is relating a fact.

What is an achievement statement?

Look at the following four examples (see also the specimen résumés in the Appendix) to get a good understanding of what achievement statements are and how they can influence an employer.

1. This is an excerpt from the statement addressing the selection criteria written by Matteo Buonopane as part of his application for the position of Assistant (Duty) Manager of a Melbourne apartment hotel:

   • With my wife, built the Welcome Nugget B&B in Ballarat from a three-room establishment to a 20-room luxury accommodation enterprise.

   • Over the past three years, achieved a 77% occupancy rate through providing exceptional customer service and off-season special events.

2. Katharina Hochstein is a teacher who, for health reasons, is seeking an administrative role in a museum. These achievement statements form part of her response to the criterion regarding administrative experience:

   • Kept detailed records of student progress against individual learning plans, developed course outlines, wrote student reports and managed the Department's budget.

   • With a colleague, developed a spreadsheet and database system for recording all the Department's records.

   • Have taken the minutes for the monthly meetings of the Korong Historical Society since being elected Secretary in 1998.

3. Don Bradley is seeking the position of Technical Services Manager with a rural municipal council. Here are some achievement statements from his response to the selection criteria:

- Under the guidance of the Manager, Engineering Services, designed and supervised a $50,000 upgrade of the East Bridlington sewerage system, 1999–2000. The job was completed two weeks early and was on budget.

- With the Manager, Engineering Services, designed and implemented a waste transfer and recycling program covering the whole shire, 2009. This program was awarded the Premier's Environmental Projects Award the following year.

- As a member of the State Emergency Service, helped prepare plans for flooding control and evacuation for the Curriedale region, 1995. Was involved in designing and directing training exercises to ensure the coordination of police, fire brigade, Australian Defence Force units and volunteers. These plans proved very effective during the massive floods of 2002.

- Initiated and coordinated emergency temporary repairs to the Belfoster Main Road within 7 hours of receiving a report of subsidence after heavy rain. Designed and implemented immediate improvements to drainage, strengthening of the embankment and resurfacing of the road. These were completed within 15 working days.

4. Sometimes achievement statements can be quite long and tell a whole story. Here is one from David Campbell's application:

- Three years ago, we had two houses accommodating seven young people. We knew that there was an urgent need for more residential care. I worked with the Board to do a business plan for building or purchasing a third house. To do this, I consulted Department officials and visited a number of residential care establishments in the State to get specifications and ideas. I then consulted architects to get suitable designs and cost estimates and I took these to the Board to choose a design. I researched possible sources of funding, put a proposal to the Board which was accepted and wrote a submission for a grant under the Cornwall Scheme.

The submission was successful and, under the Board's direction, I invited tenders for construction. The Board selected a tender and then I oversaw construction including monitoring the budget. Completion was delayed by bad weather but came in on budget.

Before completion, I worked with the Board to recruit and select staff for the house. I organised the necessary training and clearances, and the first young people were in residence within three weeks of completion.

Achievement statements describe specific events

As can be seen from the achievement statements shown in the last two examples, an element common to most is that they are specific. They talk about specific achievements, specific events, specific incidents. Generally speaking, how you performed in a specific incident is a good indicator of how you might perform in a similar incident in the future. That is convincing evidence for an employer.

When a job advertisement or position description asks for 'demonstrated' or 'proven' skills, they are asking for achievement statements, for specific examples from your past experience that clearly demonstrate or prove that you do have the skills that they are asking for.

The two-step process to compiling achievement statements

There is a two-step process to compiling achievement statements. The first is to identify the accomplishment that demonstrates the required skill or strength. The second step is working out how to express the achievement effectively; this will be discussed in the next chapter. This chapter concentrates on identifying the most relevant accomplishments.

These accomplishments do not have to be world shattering. They are just parts of the job that you did well. David Campbell's achievement statement showing how he handled a boy's behaviour while working in a residential care facility for troubled youth is a good example of how a relatively minor incident can demonstrate strong interpersonal and communication skills (see his Statement Addressing the Selection Criteria in the Appendix). You don't have to prove that you're Superman or Wonder Woman; you just need to demonstrate that you have the skills to do the job. The best way to do that is to talk about how you have tackled jobs in the past.

Three ways to identify achievements

There are three ways to identify relevant accomplishments to turn them into achievement statements. Use all three methods to build the best possible list. The longer the list is, the more material you will have to work with to create winning applications and to prepare answers to possible interview questions. Also, as the list grows, so too should the affirmation of your self-esteem — and this is a good thing.

Method 1

The first method is to record the knowledge, skills and personal qualities required for the sort of job you would like to apply for. You may find it easier if you make a table like the one below.

Knowledge, skills and personal qualities required for the job	Specific incidents that demonstrate that you have the necessary skills

In the left-hand column, record the knowledge, skills and personal qualities needed for the sort of job you would like (the selection criteria), and in the right-hand column, insert two or three keywords that will remind you of a situation which demonstrates that you have those skills or qualities. We will discuss writing the story around these words in the next chapter; this step is simply to identify where and when you accomplished something that shows you meet the selection criteria.

Method 2

The second method is going back over your work history, including voluntary work and participation in community and sporting organisations, and recording the accomplishments that you are proud of. Take each position that you have held at work, each voluntary position and each sport or hobby that you have participated in, and record them in a column on the left-hand side of the page. On the right-hand side, against each position or hobby, jot down a few keywords that will remind you of the things you did well — things you are proud of that demonstrate your skills and personal qualities.

Method 3

The third method is to go through the long list of action verbs given on pages 101–102. As you look at each entry, ask yourself if it could refer to something that you might have done in the past. 'Administered? What have I ever administered? Ah yes, I arranged the rosters for last year's squash tournament, recorded the results and gave them to the press.' It doesn't matter that the action verb has changed from 'administered' to 'arranged' — the important thing is that the action verb 'administered' triggered the memory of arranging the rosters. Make a list similar to the ones you made for methods 1 and 2 and write keywords, such as 'squash rosters' in the right-hand column.

Listing relevant achievements from outside paid employment

While everything in the written application and in your answers to interview questions must be relevant to your ability to perform in the position you are seeking, achievement statements that demonstrate your skills in the required areas can be drawn from all walks of life. The Rotary Club Regatta, helping out with the costumes or set construction for your grandchild's high school production of *Kiss Me Kate*, or playing in your local indoor cricket team or golf club all demonstrate motivation, interpersonal, team and communication skills. Therefore don't forget to look at achievements from unpaid employment or voluntary work, and from participation in community organisations and sports. It may well be that something you created at home could provide evidence of a desired skill or personal quality — the shed you designed and built or the garden produce which won you a prize at the local show. All of these achievements are evidence of your skills and your motivation.

Building self-esteem through a list of achievements

Hopefully you are starting to build a decent list from the three methods. It is not always easy to complete this in a single go, so be prepared to come back to this task. Use all three methods and include examples from outside paid employment. Work through the process several times.

As the list grows, so too should your self-esteem and self-confidence and this is essential for job search success. You need to have confidence in your ability to perform well in the job to be able to convince the employer of your skills and motivation.

Now we move on to the next step in the process, writing these accomplishments up as achievement statements.

Action Verbs

Addressed meetings
Administered
Advised
Analysed
Appraised
    performance
Appraised value
Arbitrated
Arranged
    flowers, furniture
    in a room etc.
Arranged
    meetings,
    social/sporting
    events
Assembled
Asserted
    was assertive
Assessed damage
Assessed progress
Assigned tasks to
people
Assisted
Audited
Authored, wrote
Authorised,
    delegated
Bookkeeping,
    kept accounts
Budgeted
Built
Busked
Calculated
Cared for animals
Cared for elderly,
    disabled etc.

Cast molten metal
Changed, initiated
    change
Checked
Classified
Coached a team
Coached students
Collected
Compiled
Completed tasks on
    time
Conceived ideas,
    conceptualised
Confronted people
Constructed
Convinced
Co-ordinated
Corresponded, wrote
    and answered
letters
Costed
Counselled
Crafted
Created
Critiqued, reviewed,
    criticised
Customised
Cut
Debated
Decided
Decided between
    alternatives or
    options
Decorated
Delegated
Demolished
Demonstrated
Designed things or

systems
Developed
Diagnosed
Directed
Disciplined
Dismantled
Displayed
Documented
Drafted charts,
    diagrams
Drafted reports
Drew, sketched
Drew conclusions
Drove, operated
Edited
Engineered
Entered and
    retrieved data
Established
Estimated
Evaluated
Exhibited
Explained
Expressed
Fabricated
Facilitated
Farmed
Filed
Financed
Finished
Fired
Fishing
Fitted
Flew
Forged
Formatted
Formulated
Fostered

Found information
Founded
Franchised
Handled complaints
Helped
Herded and
   controlled animals
Hypothesised
Identified
Implemented
Influenced
Informed
Initiated
Inspected
Instigated
Instituted
Instructed
Invented
Interpreted
Interviewed
Investigated
Made decisions
Maintained
Managed
Marketed
Measured
Mechanical skills
Mediated
Monitored
Motivated
Negotiated
Observed
Operated
Ordered
Organised
Originated
Overcame
Overhauled

Painted
Performed
Persevered
Persisted
Persuaded
Photographed
Planned
Planted
Played
Presented
Priced
Prioritised
Programmed
Projected
Projects
Promoted
Publicised
Published
Raised funds
Ran
Recorded
Referred
Remodelled
Repainted
Repaired
Reported
Represented
Researched
Resourced
Responsibility
Restored
Reviewed
Revitalised
Sawed
Sculpted
Serviced
Served
Set goals or targets

Shaped
Sketched
Sold
Solved
Split
Spoke
Stock control
Streamlined
Summarised
Supervised
Synthesised
Taught
Thought
Timed
Tolerated
Took control
Took responsibility
Trained
Tutored
Understood
Updated
Upgraded
Used computers
Used instruments or
   tools
Valued
Wrote

WRAP-UP

■ The things that you have accomplished in the past, the things that you are pleased to have done, these are what will convince the employer that you are the right person for the job.

■ Talk about specific events and specific incidents when compiling a list of achievements. How you performed in a specific incident is a good indicator of how you might perform in a similar incident at work.

■ Identifying achievements is an essential part of an effective job search campaign. Make compiling a list of achievements an ongoing process and don't stop once you have secured a job.

CHAPTER 6

Achievement statements and key skills spiel

Once you have identified your relevant achievements, the next step is to write them up in the form of achievement statements. To help you understand the task, here are some examples:

Ran the mile in 4 minutes 16, Caribbean Games, Barbados, 2008.

Oversaw and co-ordinated the operations of up to 43 buses on scheduled routes, Benfallen Bus Company, 2009–2012.

Directed the school musical for the past seven years. This involves motivating and directing the efforts of 20 or more students and continually thinking on my feet to solve the many problems that arise.

Usually achievement statements that describe specific accomplishments or specific events are more effective and more convincing than those that are more general. 'Ran the mile in 4 minutes 16, Caribbean Games, Barbados, 2008' would be more convincing to an employer than the less specific 'Involved in international middle distance running, 2004–2009'. As can be seen from the other two examples, this is not always possible. However, try to make your achievement statements as specific as possible.

As we said earlier, not all achievements should necessarily be drawn from paid employment. The following are examples taken from involvement in sports or community organisations. Each of them demonstrates qualities that would be highly prized by employers. They show an ability to fit well into a team, people and communication skills, responsibility, physical fitness and health, and financial skills.

> Treasurer, Westering Football Club. Responsible for an annual budget of $55,000, 2009–2012.

> Completely rebuilt an FJ Holden, Koonakurra, 2007–2008. Rebuilt engine and gearbox using parts from the wreckers. Restored bodywork and upholstery. This car won me first prize in the Koonakurra Show for Best Restored Vehicle, 2008.

> Elected member of the organising committee for East Calderwell Neighbourhood House, 2009 and 2010.

How to write five different types of achievement statement

There are no rigid rules as to how best to write an achievement statement. However, the following guidelines to five different types of achievement statement will help you start formulating your own. Once you have mastered the guidelines, there are almost no limits to the variations that can be used.

1. Experience

An experience achievement statement is often a good opening achievement statement: it can set the scene before launching into more specific achievements. The formula for a basic experience achievement statement is (1) length of experience, (2) the type of position or field of work, (3) where and (4) when:

> Eight years' experience as Works Supervisor, Gravesend Municipality, 2006–2014.

> More than twenty years' experience in clerical work, word processing, filing and reception, Cornwallis, Bendersmith and Jackson Lawyers, Templefield, 1993–present.

The second example follows the formula in this way: the length of experience: 'More than 20 years'; the type of position or field of work: 'in clerical work, word processing, filing and reception'; where: 'Cornwallis, Bendersmith and Jackson Lawyers, Templefield'; and when: '1993–present'.

There is no need to stick rigidly to the formula. There are lots of ways you can vary this sort of achievement statement. The following examples demonstrate some of the variations:

> Seven years' supervisory experience, the last three as Shift Foreman, Green Valley Engineering, responsible for a team of twelve people.

This one follows the formula except that it includes a progression from the general field to a specific position and concludes with a statement giving a graphic description of the level of responsibility.

In Jenny Barnes' statement, we find another experience achievement statement showing progression:

> Fifteen years' experience as a member of the committee of management of the Waterloo Soccer Club. Currently Secretary/ Treasurer responsible for an annual turnover of approximately $12,500, for preparing all accounts for the auditor and for complying with the rules and regulations set down by the State Soccer Association.

Tom Matlock writes an experience achievement statement very simply but it still tells the story of several years' experience in occupational health and safety:

> Fully involved in OH&S since 2002.

James Schofield starts his résumé off with an experience achievement statement:

> A cabinetmaker by trade, I have nearly 20 years' experience as Foreman at Wildwood Furniture, a high-quality furniture manufacturing plant.

To summarise, there are many ways to phrase an experience achievement statement. However, it is worthwhile starting with the formula described at the beginning of this section. Then, as you gain confidence and understanding, make the changes so that the achievement statement becomes as powerful and convincing as possible.

ACTIVITY

Write an experience achievement statement here, one that is relevant to the position you are seeking:

_____

_____

_____

_____

_____

2. Classic

The classic achievement statement is so-called because it is the type of achievement statement most frequently mentioned in books about résumés. It is also used more frequently than any other type. The basic formula for a classic achievement statement is:

    i. action verb; refer to the list of action verbs in Chapter 5. Note that they are generally, but not always, in the past tense

    ii. what; the action that was undertaken

    iii. where

    iv. when.

Here is a basic classic achievement statement from Don Bradley's application:

Completed one-week course in Park Management, Bond University, October 2001.

Don's statement follows the formula: action verb: 'Completed'; what: 'one-week course in Park Management'; where: 'Bond University'; when: 'October 2001'. Here are a few more examples:

> Ran the mile in 4 minutes 16, Caribbean Games, Barbados, 2008.
>
> Achieved favourable reports in my annual performance appraisals, Barabbas Engineering, 2010–present.
>
> Managed a highly motivated team of five part-time staff including reception/bookings and housekeeping.
>
> Captained the Southern Region Masters Netball Team, 2009–2011.

Notice that these achievements are not world shattering and they don't need to be. They indicate people who perform well in their jobs and who are therefore likely to perform well in the job that they are applying for.

Achievement statements can be strengthened by quantifying the achievement, by demonstrating the significance of the achievement through the use of specific numerals:

> Increased sales by 16% in the first 12 months after my appointment as Head of Hardware Department, Managalore General Store, 2011.

In the following examples, a second sentence has been added to describe the outcomes of the achievement:

1. Presented a paper on self-directed teams to the National Conference of Local Government Managers, Australia, in Perth, 2008. This paper was well received and was subsequently published in the *LGMA Journal*.

2. Thought out new methods to speed dispatch of outward goods, Clifton Surf Boards, 2012. Presented these ideas to management and persuaded them to adopt the new methods which have saved on average two days per order and reduced costs by about 15%.

Janet Turner went further to explain the strategies that she used to achieve her result by adding three sub-bullet points:

- Through targeted promotion, increased conference revenue by 17% over this time. This has been achieved through:
    1. Identifying higher spending corporate organisations that hold conferences.
    2. Developing a targeted advertising campaign in relevant journals and publications to build awareness and the profile of the hotel in the MICE sector.
    3. Building close working relationships with key professional conference organisers with clients in the higher yielding corporate sector and facilitating site inspections and familiarisation tours of the property.

Sometimes a classic achievement statement may mean little to the employer. The following one, demonstrating organisational skills, would not mean much to someone who did not know what organising a Scout jamboree would involve. To overcome this problem, the applicant has quantified the achievement by describing the size of the jamboree. To make it easier for an employer to fully understand, give the achievement statement a 'handle' — a way for the reader to grasp the significance of the achievement. In this example, the 'handle' is '[...] which was attended by nearly 400 scouts from interstate and overseas'.

Administered Colebrook Scouts, 2004–2009, including the 2008 Jamboree which was attended by nearly 400 scouts from interstate and overseas.

In the statement below, the 'handle' is incorporated into the 'action verb' and 'what' parts of the statement:

Saved Stonybrook Council in excess of $180,000 through inspecting and utilising existing resources, 2008, when given responsibility of up-grading the council's fire safety systems.

If you want to write about an achievement when you were part of the team, it is important to mention the other people involved. This is true of all types of achievement statement. Look at these two examples from Don Bradley's statement where all the other people involved are mentioned before the action verb:

- With the Manager, Engineering Services, designed and implemented a waste transfer and recycling program covering the whole shire, 2009. This program was awarded the Premier's Environmental Projects Award the following year.

- As a member of the State Emergency Service, helped prepare plans for flooding control and evacuation for the Curriedale region, 1995. Was involved in designing and directing training exercises to ensure the coordination of police, fire brigade, Australian Defence Force units and volunteers. These plans proved very effective during the massive floods of 2002.

Classic achievement statements don't always strictly follow the formula. In the following example, Linda Heatherton is describing her 'cheery, can-do attitude', talking about some of her experiences as a teacher at a local school:

> Directed the school musical for the past 7 years. This involves motivating and directing the efforts of 20 or more students and continually thinking on my feet to solve the many problems that arise.

The 'where' is implied through the use of the word 'school' and the 'when' is 'past 7 years'. The handle comes in the second sentence where the 20 students are mentioned.

ACTIVITY

Using the examples above to guide you, write a classic achievement statement here, one that is relevant to the sort of position you would like to work in. Describe a specific achievement for the greatest effect.

_____

_____

_____

_____

3. Position

The formula for a position achievement statement is simply the position, where (the organisation) and when (date you held the position):

Vice Captain, Toggoran Bay Cricket Team, 2007–2008.

Kesterway Council delegate on the Regional Tourist Authority, 2007–2009.

Member, Bridlington Lions Club since 2005.

Here is an example of a position statement with some additional, quantifying information:

Treasurer, Bellevue Football Club, responsible for an annual budget of $65,000, 2008.

In the following examples, a verb (*not* an action verb) has been added in front of the position.

Promoted Assistant Manager, Spare Parts, Bolton Autos, 2010.

Appointed Tasmanian delegate to the Wellsburn Committee, planning the establishment of a statewide junior football development program, 2009.

The reason the verb is not an action verb is that it wasn't the applicant who did the promoting or appointing.

ACTIVITY

Write a position achievement statement here:

_____

_____

_____

_____

4. Testimonial

This sort of achievement statement involves a comment made by someone else about your work, perhaps a quote from a written reference or perhaps something that someone said. The following examples follow the formula (1) 'who said it', and (2) 'where was it said' followed by the words themselves:

- A regular customer at the Welcome Nugget wrote in a letter: 'We have really enjoyed staying at your B&B because of the outstanding customer service you and your wife always provide.'

- In a company press release published in November last year, I was described by the Manager as 'one of the leading minds in renewable energy research in Australia today'.

- After the railway line had been restored within 4½ days, State Rail General Manager, William Farmer, thanked me and told me that I had achieved 'the impossible' through my determination, excellent organisation and ability to motivate others to 'give their all' to the project.

In this last example, the applicant is quoting a spoken testimonial and, except for the words in quotation marks, the exact words have been forgotten. There is no problem with writing a testimonial of this sort as long as the spirit of what was said is preserved.

If an employer asked Mr Farmer if this statement is accurate, we would want him to say yes. Therefore it is very important to resist any temptation to exaggerate the words, to 'gild the lily'. You know that you are right for the job so there is no need to exaggerate and, if you do so, it's quite likely that the employer will get a whiff of it.

Once this happens, your credibility and job chances are blown.

ACTIVITY

Write a testimonial achievement statement here.

_____

_____

_____

_____

_____

_____

5. SAO (Situation, Action, Outcome)

A SAO (Situation, Action, Outcome) is usually longer than the other types of achievement statement. It can comprise up to six or seven sentences. It is very useful when you have quite a story to tell, one that wouldn't get proper treatment in a classic statement.

Let us use an example from Don Bradley's application for a municipal council Technical Services Manager position. As its name implies, a SAO begins with a description of the Situation: 'A local dairy farmer sought planning permission to set up and operate a boutique cheese factory in 2012 while I was Assistant Manager, Engineering Services.'

The second part describes the Action taken: 'I took the farmer through the whole process, ensuring that his proposals met all local government requirements as well as State and Federal regulations. This included checking his building plans for structural soundness, food hygiene requirements, OH&S factors, water and sewerage, and transport access.'

The final part tells the Outcome: 'The factory has now been built and the cheeses produced there have already won medals at agricultural shows.' Here is another example:

> A major fire destroyed a large part of the manufacturing capacity at the Yankalilla factory in 2007 when I was the factory's Commercial Manager. Damage to the plant and loss of profit totalled $10 million. Without any prior training, I set in motion the process to claim this amount from our insurers as quickly as possible to enable the rapid restoration of production. These actions resulted in:
>
> - An interim payment of $4 million within 48 hours of the fire.
>
> - Loss assessors on site within 24 hours.
>
> - Partial production resumed within four days; full production within six weeks.
>
> - Full settlement of the claim within four weeks.
>
> - Commendation both from the insurers for the way I had managed the claim process and from senior management at the company's national headquarters in Sydney.

These examples both talk about fairly major achievements but SAOs, like other types of achievement statement, can be just as effective with relevant achievements that are far less dramatic. Here is one from David Campbell's statement:

> - Three weeks ago, counselled a 17-year-old boy who had been suspended from school because of fighting. He had been doing well and was in line for a traineeship but his suspension could jeopardise his chances. He told me that he fought because he was being bullied by a number of students about being in residential care. Explained the situation to the school principal

and arranged for details of all the work that he would miss during his suspension to be sent to the group home.

Helped him learn the material and complete the assignments as well as assisting him to develop strategies for coping with the bullying. The principal also agreed to speak to the students who were bullying him.

The result is that he is now back at school; he is no longer being bullied, his studies are going well, and he has every likelihood of getting the traineeship.

ACTIVITY

Write a SAO here. Tell the whole story in a way that would interest the employer. For the sake of this exercise, break it up into the three sections: Situation, Action, Outcome.

Situation: _____

_____

_____

_____

Action: _____

_____

_____

_____

Outcome: _____

_____

_____

_____

Start a 'directory' of achievement statements

We have discussed the 'rules' of how to write five types of achievement statement. These 'rules' are not designed to restrict you in any way — in fact, the opposite is the case. The five different ways of demonstrating your skills and achievements that have been discussed are to help you get started. There are many, many other ways of writing them. Use the 'rules' to compile your achievement statements but don't be afraid, later on, to alter them or to use other styles if you think that this will be more convincing.

One point to emphasise is that as you start to make changes to the rules, you may be tempted to be more general in your statements. Be as specific as you possibly can. This is especially important when writing classic and SAO achievement statements. The more specific your statements, the more convincing they will almost certainly be.

Achievement statements are probably the most important ingredient in any successful application. They are also extremely effective when answering interview questions. Yes, they are hard work but that hard work will be repaid by the success you will enjoy in your job applications. So don't allow yourself to be tempted to skip the process of writing them. Keep working on them until you have more than enough for the next application. You won't regret the effort in the long run.

To begin, choose ten achievements from the list you made from the three methods in Chapter 5 — achievements you consider the most important or the most relevant for the sort of job you want. Practise writing achievement statements for these ten. It may take you several attempts to get it right but the more you do it and the more determined you are to write them in the most effective way, the easier it will become.

Once you have completed the first ten to your satisfaction, do the same for another ten and so on. Revisit your list of achievements on a regular basis and add new ones whenever you accomplish something worthwhile. Then write each one up as an achievement statement and add it to your 'directory'. If you do this on a regular basis, you will always have an up-to-date directory of achievement statements to work from when you need them.

You can use this growing 'directory' to provide material for your résumés and job applications, and for preparing answers to possible interview questions. The more entries in your 'directory', the more achievement statements you will have to choose from.

You should find as you write these achievement statements that your self-esteem is being given a boost. That is just what should happen. Whenever you feel rejected, go back to your list of achievement statements and get your self-esteem back up to where it ought to be.

Your 'key skills spiel'

Another important marketing statement is your 'key skills spiel'. It is similar to an 'elevator pitch', which is a short statement aimed at marketing a particular product or idea in the time it takes for an elevator ride. Your key skills spiel is a short, persuasive line aimed at marketing you. You can use it to attract the interest of someone you would like to meet to advance your job search. In your networking, you will be talking to a lot of people who don't know you and you have a very short window of opportunity to persuade them to listen to you.

If you work on creating a spiel of about 30 seconds, you will need about 65 words.

To prepare your key skills spiel, you need to remember the three things that every employer is looking for in every applicant for every position (as covered in Chapter 1):

1. The *skills* to do the job.

2. The *motivation* to do the job well.

3. The *ability to fit well* into their team.

You need to show your attributes in a brief, interesting and positive way. Look at this example from someone seeking a role in sports administration and find evidence of skills, motivation and team. In your opinion, what are the words or phrases that imply the relevant skills, motivation and working well in a team?

> I have been actively involved in sports administration through Little Athletics on a voluntary basis for the past five years — and I have really enjoyed it.
>
> For the past three years I have taken on responsibility for public relations and promotion and, I'm pleased to say, we now have more than 600 young people attending.

When it comes to writing your own spiel, the first step is to jot down all the reasons that make you worth talking to in these particular circumstances. What are the relevant knowledge, skills, experience, personal qualities and motivation that you would bring to their organisation?

Let's take James Schofield. His background is as a cabinetmaker and Foreman in a furniture manufacturing company and he is applying for the position of Factory Manager for a business that designs and makes shop displays and point-of-sale fittings.

The criteria for selection for the position are safety, quality, accurate record-keeping, good maintenance and leadership skills.

James can list his current employer's name for high-quality furniture, his occupational health and safety training, his participation in stocktakes and inventory control, his participation in management meetings involving sales, budgeting and performance measures and the rapport he maintains with all the people he supervises on the shop floor.

From this list, he could compile a spiel something like this:

> I have been Foreman at Wildwood Furniture for the past seven years. Over this period we have built a strong team spirit and this has led to improvements both in quality control and in safety. I participate actively in management meetings, inventory control and budgeting.

In 45 words, he has covered all the selection criteria except maintenance and he will have grabbed the employer's interest in perhaps just 25 seconds. Here are some other examples:

- I've been a Management Accountant and Commercial Manager for Australian Farm Products in this state for the past ten years. The experience has been great. During this time I've had many challenges including managing the financial ramifications of a $10 million fire, and these challenges really stimulated me.

- I've always been passionate about children. As a result I taught for twelve years before I decided to be a stay-at-home mum. Since 2004, I have served on the committee of the Waterloo Soccer Club, organising children's competitions. My role with the club has involved some very successful lobbying, marketing and fundraising and I would love to be able to do the same things for children's safety.

To compile your key skills spiel, identify the sort of position you are seeking, list the knowledge, skills, experience and personal qualities that employers are looking for (i.e. the selection criteria), and then list your own knowledge, skills, experience and personal qualities to match what they are asking for, including your motivation for that sort of work and the personal qualities that show you would be a good member of their team. Remember that job ads do not always specify the required competencies and it is sometimes only by researching the position descriptions for similar jobs or by talking to people in that occupation that you can find out exactly what it is that the employers are looking for.

ACTIVITY

Using the steps below, write a key skills spiel that is relevant to the position you are seeking.

Step 1: The knowledge, skills, experience and personal qualities being sought are:

_____

_____

_____

_____

_____

_____

_____

_____

_____

Step 2: The knowledge, skills, experience and personal qualities that you will bring to the position — and evidence of motivation for the job and your ability to be a good team member:

_____

_____

_____

_____

_____

_____

_____

_____

_____

_____

Step 3: Now write your key skills spiel:

_____

_____

_____

_____

_____

_____

_____

_____

_____

_____

_____

WRAP-UP

■ Achievement statements are probably the most important ingredient for résumés and job applications. Because they describe specific things you have done, they are interesting to an employer and far more convincing than saying that you have the skills to do this or that. They are also what the employer is looking for when the position description asks for 'proven ...' or 'demonstrated ...'. Achievement statements are also extremely effective when answering interview questions.

■ Continue to add to your 'directory' of achievement statements after you get the job. Think of this as part of your marketing strategy for your micro-business. It may seem like a lot of work but you will be very grateful for it if you need to embark on another job search.

■ Formulate a key skills spiel to complement your achievement statements. A key skills spiel is a short, persuasive line aimed at marketing you. It needs to be about 30 seconds long or 65 words in length. To create your own key skills spiel, identify the sort of position you are seeking, list the knowledge, skills, experience and personal qualities that employers are looking for, and then list your own knowledge, skills, experience and personal qualities to match this.

CHAPTER 7

Documents to support your application

This chapter is about compiling all the documents that might need to be part of your application other than your résumé. If the position is advertised, the advertisement or position description will usually dictate what documents are required. These could include a cover letter, an expression of interest (EOI), a statement addressing the selection criteria and an application form.

Before writing any of these documents, you need to be applying for a specific position. Like the final résumé, these documents need to be tailored for each position you apply for. If you haven't yet identified a definite position to apply for, leave this chapter for the time being and come back to it once you have that specific job in mind.

Let's start with cover letters. These should accompany almost every application.

Cover letters that sell

My clients often ask me, 'Do I need to send a cover letter?' My advice is always to include a cover letter in a job application. The exception is when there is no facility to attach a cover letter for an online application.

Some employers read the cover letter first. Others may hardly glance at them. A survey in the US carried out by résumé guru Wendy Enelow in 2006 found that 12 per cent of the employers who responded said that they didn't even look at cover letters, however, 39 per cent reported that they believed the cover letter to be 'among the important factors' and a further 7 per cent stated that they considered the cover letter to be 'very important: it can clinch the job'.[1]

What all this means is that, unless you have been specifically told not to include one, it would be unwise not to include a cover letter in your application. You don't know whether the employer you are applying to is one of those who disregards cover letters or one who considers cover letters to be important. It's not worth taking the chance. Also a cover letter gives you an added opportunity to market yourself — so take advantage of it.

Standard cover letters

Cover letters should not be long. Usually three paragraphs containing four or five sentences in all and totalling approximately 150 words is about right. Sharp and succinct is the key. A cover letter should summarise what makes you right for the job, and especially show your motivation.

A note of caution: some employers ask for a cover letter addressing the selection criteria. This is not the sort of cover letter that we are talking about. We will discuss addressing the selection criteria on page 130, later in this chapter.

The letter should be written under the same masthead that you used for your résumé. This ensures that all your documents have the same style and that you are creating for yourself a personal brand.

As for any business letter, write the name and address of the person you are sending the application to and then, beneath that and in bold type, write the position title (including position number if there is one) and then, in brackets, where you saw it advertised. This is how Don Bradley did it:

Don Bradley

Bridlington, SA 5678
08 3462 1792 (h)   08 3460 8879 (w)   0434 220 187 (m)
bradleyd@wellington.sa.gov.au
au.linkedin.com/don_bradley

Tuesday, 20 January 2015

Bernie Conningham
General Manager
Broadhurst Shire Council
PO Box 567
Broadhurst, Vic, 3456

Technical Services Manager (*Western Mail*, 10/01/15)

Use the name of the person to whom you are applying. If this is not mentioned in the advertisement or in the position description, ring up and find out what it is and how to spell it. 'Dear Sir or Madam' is, in my opinion, a big put off. If people write to me but they can't be bothered to find out my name, I usually read no further than the

Dear-Sir-or-Madam bit and bin the letter.

The first paragraph of your cover letter should state your motivation for the job. Forget that old formula, 'I wish to apply for the position of XXX which was advertised in XXX'. That approach is boring — and we want to grab the employer's interest with this paragraph.

Don Bradley applied for the Technical Services Manager position mentioned above. This is how Don wrote his first paragraph:

> Dear Mr Conningham,
>
> I would love to be part of your dynamic, progressive team and I would welcome the opportunity to place a positive stamp on the municipality. I do have vision and drive and I am stimulated by challenge. Here is my application for this exciting position.

Notice how he has used the keywords from the advertisement to show that he does understand what is required and notice how he is not ashamed to say, 'I would love to be a part of your [...] team', a sentence that immediately shouts motivation.

The second paragraph lists as dot points the key skills, experience and qualifications that show how you match the selection criteria. In his cover letter, Don wrote them like this:

> I will bring to the position:
>
> - Twenty years' experience as a graduate civil engineer, including fourteen in local government and the past five in senior management.
> - Excellent human resource management, motivation and leadership skills.
> - Highly developed interpersonal and communication skills.

If the employer reads the cover letter first it will whet his appetite for the rest of the application. In a very short space, Don has outlined why he is right for the job.

The third, and often final, paragraph refers the employer to the résumé and, in this case, to the statement of claims against the selection criteria. Then it mentions a personal quality that is worth emphasising and which might not otherwise be so easily picked up:

> My résumé and statement of claims against the selection criteria will provide details of the relevant skills and achievements that I would bring to the position and an understanding of my determination to complete all projects to high standards, on time and on budget.

If you have anything further that should be covered in the cover letter, a good place to insert it would be immediately before the final paragraph. Linda Heatherton has written an EOI letter for the position of Tour Guide, *The Lord of the Rings/The Hobbit* film locations and we will see more of this letter shortly. An EOI letter usually ends the same way that a normal cover letter would end. However, Linda has inserted an additional paragraph with regards to applying for a P licence (New Zealand passenger licence). This is because the ability to obtain a P licence is listed as an essential requirement for the position. Here are the final two paragraphs of her letter:

> I have researched the requirements for a P licence and I am confident that I would be quickly able to obtain one. I am a good, careful driver and a 'fit and proper person'.

> My résumé gives a more detailed outline of my background and the qualities and qualifications that I would bring to the position and an insight into my bright, cheery, can-do attitude.

Note also how she has mentioned her 'bright, cheery, can-do attitude', which were the words used for one of the highly desirable qualities for the position.

Cover letters that address the selection criteria

Sometimes you may be asked to write a cover letter that addresses the selection criteria. This will mean a document that is not as long as a statement addressing the selection criteria but one that is considerably longer than the 150-word standard cover letters that we have already discussed.

As in the standard cover letter, the first paragraph should indicate why you are interested in the job and what especially attracts you to this position. Write it in the same way you would write the first paragraph of a standard cover letter. Here is what Tom Matlock wrote in response to an advertisement for a Senior Safety Consultant.

Senior Safety Consultant

Dear Tony,

I have enjoyed 12 years' managing OH&S in the RAAF, and I would love to be able to provide effective OH&S policies for Cuthbertson Roofing. I notice that, although risk is inherent in the roofing industry, you have an enviable safety record. I would like to help you maintain that record.

Then, instead of the dot-point list of the 150-word letter, write a paragraph on each of the most important of the selection criteria. Here, again, is what Tom Matlock wrote:

I have developed policies, negotiated with management to change procedures to reduce risk, and run training programs for supervisors, for operative staff and for contractors. I wrote from scratch the OH&S policies and procedures for Messing Services, RAAF Glenbrook, and these now form the basis for OH&S practices for most of the other sections on the base.

My management skills have been developed when I was responsible for eleven facilities providing catering, accommodation and recreational services and through my supervision and coordination of 70 permanent civilian and Defence Force personnel and looking after the requirements of up to 2000 people at peak times.

Through lateral thinking and careful negotiation, I was able to provide alternative transport facilities. I ensured that all personnel on the base were aware of the new transport arrangements and, as a result, I was able to virtually eliminate fuel fraud and the misuse of service vehicles at RAAF Balberra. This has resulted in an annual saving of about $10,000.

He finishes with a typical final paragraph referring to the accompanying résumé followed immediately by 'Yours sincerely'.

My résumé provides further details of the relevant skills and experience that I would bring to the position and an understanding of my determination to do the job properly.

Yours sincerely,

Expression of Interest or EOI letters

An Expression of Interest (EOI) letter is similar to, but not quite the same as, a cover letter addressing the selection criteria. It is a usually a letter introducing yourself, indicating your interest in the organisation and how you could contribute to a particular role or position.

An EOI is often requested for a temporary position but it can also be asked for when an enterprise is recruiting a new team and so is seeking EOIs to pull in skill sets rather than have candidates applying for a specific job.

No specific format is required. However, care must still be taken to grab the employer's interest with the first few lines and then to hold that interest through describing motivation and skills that are relevant to the organisation. The EOI is usually less formal than a full job application, so the employer or a selection panel will not be expecting anything too long. One or two pages are usually sufficient — the important thing is to hold the employer's interest through to the end.

Begin your EOI as you would a standard cover letter, expressing clearly your motivation for the position or, in the case of a prospecting EOI, for the sort of position which you would like. Let's have a look at how Linda Heatherton, applying for the position of Tour Guide with Lord of the Rings Tours, started hers:

LOTR/Hobbit Tour Guide – Expression of Interest

Dear Mrs Carmichael,

I would love to help visitors experience the filming locations for *The Lord of the Rings* and *The Hobbit*. I have a passion for the writings of JRR Tolkien and I loved the way these great books were transformed for the screen.

Then, in the second paragraph, give two, three or four key qualities that would enable you to make a solid contribution to the organisation. Linda has done this with dot points as she might have done in a standard cover letter:

I will bring to the position:

- A thorough knowledge of both books which comes from using them as major texts for secondary English and Drama classes for more than 10 years.

- A commitment to providing the highest possible level of customer service.

- The ability to think on my feet and to solve problems quickly and decisively as they arise; a can-do attitude.

- The people and communication skills to engage and motivate people to participate enthusiastically in the programs that I lead.

Expand on these in subsequent paragraphs; don't go into a lot of detail but the use of an achievement statement for each of the key criteria can be very effective. You will notice that Linda's achievement statements include quite a lot of explanation of how they are relevant to the position. Here are the first three paragraphs of this part of her EOI:

My thorough knowledge of *The Lord of the Rings (LOTR)* comes from reading it at least five times and *The Hobbit* three times just for my own pleasure and from using *LOTR* as a major text for years 9 and 10 English and Drama since filming began in late 1999.

Customer service in the teaching profession means providing excellent teaching service to students and advice to their parents. I have an absolute commitment to both and my success in this area is demonstrated by the excellent rapport I have with both students and their parents.

The best example demonstrating my cheery, can-do attitude and effective problem-solving skills is probably the fact that I have directed the school musical for the past 7 years. This involves staying calm and positive when things go wrong, motivating the 20 or more students in the cast and stage crew, and encouraging rather than chastising them when they make mistakes. It also requires quick thinking to resolve the frequent problems inherent in such a venture.

Make the last paragraph like the final paragraph of a cover letter, mentioning your enclosed résumé. Here is Linda's last paragraph again. Notice how she has picked up the keywords 'bright, cheery, can-do attitude' to confirm that she is the right candidate for the job:

My résumé gives a more detailed outline of my background and the qualities and qualifications that I would bring to the position and an insight into my bright, cheery, can-do attitude.

Yours sincerely,

A prospecting or inquiry letter

Similar to both the EOI and cover letter addressing the selection criteria is a 'prospecting letter'. A prospecting letter can be used when you have identified an organisation which you would like to work for but where you haven't managed to contact anyone personally. It is especially useful if the organisation is a long distance away.

Begin by saying how you found out about the organisation and why you are interested in working there. As with every other job application document, you need to grab the employer's interest with the first few lines, so your motivation for working in that organisation must be shown.

In the middle part of the letter, you could either use the dot-point approach of a cover letter or separate paragraphs describing how you meet each of the main criteria for the sort of position you are seeking.

The next paragraph is the one about the résumé and the key personal quality that you would like to emphasise. Finally, add a closing, one-sentence paragraph saying that you would like to meet with representatives of the organisation to further discuss how you could help the organisation achieve its objectives.

I do not recommend thanking the addressee for taking the time to read the letter — that smacks of job begging. Don't say 'I look forward to meeting you ...' because it sounds presumptuous and would annoy the person reading the letter. Just finish 'I would like to meet with you to discuss how I could help [the organisation achieve its objectives]'.

If you get a response, follow-up immediately with a telephone call or email to arrange a time to meet. If you don't get a reply, follow-up with a phone call about two weeks after sending the letter.

Addressing the selection criteria

Studying the position description and addressing the selection criteria are among the most dreaded tasks facing a job seeker. And it's not easy. It's a fairly long, hard slog, but it's not rocket science and it can be very satisfying. You should get a boost to your morale when you read over your completed statement and see that you have created a convincing document describing your skills and achievements in a really interesting and effective way. It does require hard work but if you break it down into the smaller steps suggested here, you will create a marketing document that you are proud of. If you really want the job, your application needs to be better than everybody else's so you need to be willing to put in the necessary work.

Position descriptions are an extremely valuable source of information for the job seeker and they need to be studied carefully to get the most out of them. This study takes a lot of time and you may well be thinking halfway through the process that you want to get straight into writing the statement. Careful study of the whole document will help you create an application that is effective in conveying your skills to do the job. And it is less work to produce one really successful application and to get the job than to slave away over dozens and not get anything.

To be able to develop an effective application, you need to know what the job is all about. The position description should give you a good understanding of the position but you need to squeeze hard to get out all the information it can give you.

Position descriptions generally have three main parts: the first part usually describes the organisation; the second outlines the key tasks and responsibilities of the position; and the third part, the knowledge, skills and experience required of applicants, in other words the selection criteria.

Some applicants go straight to the selection criteria part and start addressing this section without carefully studying the key tasks section. This is a serious mistake. The key tasks section can provide meaning to the selection criteria. If you notice that one of the key tasks is to liaise with key stakeholders, you can then use examples of your liaising under the criterion (the word 'criterion' comes from the Greek; the singular form is 'criterion' and the plural, is 'criteria'; one criterion, two criteria) on communication skills.

Surprisingly, there are sometimes key tasks and responsibilities that are not reflected in the selection criteria. Unless you make a thorough examination of the key tasks first, you could well leave out of your application any mention of your skills to carry out this key task and responsibility. For instance, there is no mention of financial management skills in the selection criteria for Don Bradley's position. Yet financial management is one of the key responsibilities. Don has demonstrated his financial management skills in a sub-section to his response to criterion 1 (see specimen résumés in the Appendix).

To see how to do this, let us first look at a typical position description. This one is for the position of Chief Executive Officer for a government-funded community organisation. It has been taken from the position description for a real position and it is fairly typical of all position descriptions except in that it has a relatively high number of selection criteria:

POSITION DESCRIPTION
Star Futures Youth Service

Chief Executive Officer

Overview

Star Futures Youth Service is not-for-profit community organisation based in Wangaratta, Victoria with an office in Seymour and delivers services throughout the Rural City area. Star Futures employs fourteen staff, a number of volunteers and has an annual turnover of $800,000.

Star Futures is a dynamic and respected youth service and is financially secure having recently purchased new offices in North

Wangaratta without incurring any debt to the organisation. The organisation is in excellent health in terms of human resources.

The position of Chief Executive Officer is suited to a dynamic, energetic and visionary person with a keen understanding of the challenges facing young people in contemporary culture. The incoming CEO will work in comfortable and well-equipped facilities.

The ideal candidate will have demonstrated experience and knowledge in business and financial management, excellent leadership and people management skills, including effective management and motivation of staff, superior interpersonal and communication skills, both written and oral, along with excellent negotiation, presentation and consultation skills.

The successful candidate will enjoy the many benefits of living in Wangaratta. The Rural City has a population of 26,000, has a temperate climate ideal for outdoor activities, and offers fine food, wineries, native forests, and tranquil waters. Wangaratta is just two-and-a-half hours' drive from Melbourne, and just half-an-hour from Beechworth in Victoria's High Country.

For more information on services provided by Star Futures Youth Service visit: www.starfuturesyouthservice.org.au

Our Vision
A community where all young people have the opportunity to reach their full potential, where all young people are valued, and where families live in harmony.

Our Mission
To stand for opportunity and empowerment for all young people in the context of their families and communities.

Areas of Responsibility

Key responsibilities include:

1. Management, oversight and development of program areas.

2. Human resource management.

3. Management of external relationships and partnerships.

4. Development of the organisation's profile, including promotional strategies.

5. Organisational development and growth.

6. Board reporting and accountability.

7. Financial, business and asset management, including sourcing funding.

8. Implementation of the organisation's Strategic and Business Plans.

9. Maintenance and development of Continuous Quality Improvement processes.

10. Organisational compliance with relevant legislative acts.

Performance Indicators

Performance standards include:

1. Program targets met; funding contractual requirements met; Board reports meet required standards; evidence of program review, evaluation and development.

2. High levels of staff satisfaction; risk management strategies implemented; evidence of professional development across all staffing areas; regular supervision provided to the management/leadership team.

3. Evidence of well-maintained relationships/partnerships with relevant government departments; collaborative partnerships

with other agencies; cultivation of strategic alliances and consortia.

4. Regular, positive media exposure; service/program promotional material maintained to a high standard and appropriately disseminated.

5. Policy review systems implemented and maintained; inter-organisation collaborative program implementation; evidence of continuous quality improvement; sustainable organisational growth.

6. Financial and operational reports provided monthly to the Board; productive and transparent relationship between Board and CEO; strategic plan KPI review provided to the Board quarterly.

7. Budget targets achieved; growth in the future development fund; accounting standards met; financial reporting requirements to funding bodies met; asset management systems implemented and maintained; evidence of funding submissions to government, trusts and community; efficient IT, information management and filing systems.

8. Achievement of KPIs indicated in the organisation's Strategic and Business Plan.

9. Achievement of accreditation as required by government funding bodies; evidence of active continuous quality improvement systems and CQI committee.

10. Evidence of the organisation's compliance with relevant acts and systems ensuring ongoing review and compliance.

The Chief Executive Officer will at all times work within the philosophy, policies and procedures of Star Futures Youth Service.

Accountability and Extent of Authority

The CEO has authority to act within the objectives and policies defined by the Board and the provisions of relevant Acts, regulations, codes, approved arrangements, standards and policies.
The CEO is accountable to the Board for the:

- Effective and efficient management of Star Futures Youth Service's staff and resources and the achievement of the objectives identified in the organisation's Strategic and Business Plan, Annual Budget and other plans where applicable.

- Successful achievement of the annual financial and performance targets identified by the Board in its plans and as required through Funding and Service Agreements.

- Successful establishment of cooperative relationships with key stakeholders including partner organisations, service users, community groups and funding providers.

- Ethical application of procedures.

Key Selection Criteria

1. Understanding of the issues and challenges facing young people in contemporary culture, including the impact of social policy. Ability to engage with and communicate effectively with young people.

2. Demonstrated leadership and motivational skills.

3. A record of success in working effectively with a Board of Management.

4. A proven record at a senior level of policy development, management, strategic and business planning and evaluation within a human services/community services organisation.

5. Highly developed communication and public relations skills.

6. Knowledge of legislation, regulations and the economic and political environments relating to the human services sector.

7. Evidence of successful involvement in change management processes.

8. Proven capacity in budgeting, financial monitoring and reporting to achieve organisational goals.

9. Understanding and commitment to continuous quality improvement and best practice in the human services field.

10. Information Technology skills.

11. Ability to lead, manage, supervise and motivate staff in achieving desired goals.

12. Ability to develop and set objectives, performance and development criteria, targets and establish priorities.

13. Strong, clear and concise interpersonal skills including oral and written report presentation.

14. Negotiation and conflict resolution skills.

15. Understanding of and commitment to contemporary HR principles and practices.

16. A current driver's licence.

17. A full pre-employment security check (including identification, national criminal history check and working with children check) will be required by competitive candidates prior to any offer of employment.

To make sure that you include in your statement all the skills and personal qualities that the employers are looking for, it is important to allocate the key tasks, here called Performance Indicators, and responsibilities, here called Areas of Responsibility, to the criteria that they have listed, here called Key Selection Criteria. An easy way to do this is to take one sheet of paper for each of the selection criteria. Usually there are somewhere between five and eight selection criteria. In this case, there are seventeen criteria, which is quite a number, so seventeen sheets of paper — except you won't need a whole sheet of paper for criteria such as driver's licence and police check.

Write the criterion in full across the top of the page. Then divide the page like this:

3. A record of success in working effectively with a Board of Management.	

The next step is to identify the key tasks and responsibilities that are relevant to this criterion and to write them into the left-hand column like this:

3. A record of success in working effectively with a Board of Management	
Productive and transparent relationship between Board and CEO	

You will find that many of the key tasks are relevant to more than one criterion. In such cases, only write the part of the key task that is relevant to the criterion being looked at.

It is important to make sure that all key tasks and responsibilities are allocated to at least one criterion. If a key task is not allocated to a criterion, it is very likely that you will not think to mention that you have the skills necessary to perform that task.

The third step is to identify events and achievements from your experience that show that you have the ability to carry out the task and do it well. Enter these into the right-hand column. When David Campbell applied for this position, he put '3rd house'. These are the keywords that remind David of his achievement in organising the construction of a third house for the residential care facility that he wants to use to demonstrate how he meets this criterion. You can see the full achievement statement under criterion 3 in David's statement addressing the selection criteria on page 290 in the Appendix.

3. A record of success in working effectively with a Board of Management	
Productive and transparent relationship between Board and CEO	3rd house

Your final statement addressing the selection criteria should be full of achievement statements. If you look through the specimen résumés in the Appendix, you will see how effectively they demonstrate skills and motivation without being too wordy or too boastful.

Once you have completed this step for all of the selection criteria, the next step is start preparing the final document.

Copy across the masthead of your résumé into a new document. Write the position title underneath in the same style that you have used for your name. The visual similarity between your name and the position gives an impression of connectedness, an impression that you are right for the job. This is how David Campbell did it:

David Campbell

149 Cribbes Road
Sudbury Vic 3745
03 5922 3562 (h)
0457 654 927 (m)
david.campbell33@gmail.com

Statement addressing the selection criteria

Chief Executive Officer
Star Futures Youth Services

Underneath this, write the first criterion in full:

Understanding of the issues and challenges facing young people in contemporary culture, including the impact of social policy. Ability to engage with and communicate effectively with young people.

David starts his response to this criterion with a positive statement of claim that he does have the knowledge, skills and experience to meet this criterion:

> Almost seven years as Residential Care Worker, five as Supervisor and three as Group Manager, at Widdicombe Downs Residential Care have given me an excellent understanding of the issues and challenges facing young people in today's culture and developed my ability to engage and communicate with young people.

He then backed up his claim with an achievement statement, a SAO:

- Three weeks ago, counselled a 17-year-old boy who had been suspended from school because of fighting. He had been doing well and was in line for a traineeship but his suspension could jeopardise his chances. He told me that he fought because he was being bullied by a number of students about being in residential care. Explained the situation to the school principal and arranged for details of all the work that he would miss during his suspension to be sent to the group home.

  Helped him learn the material and complete the assignments as well as assisting him to develop strategies for coping with the bullying. The principal also agreed to speak to the students who were bullying him.

  The result is that he is now back at school; he is no longer being bullied, his studies are going well, and he has every likelihood of getting the traineeship.

Because there are a lot of selection criteria for this position, each response needs to be kept fairly short. As a result, David has left his statement of claim to just that one, quite long sentence and one long achievement statement. Sometimes, however, you will find that you need to enlarge on that first sentence of your statement of claim.

Steve Burton, who is applying for the position of Contract Services Manager with a government housing department after a career in the Navy, started his statement of claim in response to the criterion like this:

> Demonstrated experience in contract management, maintenance management and a sound understanding of warehousing freight distribution and operations under a defence contract. My contract management skills were highly developed through my work as Facilities Contract Manager, RAN Allanstown.

He then expanded the statement of claim with more detail:

> In this position, I was responsible for the contract maintenance of the buildings, plant and equipment worth approximately $100 million and I established a reputation for getting things done fast, efficiently and to a very high standard. I supervised maintenance contracts and the contractors performing planned and breakdown maintenance required for the 24/7 operation of the two multi-storey headquarters buildings.

Give sufficient information to allow the employer to form a general impression of your skill level but do not make this paragraph too long. Steve backs up his statement of claim with an achievement statement:

> I proposed, planned and managed a $200,000 contract upgrade of the heating, ventilation and air conditioning (HVAC) chiller control

system at Maritime Headquarters within budget and ahead of schedule. This project made a significant reduction in energy consumption and extended the life of the machinery. For this project, I was awarded the Maritime Commander's Commendation (Admiral's Commendation).

Addressing selection criteria is a lot of hard work and, to do it properly may take you five or six hours, or maybe longer. But if you really want the job that you are applying for, it's worth doing it as thoroughly as you can.

Online applications for each criterion with a strict word limit

A typical online limit for each criterion could be 500 words or even as few as 200. This means that you have to make each word count. Don't work in the online window provided. Instead draft your response in a word-processing program such as MS Word because, in this way, not only will you have an instant word count, but you will also find it much easier to make changes.

Approach each criterion in the same way as you would if you were writing a statement addressing the selection criteria, including the use of achievement statements. Remember that achievement statements are not only more convincing and more interesting than a bare statement of claim but they often require fewer words to get the point across. Write until you feel that you have fully addressed the criterion and then check the word count. If you are over the limit, try to cut the number of words without reducing the impact of what you want to convey. If you are under the limit, consider strengthening the achievement statement(s) that you have used or think about adding another achievement statement. However, avoid the temptation to stuff in more words just to bring it up to the limit. Often 350 words will convey very effectively how you would meet one criterion and the person reading your application is much more likely to be impressed with 350 well-chosen words than 500 words, half of which are waffle.

Once you have created the response that you want, copy and paste it into the relevant online box.

Application forms

Application forms, whether online or on paper, do not make it easy to demonstrate your skills effectively because they are rigid in the way the information is required to be presented. The rigidity is in order to make it easier for Human Resources staff to compare specific information of all applicants. Fortunately, on most application forms, much of the information needed is personal data, contact details and referees. However, if they do ask you to describe your qualifications and competencies for the position, you will need to think carefully about how best to do it.

In order to present your skills on an application form in the most impressive way, it's important to practise. If it's a paper form, make several copies of the blank form and practise completing them so that you do present the reasons why you are right for the position as effectively as possible. Don't try to cram everything into the small space allocated for each particular topic; write legibly and neatly in the normal size you use for handwriting.

If you are required to complete an online form, try saving it as a document on your hard drive to practise with. For online applications, there may be a word limit. The secret is to choose your words carefully in order to be as effective as possible while still fitting the allocated space. Remember while doing this to just focus on the skills and personal qualities that the organisation is looking for.

The last word

Writing these documents is hard work but if the position is worth applying for, it's worth applying for properly. To win the position means putting in a better application than other candidates and that means hard work. If you follow the steps that I have outlined, it is not too difficult.

Once you have written and sent off your application you might think that now all you have to do is wait for the invitation to attend an interview. But that's not the way it works. Start preparing for the interview by further researching the organisation and consider your online presence. Most employer organisations from large to small, when they receive your application, will Google your name to discover how you appear on social media. Creating a positive online presence might therefore be crucial to your success. This is the topic of the next chapter.

WRAP-UP

- Make sure that all documents in your application are of the same great quality as your résumé and are tailored to the position you are applying for. Don't be tempted to omit a cover letter for a posted or email application. Recognise that it's another good opportunity to market your services and to show your motivation.

- These other documents, including statements addressing the selection criteria, require a lot of careful work. However, if the job is one you really want, that careful work is well worthwhile. Remember to always include in your statement all the skills and personal qualities the employers are looking for and make sure each criterion is addressed.

CHAPTER 8

Using social media

Y ou may have heard stories of job applicants who were unsuc-
cessful because of information that employers had found out
about them through looking them up online. This can be a risk but,
on the other hand, social media can be a very big help to you in the
job search. In fact, having a positive and professional online presence
can be a deciding factor in securing an interview.

Social media has advanced rapidly since the first platforms were
launched in 2003. A positive presence on one or more social media
platforms is now seen as extremely beneficial to winning professional,
technical, supervisory or management positions in many sectors of
the workforce. In addition, if employers see that you are using social
media, they will get the impression that you are reasonably IT savvy
and that you are willing to move with the times.

According to a recent blog, there are now more than five million members of LinkedIn in Australia.[1] Membership especially among professional, para-professional and business people is high. If many of the candidates looking for similar jobs to you are on LinkedIn and you are not, you need to consider whether you are putting yourself at a disadvantage.

There are three major advantages to developing a positive social media presence. First, social media allows you to present a lot of background information supporting your applications, information that would help prospective employers see what sort of a person you are and how you would fit into their team. Second, it can be a useful tool for undertaking the all-important research into the organisations you may wish to work for. Thirdly, social media enables you to more easily build a network of contacts within the field where you are hoping to find employment.

ADVANTAGE 1:
Helping prospective employers see what sort of a person you are

Most employers nowadays look online to find out a bit more about candidates who appear to have the potential to be good employees. Organisations are keen to ensure that the people they hire will fit into their team and the organisation's culture. If you have a social media presence which indicates that you are likely to be a good 'fit' with the organisation, there is a good chance that you will be invited for an interview. If, on the other hand, employers cannot find anything about you online, they may well disregard your application.

Your profile on social media is not an online résumé. Your résumé demonstrates how you meet the needs of a specific position and it enables the employer to envisage how you would perform in the job. Your online presence allows the employer to envisage how you would fit into the organisation. While your résumé shows what you can do, your social media profile shows what sort of a person you are.

Posting photos on Facebook describing a holiday travelling through South-East Asia or Europe can tell an employer a lot about you. Assume that you are an employer and you have advertised a position. Two applicants have very similar qualifications for the job and now you want to see how each would fit into the organisation. One of the applicants does not have an online presence but the other does. Her social media pages include some photos of her sporting, social and leisure interests. These pages create a positive picture of her in your mind and you may well select her in front of the candidate with similar qualifications and experience but with no social media presence. If the employer finds you interesting, he is more likely to employ you than someone he knows very little about.

ADVANTAGE 2:
Undertaking research into your target organisations

If you are considering yourself to be self-employed, the CEO of Yourself Pty Ltd, as discussed in Chapter 1, and you are looking for 'clients', you cannot afford to skimp on market research. The more you know about an organisation, the better you can tailor your application.

Social media is a wonderful resource for helping you research target employer organisations. After reading carefully all you can find on the organisation's website, including its annual report, look to see if the organisation is also on Facebook or Twitter or other social media platforms. If so, go to those sites and look through them. They may give you a picture of the organisation that is slightly different to the one you got from their main website. If you then interact with the organisation by 'liking' it on Facebook or following it on Twitter, you will then be on the organisation's 'mailing list' and receive all their latest posts. This will keep you up-to-date with what is happening and the most recent developments, which is invaluable information for your market research and very useful for preparing answers to possible interview questions.

Some organisations on social media provide an opportunity for comments from members of the public. Some comments may be positive but some may be negative and it's useful to be able to see the 'warts and all' picture of an organisation.

If on Twitter you enter your chosen occupation in the search button, you will get a list of names of organisations, groups and individuals related to that occupation. This then gives you the opportunity to research these names and to select a few to follow. And once you are following a person or a group, you can join in their conversations, make comments and so become known and respected for your knowledge and ideas.

LinkedIn has a Companies tab and this leads to more information written not by the organisation itself but by LinkedIn members. The information is often fairly brief but, much more important, it provides a list of LinkedIn members who are currently employed at that organisation or who have been employed there in the past.

ADVANTAGE 3:
Building a network of contacts

Building a face-to-face network is the subject of Chapter 9, but this process can be greatly helped by having an online network as well. Your online connections can help you find prospective members for your face-to-face network.

LinkedIn is an excellent resource for building your online network. It gives you the opportunity to look at the profiles of '2nd level connections', that is those people who share connections with you, or in other words people who know people whom you know. Using LinkedIn, you can contact these 2nd level connections and invite them to connect with you.

You can also connect with other people on the LinkedIn list of people in the selected organisation, people who are not 2nd level connections. However, at the time of writing, you are not able to look at their profiles and so it would be difficult to know how they would be able to help you.

Anyone you invite to connect with you, whether 2nd level connection or not, will almost certainly check your profile before accepting your invitation and, if what they see there is professional and positive, they are likely to accept. Once you are connected, you can then start a dialogue with them and so gain valuable insights into the organisation. Your communication with these people may be restricted to emails or InMails (communications using LinkedIn) but, if they live or work locally, you will be able to invite them to have a coffee with you and so develop a face-to-face relationship.

Face-to-face meetings are more effective than 'virtual' meetings on social media and you should make every effort to build your relationship with these new connections to the extent that you can email them, then telephone and hopefully meet face-to-face. It is important not to allow yourself to be tempted to spend too long on the computer instead of going out and meeting someone in person. For this reason I suggest that you restrict your time on social media to an average of one hour a day.

Taking part in professional discussion groups on LinkedIn or tweeting and re-tweeting on Twitter are also good ways of building an online network. I have received a number of invitations to connect from some well-known and highly regarded career practitioners from not only Australia but from around the world who have read and agreed with comments that I have made in this sort of discussion.

How to create a social media presence

Create a profile in each platform that you intend to use. In Chapter 3, I recommended that you not use a photo in your résumé but I strongly recommend that you use a good photo on your social media platforms, a photo that shows you in a way that you would like prospective employers to see you.

The LinkedIn profile is professional in nature and is designed to show your career history but, even with LinkedIn, you can show some of your outside interests. Include any roles you may have had with Lions or Rotary or other service clubs, the voluntary work you may have done for a charity or the local men's shed or church. If you have been the treasurer for a dancing club, or coach for a sports team, put this in because this sort of role demonstrates interpersonal skills, commitment, reliability and a bit of get-up-and-go. The employer is thus likely to get the idea that you are the sort of person who could have a positive influence on the team.

Include photos of your interests, activities and projects on Facebook or Instagram. Photos of you sailing, or bushwalking, or working on a Rotary project all help to give prospective employers an all-round picture of who you are and enable them to see how you would fit into their team. Instead of being an unfamiliar applicant, only known by the information given in your written application, you can be seen as a whole person, someone with a life and interests and someone who would be interesting to talk to.

How to clean up your online image

If you are concerned that there might be material on social media that could jeopardise your chances of getting that new job, you need to clean up your social media sites. Delete any photos or comments that you would not like to see on the front page of the local newspaper. If there are photos which could embarrass you and which are tagged with your name on other people's sites, ask if they would consider removing the photos or comments or, at least, removing the tags. And, if you are not successful in getting all embarrassing material removed, 'bury' it; put so much new, positive material up that the older, more embarrassing material only shows up after an exhaustive search, which most employers would be unlikely to do. Once they have seen some of the positive information that you have posted on your site or sites, most of them would be unlikely to continue searching until they find something not so good.

Keeping in touch with your support network

You can use social media to keep your support network up-to-date with your progress. This support network includes your family and friends, the 'Board' of Yourself Pty Ltd, (the concept of creating a 'Board of Directors' to support you through the job search is discussed in Chapter 10) and all those who most want to support you through the job search process.

If you choose to use a platform like Facebook to keep a daily log of what you have achieved in the job search each day, your family and friends who are active on social media will be able to keep up-to-date with your progress. When they know how you are faring, they are much better placed to provide the support you need.

People like to help people who are making an effort and by showing the effort that you are making towards getting a new job, you will be encouraging your support network and any others who see your posts to assist you. They will see that you are serious and that you are worth helping.

However, if you are currently employed and you don't want your employer to know that you are seeking another position, unless you have set tight security settings, you may need to find another way to keep your support network informed.

Without tight security, what you post online can be read by anybody — including prospective employers! This may not be a problem as long as everything you write is positive. Never say anything derogatory about anyone because the remark could come back to bite you. Keeping a record of your job search progress on a site like Facebook is almost like having it published in the local newspaper.

If you had an interview with someone who was hostile and would not listen to what you had to say, do not post that he is an idiot or a pig. Remember that he may be well respected by others in the industry. You could say instead that you had a challenging meeting with a marketing person. Never mention the name of an individual or an organisation in your posts unless you have their permission to do so. You can say how you could have handled the meeting better. That would show that you are working on improving your job search skills, that you are resilient and that you are learning to overcome obstacles. Your support network will want to help you and so will appreciate the update and, should someone from a prospective employer organisation come across your post — and this is always a possibility that you need to keep in mind — they may well be impressed by your tenacity.

Another, possibly safer, method of keeping your support network up-to-date with your progress is to send a regular email bulletin to all members of your support network. This will keep you in the front of their minds and enable and encourage them to give you advice and support when you need it most. And neither your current nor your prospective employers will know anything about it.

WRAP-UP

■ To be successful in gaining employment in many fields today, it is necessary to develop a social media presence. Increasingly, employers Google candidates' names to try to find out how they would fit into the organisation's team.

■ Take a proactive approach and make sure that your online profile is professional and demonstrates the qualities that you believe employers would most want to see. Also, through using social media, you can research possible employer organisations and get to know key people there and so build a network of contacts.

- By using social media, you can demonstrate that you are up with the times and confident using technology. The activities you show on social media provide a clear picture of who you are and how you would fit into an organisation.

CHAPTER 9

Networking and research

Once you have identified the career path you want to follow, developed your marketing materials — your résumé — and learnt how to build your online presence and create an online network through social media, it's time to get out onto the road and start creating a network of people you can meet face-to-face or at least over the phone who can help you to find and win the sort of job you are seeking.

You may already have an extensive network of colleagues, clients and/or suppliers from your previous jobs. Hopefully some of these people will be relevant to your new, specific, job search network. If this is the case, you're in luck. If, however, you are changing career direction or moving to a different geographic location, you might have to start from scratch. Whatever the case, it is likely that you will have to add people currently unknown to you to your network as your job search progresses.

Networking is not an 'optional extra'

Whether you like it or not, networking is essential to not only job search success but also to your future career success. Adelina Chalmers, a guest lecturer at Cambridge University's Judge Business School, wrote: 'You should consider networking as a long term investment in your business/life/career where the key purpose is to build meaningful, mutually beneficial relationships with other people.' She quotes American business philosopher Jim Rohn, who said: 'Your net-worth is your network.'[1] You might consider that to be a slight exaggeration but you are certainly more likely to be viewed favourably by a potential employer if you become known by people working for that organisation. You will have insider information that will put you streets ahead of those who don't have that information and you will have people on the inside who can speak well of you.

Even if you have found an advertised position, networking will greatly enhance your prospects of winning the position. Getting in touch with the contact person mentioned in the ad is the barest minimum; failure to do so can lead to your application not being considered simply because you haven't taken the trouble to make that contact. And, if you want to make a good first impression, before you make contact, (1) research the organisation, and (2) prepare a list of questions that you want to ask.

But if you really want to improve the likelihood of winning that job, you should take your networking a lot further than that; see if you can find someone who works in that same organisation through your existing contacts or through using LinkedIn. Telephone to set up a meeting — an information interview — and prepare for that interview using the processes described in this chapter and the next. Not only will you be seen by the employer organisation as someone who is motivated, but the information and advice that you receive through the interview will boost your confidence as well as helping you tailor your application and answers to job interview questions more closely to the position. (The terms information interview and network interview are virtually synonymous. Both terms are used to describe interviews for which the objectives are to build your network and to gain information that would be useful in helping you find and win the sort of job you are seeking. In this book, the term 'information interview' is used.)

However, in good networking the quality of your interviews is more important than the number you do. Your aim is to get your informants to like you and to want to supply the information and advice which you need. To make this happen, each interview needs to be carefully prepared and this takes time. Trying to undertake too many interviews in a short period of time could mean that the quality of each interview is jeopardised. Unless you are very confident, start with just one interview per week. This should allow it to be very well prepared and therefore achieve the results you want. Then, as you get more experienced, you could increase this to two or more a week. Remember that quality beats quantity every time.

What is a network?

A network in this instance comprises the people who can help you find out about and win a good job. This is your job search network. Once you have the job, you should continue to collaborate with members of your network so that you can help them in their careers. Then they, in turn, will still be there to assist you in your next career progression. So, what started as your job search network becomes your career development network.

Networking can be described as developing long-term relationships for mutual gain. As long as you demonstrate that you are someone worth knowing, the people you network with will not see you as imposing on them.

When you are setting up an information interview, you must have that mutual advantage in mind. It is quite possible that in the future some of your contacts will, in their turn, seek your help. By showing at the outset that you are ready and able to offer assistance, you will create a lasting impression with them so that they think of you positively and will speak of you positively when an opportunity arises.

Recruitment firms

Recruitment firms can be useful in helping you find the position that you want. However, you need to be aware that recruitment firms are agents for employer organisations and not for you. It is the employers who pay them and it is with the employers that their first loyalties lie.

Select two or three recruitment firms that cover the industry or occupation that you want to work in. Research the firms thoroughly and, once you have the name of someone in that firm, find out all you can about her. Then establish a good rapport with her and treat her as a member of your job search network. This means making contact with her at least once every two weeks. Invite her out for a coffee every so often so that, to her, you become more than a name on her books; you become someone with initiative and drive, someone who is motivated to get ahead. She will want to find a position for you fairly quickly because she will realise that you are someone who is going to get a good job anyway and she might as well try to get her commission for putting your name forward. Keep the relationship going once you get your job because you may be able to help her in the future and she may be able to help you if, in your new position, you need to recruit and select someone or if, for some reason, your newfound employment eventually comes to an end.

If you are an introvert

Introverts are people who prefer to think before they act, people who prefer to have a few close relationships rather than a large number of casual contacts. However, these behaviours are just preferences: according to the Myers & Briggs Foundation, everyone spends some time acting as an extrovert and some time acting as an introvert.[2]

There is nothing wrong with being an introvert. In fact, research has shown that introversion increases with intelligence.[3] Regrettably, that on its own doesn't make it any easier for an introvert to go out and network. If you are an introvert, here are some strategies that you might like to consider to make networking less of an ordeal.

In the structured networking process that I am suggesting, you will only be talking with one person at a time. To make it easier when you first meet the person face-to-face, find out as much as possible about her and about her organisation before telephoning to set up a meeting. Try to see the world from her perspective; envisage what you think her goals and motivations might be and how you think she might view you. If you can find her on LinkedIn, see what discussion groups she belongs to and join one or two of those groups. The discussions will help you develop a good understanding of her interests and provide you with topics to talk about. It may even stimulate you to send her an email, which some find a good way to break the ice and ease into a relationship.

Information interviews: what are you going to talk about?

Before setting up an information interview, you need to plan your questions. The purpose of these is to get the information you need to start planning your first few weeks in the sort of job you are targeting (a time when you are finding your feet, getting to know your colleagues and becoming productive in the position). Obviously, you won't get sufficient understanding from one interview to be able to create such a plan. In fact, there will probably still be gaps in your knowledge after interviews with several different people. But the more detailed your knowledge and understanding of the industry and, later, a particular enterprise, the better you will be able to prepare a well-tailored résumé and to go into an eventual job interview with the confidence that will show that you're going to hit the ground running. If you have established a network within an organisation and if, as a result, you have detailed knowledge of the organisation and possible positions that you may be seeking, you will have a significant competitive advantage over other applicants who have not been as thorough as you.

There are five topics or areas of information that you need to cover over a series of information interviews. While working out the questions to ask, keep in mind the information that you need to create the plan of your first few weeks. The five topics are:

1. **The work: the tasks and responsibilities of the job
   — what your informant does from when she first gets
   in until she knocks off, the best bits and the worst, the
   chain of command, what the boss is like, the corporate
   culture. What resources does she have? Who does she
   work with? Who does she report to?**

2. The prospects: the prospects for the industry — is it likely to continue for some time into the future or is it at risk of competition from overseas or technological change? The prospects for the company — is it growing or in financial stress? A target for a take-over or merger? The prospects for the position — would it survive a restructure? And, finally, the prospects for the way you want your career to progress should you get this sort of job — would it help you to achieve your career and personal goals?

3. The knowledge, skills, qualifications and experience required for the position: what are the employers looking for?

4. Possible job openings now or in the near future, in this organisation or another in the same industry.

5. Referrals: 'Is there anyone else you would suggest that I contact to get further information?'

To start with, your interviews may be across several enterprises or organisations within your chosen industry. In your interviews with the first two, three or maybe more informants, you would be advised to stick to asking questions about the first topic, the work, and, at the end of each interview, requesting a referral. It's a great help when first contacting someone new to be able to say, 'Stephanie Palmer suggested that I contact you.' If your new contact knows and respects Stephanie, he will expect you to be someone worth talking to.

Once you have a good understanding of the work involved, and provided that you are still just as keen to win this sort of job, you can start asking questions on the second topic, regarding the prospects. You need to be confident that this sort of position is likely to last a reasonable length of time and that it would help you achieve your personal and career goals. If this information satisfies you and you are getting excited about the possibilities of such a job, you need to find out what key things employers are looking for in applicants for that sort of work so that, when the time comes, you can more finely tune your résumé and application to their needs. This is the third area of questioning.

The fourth topic, possible job openings, is one that needs a bit of care. You will have told your informants that you are not asking them for a job. This is important because no one is going to offer you a job until they have developed a good idea of how you would fit into their team. But, if you are not asking them for a job and suddenly you ask if there are any job openings coming up, it can seem as if you are breaking your word — and this is not likely to win you any favours! Integrity is essential. So, be careful and say something like, 'I told you that I was not asking you for a job and I'm not. But what you have told me has helped confirm that this is an area where I would love to work, so I am wondering whether you know of any possible openings that might be coming up in the near future, either here or in other organisations.'

The fifth and final type of question you will ask, preferably at the end of every information interview, is for a referral.

To start planning your questions, imagine that on Monday you are going to start in the sort of job you are seeking. What would you need to know beforehand? You will be able to find the KPIs (Key Performance Indicators) from the position description for a similar job. You can often find a similar position on an online jobs board or on a company website. Sometimes you will find the KPIs in the text of the ad but sometimes you may have to download a position description.

In Chapter 8, we looked at how social media and the internet can be used to research industries, organisations, specific positions and some of the key people you would like to talk to. An organisation's website may include a press release page and an annual report. Also look for brochures, advertisements and newspaper or journal articles. These can all give you a good background picture of an organisation and help you to start envisaging what it would be like to work there. With this minimal information, start trying to envisage what you would be doing on Monday. What would your main tasks be? Who would you be working with? This envisaging, while based on insufficient evidence, is a good start to planning those first few weeks in the job and to guiding you in planning your questions.

To gather your information, use a good quality A4 compendium with no zip. Write your questions onto the pad leaving plenty of space for answers. Using a compendium this way has a number of advantages: it looks efficient because it is efficient; you ask the questions you need to ask; and, if you are feeling a bit apprehensive, it will give you added confidence. The compendium will also be useful when you attend a job interview.

How to identify a possible contact

If you are interested in discovering employment opportunities in an organisation and you don't know anybody who works there, you will need to ask around to see if there is anyone who might know someone there. This could be through colleagues, friends and neighbours or through attending a meeting of a professional association.

Some organisations have a staff profile page on their website. Or you can find contacts in an organisation through LinkedIn. Enter the name of the organisation in the LinkedIn 'Search for people, jobs, companies and more' button on the tool bar at the top of the screen and you will get a list of people in the organisation who are connected directly or indirectly to you or your contacts on LinkedIn. From there, you can see their profiles and invite them to connect with you.

Once you have a name, find out as much as possible about that person. If he's not on LinkedIn, his employer's website is a good place to start. Another possible source of information is to look through press releases displayed on the website. Google the name and you may be rewarded with referrals to articles written by him or mentioning him or to other social media sites where he may have a profile.

If you join all the online discussion groups relevant to the position you are seeking, you may find a comment by him there. If so, join in the conversation by making a comment yourself. This can help considerably in breaking the ice and it also demonstrates your keen interest in the area.

If you can't find out anything about the person, and that is quite possible, don't worry. You will still be able to show interest in him by asking about him and his work.

Planning the first phone call

Now that you have planned the questions you want to ask and identified the person you want to contact, the next step is to contact him. If you have been able to establish some sort of online connection with him, so much the better. In this case, you might feel confident to send an email to ask him if he would like to join you for a coffee.

However, if it's someone you have not made contact with before, probably the surest way to get the results you want is through a telephone call. Letters can easily be binned and emails deleted but it's harder to put the phone down on someone who is polite and asking reasonable questions — especially if you have a connection in common.

Some people dread making this first phone call but it's not that difficult if you plan it out beforehand. To plan your first phone call, I suggest that you use a communication planner like the one below (blank PDF communication planners are available to download for free from www.jobwinnersguides.com). In this example, Kevin Drew is trying to contact the Production Manager at Bulls Eye Bearings, whose name he does not yet know.

Name		Tel 1 9551 5432
Organisation Bulls Eye Bearings		Tel 2
Position		Mobile
Address 413 Cotterslea Road		Email
Town Glenfield	P/code 0629	Receptionist's name Tricia
Subject		Response
Introduce myself		
Name of Production Manager		
Reason for call		
Key skills spiel		
Ask for meeting		

Note the box for the receptionist's name. The receptionist is a hub of communication and in order to establish a good rapport with her, it is important to know and use her name. Write it in the box as soon as you know it. By the same token, it is important that you introduce yourself to her. If you establish a good rapport with her, she can open a lot of doors for you. If you don't, she won't.

If you don't know the name of the person you want to speak to, it is important to ask the receptionist for the name. When she gives you the name, she may ask if you want to be put through immediately. It is sometimes best to ask what would be the most convenient time to call and then to ring back at that time. This will give the receptionist a chance to let your informant know to expect a call from you and this can be of benefit to you. If he doesn't want to talk to you, he will ask her to tell you that he is busy. In this way, you won't have put him offside. If, on the other hand, he is prepared to talk to you, your call won't come as a complete surprise. The ice will be broken.

It is to be expected that the receptionist would ask what you want to talk about. That is part of her role of protecting her employer from nuisance calls. It is essential that you are honest but you don't want to give the impression that you are seeking employment which, in fact, you are not yet doing. Just say, 'I am seeking some information and advice.'

When you do get through to the person you want to talk to, get to the point quickly. Give the reason for your call and then use your key skills spiel, which we discussed at the end of Chapter 6. Kevin's goes like this: 'I have been working in the production of machine tools for a number of years. You may have heard of the Spoode cam system. I was part of the engineering team that designed and managed that project. Now I am at a career crossroad and I am very

interested in learning something about the processes you use to man-
ufacture precision bearings and to assess whether a move into this
field would help my career. I should add that I am not asking for a
job. At this stage, what I need is information and advice to help me
make a decision.'

Kevin's statement is a bit of a mixture of what he wants to get out
of the meeting and sufficient background information in the key skills
spiel to whet the Production Manager's interest. That's fine. You
know your key skills spiel and you know what you are asking for. Put
the two together in the way that is most comfortable for you.

Asking for the meeting

As soon as you have given your key skills spiel, ask for a 20-minute
meeting. Have confidence you are worth talking to. Kevin Drew simply asked, 'Would you be able to spare me twenty minutes to give me
some information and advice?' (Performing well at information and
job interviews is further explored in Chapter 11.)

'There aren't any jobs here'

In spite of your saying that you are not asking for a job, it is always
possible that your informant will jump to the conclusion that you are.
If he replies that there aren't any jobs at the moment, you can reply:
'That's all right. I'm not seeking a job just yet. What I would like is
some advice and information so that I can start planning my next
steps. Because you are working in the field I'm interested in, the information you could give me would be very useful to me. Would it be
possible to meet sometime next week?'

What to do if they say 'No'

It happens. Some people are too busy and some others are just reluctant to talk to anybody they don't know.

When it happens, accept it with good grace. Remember that your primary aim is to get employers to like you. If your informant seems very reluctant, ask if instead he could suggest somebody else you could talk to, to get the information that you need. And thank him for taking the time to talk to you on the phone. He may be reluctant today but once you have interviewed a few people in his organisation or industry, he may get to hear good stories about you and want to talk to you himself.

This is because every team worth its salt is always on the lookout for new talent. If he later hears that you are someone with get-up-and-go as well as having the qualifications and experience needed, he would probably prefer to have you working on his team than working for the competition. People are generally willing to help others they see as worthwhile, and organisations are always seeking new people with motivation and team skills, so don't feel that you are imposing on others by asking to meet with them. If you were an employer with a possible opening and someone had the initiative to come and see you and to ask intelligent questions, you would probably prefer to employ that person rather than advertise the position, go through dozens of applications and then interview a whole lot of people you had never met.

Building your network

The key to building your network is to get the people you interview to like you and therefore to want to help you. If your informants like and respect you, they are likely to give you referrals to other people.

Suppose that you have identified someone who is likely to have useful information. We'll call him Alan. You phone him, set up an appointment and then go and interview him. Because you are well prepared and ask sensible questions, he likes you and he refers you to a colleague, Becky, who may be able to give you more information.

After the meeting, you write a thank-you note. Then you call Becky and make an appointment with her and then have an interview with her. Once again, you are well prepared and Becky likes you and she refers you on to another colleague of hers, Craig.

You send a thank-you note to Becky and an email to Alan thanking him once again for the referral to Becky and telling him how the interview went. After your meeting with Craig, you could well send Alan an email to let him know how you are progressing and he might think of another person you might want to contact.

You should be in touch with each member of your job search network regularly, preferably at least once a fortnight. Sometimes, of course, you will talk to one or more members of your network several times in a single day. But the important thing is that you keep all members of the network up-to-date with progress, and you involve all relevant members of the network in discussing issues that occur in the job search.

In the course of your job search, some of your earlier contacts may cease to be as relevant, and therefore less able to actively help you than they were at the beginning. However, don't abandon them. They did help you and they might be able to help you in the future, so keep them in the loop. Email a progress report perhaps once a month or so and certainly let them know once you have scored that sought-after position.

WRAP-UP

- Many job seekers dread networking and information interviews. However, these are an essential part of a successful job search and they need to be done. If you interview well, for information as well as employment, you will quickly gain confidence and start to enjoy the interview process.

- The more thoroughly you have researched the organisation and, if it is possible, the informant you are going to interview, the more confident you will feel. Thorough research before each meeting will enable you to ask intelligent questions and to understand your informant's answers. This preparation will also ensure that your informant does not consider the time required for the meeting to be time wasted and he will be impressed by the motivation that you have shown in the thoroughness of your research.

- Many people dread that first phone call to an informant. Careful planning and a bit of determination builds confidence and most people are soon able to tackle these calls with assurance and even enjoyment.

CHAPTER 10

Building and maintaining a positive self-image

Self-confidence and self-esteem are essential to job search success. If a job seeker doesn't have the confidence he could do the job, how is he going to convince the employer? In this chapter, we explore practical strategies for maintaining self-confidence and self-esteem. Job seekers are all different and all have different needs; some may need to use all the strategies suggested to build a positive self-image, while others may not. I recommend that you read the chapter before deciding which strategies you will use, so that you have a knowledge of those available to choose from.

Envisage success

'Success breeds success' as the saying goes. The more someone experiences success, the more that person tends to be successful. Some sports coaches say that winning becomes a habit. Each win builds confidence and with confidence comes the ability to succeed in ever bigger challenges.

To be successful, you need to see yourself being successful. What we see is what we get. The mind is a powerful influencer, as anyone who has an interest in elite sports knows. This is why teams use sports psychologists.

Success in the job search requires us to see ourselves being successful; successful in the job search, successful in the interview and successful in the job itself. The research that you have already done and the planning of your first few weeks in the job will help enormously in this regard. Just by running through that plan in your mind will help you see yourself being successful in the job and this will boost your confidence accordingly.

In order to maintain belief in your success in the job hunt, make sure that you record the progress you make each day and that you 'celebrate' each little success, reward yourself for undertaking a task that made you feel nervous, an information interview for example, and for doing it well.

Dress for success

One strategy that is essential is to dress for success. If you want a job in marketing or tour guiding, dress as if you already had the job. This is especially important for interviews, both information and employment, but it is also effective if you are dressed to the same code every time you are in public simply because of the way other people will react to you. If you are dressed as a marketing executive or a tour guide, others will see you as a marketing executive or tour guide and will treat you accordingly. This, in turn, will help feed your confidence in your ability to do the job.

Some years ago, I watched a top telephone salesperson presenting on a training video. Before lifting the phone to make a call, he always checked that his tie was straight because knowing his tie was straight gave him confidence. That may not apply to everyone but it certainly boosts your confidence if you look the part.

One of the best ways to find out about the dress code in the organisation you are researching or where you are being interviewed for a job is to visit the organisation beforehand — a reconnaissance visit (see Chapter 11).

Be fit and healthy

Maintaining good health is important. The job search can be a very challenging time and to successfully meet that challenge, you need to be able to perform at your peak. What you eat is an important component in keeping fit. When stressed, some people compensate by eating unhealthy snacks. This does not help you achieve peak performance, so resist the temptation.

The Victorian Government's website 'Better Health Channel' states that good diet and good nutrition can enhance sporting performance.[1] It can also enhance your performance in the job hunt. Make sure that you have a varied, healthy diet to sustain your energy and feeling of wellbeing. This, in turn, will help to maintain your positive self-image and self-confidence.

Make time during the whole job search process to get some aerobic exercise. Half an hour each day is very beneficial. If you regularly do some aerobic exercises, you will develop a healthier and stronger body. Physical fitness gives a significant boost to self-confidence.

Stand tall, walk tall

Maintaining good posture is another way to boost your self-confidence. A study by Pablo Brinol and others, published in the *European Journal of Social Psychology*, found that posture had a marked effect on confidence.[2] An earlier study in 1982 by John Riskind and Carolyn Gotay found that 'subjects who were placed in a slumped, depressed physical posture later appeared to develop helplessness more readily than did subjects placed in an expansive, upright posture'.[3] So, the message is to stand tall and sit up straight as well. Make it a habit and keep your self-confidence high.

Walking briskly with your head up and shoulders straight can also have a similar result; people who feel confident tend to move in an energetic way and, through emulating them and walking a little more briskly, you will start to believe in yourself more strongly.

Promote the 'feel good' neurotransmitters

Clinical research has shown that happiness and a sense of wellbeing are important ingredients in success and that serotonin, a 'feel good' neurotransmitter, is widely considered to be a contributor to this sense of wellbeing.[4,5]

Simon Young, Professor of Psychiatry at McGill University in Canada, has identified practical and natural ways to increase serotonin in our brains and, in this way, improve our level of happiness and confidence. These include being in bright light and remembering happy events as well as exercise and diet.[6]

We can expose ourselves to bright light by walking outside. We all know how good we feel when first going out into the sunshine and this is because of the serotonin the sunshine stimulates in our bodies. Even if the sun is not shining, the light is usually brighter outside than it is indoors. So, get out and get walking.

Endorphins are the other 'feel good' neurotransmitters. These are released into the body by physical exercise and by smiling and laughter.

Laughter

Smiling and laughter are important to our sense of wellbeing and, therefore, to our self-confidence. Smiling is good for our health, it improves our mood and it can help increase the likelihood of success according to US health and fitness enthusiast and author Charlie Pulsipher.[7]

Laughter has been proven to be very effective in improving our physical, emotional and social wellbeing. Therefore it should be an important component of our job search strategy. Laughter decreases stress, increases the production of serotonin and endorphins and boosts blood flow.[8] Laughter and smiling can also help to make us look younger. The facial muscles that work together to make us laugh or smile increase the blood flow around the face and this can make us look younger and healthier.

So, make sure that humour is part of your daily routine. This can be achieved by making time to swap jokes with friends, by going to see a comedy at the movies or a stand-up comedian. If you are on your own, tuck a good cartoon in your job search file and when you need a boost, take a look at it. Part of the routine of a successful Job Club program that I ran was to start each day with a fifteen-minute joke swapping session. The laughter eased tensions and made participants open and ready to receive new ideas and gave them the confidence to carry them out.

Relationships are important

It is important to look after your relationships with those closest to you. Career transitions and joblessness do cause stress and frequently put strain on relationships.

To minimise the risk of your relationships suffering involve those closest to you in your job search. Tell them about your plans and your progress. Discuss issues. Ask for opinions and advice. With this will come support. You might consider creating a 'Board of Directors' for your 'micro-business' (see chapters 1 and 9) and appointing your partner, family and some close friends to it. This 'Board' is not the job search network we discussed in Chapter 9. The 'Board' is your support network and consists of just close family and friends, the people best placed to provide you with the encouragement and support necessary to keep you performing at your best.

Schedule regular, perhaps weekly, meetings over a coffee or a meal with all or some 'Board' members to discuss progress, hurdles that need to be overcome, issues and possible options.

When you need special help or advice, discuss the problem with one or more of your 'Board' members. It is much easier to manage an effective job search campaign when you have support from the people you care about and trust.

Collaborate with other job seekers

It can also be incredibly helpful to find other people who are looking for work and to collaborate with them. Not only will you be sharing your experiences, your successes and failures with them, and they with you, but you will be encouraging each other and providing that motivation and determination to succeed. Also, through helping, advising and counselling others, you will be further developing your own job search skills and you will be achieving great things for your own self-esteem. You may not decide to appoint these people to your 'Board' but they can certainly be collaborators.

Even if there are two of you going for the same job, don't stint on helping each other. You would both be happier if one of you gets the position rather than if it goes to someone else entirely. There is the chance that, if you both put in outstanding applications, the employer will create a second position and employ you both. If you were the employer and you had two great candidates for the one position, would you prefer to see one of those good candidates working for the competition or would you rather have him or her on your team? Yes, extra positions are created for exceptional applicants — not every time, certainly, but often enough for this to be considered a possibility.

And, very important, if you get a job before your job-seeker friend, don't stop helping. Stay in there providing support until he or she too has a job.

Volunteering

Another strategy to boost your feelings of self-worth is to volunteer. This gives you a sense of purpose and the self-esteem that comes from having a positive and valued role in the community. Helping others makes you feel good about yourself and significantly boosts your morale. Find a cause that you are passionate about so that you get not only great satisfaction but also immense pleasure. Getting pleasure from your voluntary work may be particularly important during the job search, which has limited opportunity in itself to provide that pleasure.

The risk of rejection

The risk that many people fear most in the job search is the risk of rejection. You face the risk of rejection when you telephone to set up an information interview. If you don't take that risk, the information interview will not happen and you have no chance of establishing a possibly beneficial relationship and building your network. It is important both for the effectiveness of your job search and for your self-esteem that you are proactive. Don't be afraid of taking risks. Almost certainly you will contact people with whom you don't get along, people who are not as helpful as you would have wished. That's life. But there are also people out there who would enjoy helping you in the job search and you need to find these people and contact them. And, when you do, you will find a lot of comfort and pleasure in their company.

One of the hardest blows to bear is rejection after a job interview. You have worked so hard to get that interview and now it seems as if it was all for nothing. To counter this feeling of rejection, once the interview is over write that job lead off because there is nothing further that you can do to progress it. Then find another job lead or prospect to take its place. Always have a minimum of two job leads on the go at once so that, when you do get a knockback, you can say to yourself, 'That's all right. I still have two job leads that I'm working on.'

As we said in Chapter 1, however, don't have too many job leads. Two or three is about the right number. With two or three, you can put sufficient energy, research and networking into each one to ensure a really good application performance.

WRAP-UP

- The job search process can be a difficult and depressing one. It is unlikely that you will get the first job that you go for and you may get a number of rejections before you win a good job. Each rejection hurts and it knocks your self-confidence, however, self-confidence is essential to persuading employers that you are the right person for the job. Therefore envisage success, dress as if you already had the job, be fit and healthy, and do whatever it takes to maintain that important positive self-image.

- Be determined that you are going to be successful, that you are going to get satisfaction from the job search and that you are going to take care to maintain your relationships with family and friends. Invite family and friends to support you during the job search and keep them informed of your progress. Collaborate with other job seekers or perhaps volunteer for a cause or organisation that you believe in because, through helping others, you will build your self-esteem and self-confidence. Look for ways to find enjoyment, keep a record of your achievements and find things that make you laugh.

CHAPTER 11

Performing well in information and job interviews

Interviews are something that many people dread. Yet virtually everyone can learn to perform well at interviews, whether information interviews or interviews for a job. The key to successful performance at interviews is thorough preparation. The strategies for effective interview preparation described in this chapter can bring success to most job seekers. What is more, if at the moment you dread interviews, you will find that as a result of thorough preparation you will quickly become skilled and you will start to enjoy them.

If you are already quite confident, some of these strategies may seem 'over the top' and you may want to leave them out of your job search campaign. Being successful is what is important; if you find that you are not being as successful as you would like, you can always reconsider your decision.

Interviews are meetings

Essentially, interviews are meetings between two parties, and most of us like meeting people. What puts us off is the stress that almost invariably seems to accompany an interview, especially job interviews but also those for information. I can't promise that you won't be nervous when you attend your first few information interviews to gain specifics from someone who would be useful to you in finding and winning a job and in building your network, but I can just about guarantee that when you have completed a few, you will start to find them easier and less stressful. Once you have gained some confidence in information interviews, you will discover that you perform more confidently in job interviews as well. As you become more confident in interviewing, you will find it easier to get your informants and prospective employers to like you and this has to be the prime objective of any interview, whether for information or for a job.

Preparing for information interviews

There are four parts to preparing for information interviews:

1. **Prior research: As we said in Chapter 9, the more thoroughly you research the target organisation, the more confident you will be at the interview.**

2. **Preparing questions to ask: We discussed the questions to ask in an information interview in Chapter 9. Questions to ask at a job interview are covered in Chapter 12.**

3. **Reconnaissance: Visiting the place for the network interview beforehand so that you are not in unfamiliar territory.**

4. **Psyching yourself for success so that you can establish a good rapport with your informant at an information interview or be successful at a job interview.**

The same four parts also apply for job interviews as well as the major task of preparing answers to possible interview questions.

Prior research

Hopefully, by the time you have reached the interview stage, whether for information or for employment, you will have already carried out extensive online research. Research is crucial. The more thorough your research into the organisation, the more confident you will be at the interview itself. This is just as true for information interviews as it is for job interviews. In part, this will be because you feel so much better prepared.

Research annual reports, marketing documents, newspaper and magazine articles. Find out what are the organisation's services or products. How well is the organisation thought of in its industry? What are its goals, its vision and mission? This, of course, is easier to find out for large organisations; for smaller ones, you may need to talk to neighbours, customers, suppliers or competitors.

If you are undertaking an information interview, you will quickly become aware of the respect with which your informant regards you if the research that you've carried out is thorough and detailed. This respect will make you feel a lot more confident and comfortable in the interview, especially if you still harbour lingering fears that you might be trespassing on your informant's time.

Remember that, even in times of downturn, most organisations are still looking out for new talent for the team. If they discover someone who has shown the initiative and motivation to undertake thorough research, someone who is keen to be a part of their organisation, they will want to talk to that person whether or not there are any positions available.

And if it's a job interview that you are attending, the interview panel is likely to take greater interest in you because of your knowledge and understanding of the position and the organisation.

Reconnaissance

The idea of making a reconnaissance trip a couple of days before an interview may seem to some people to be overkill. However, such a reconnaissance trip can significantly reduce the stress that the interview imposes. Reconnaissance is especially beneficial if the interview is to be held in someone's office; a bit less so for an informal meeting in a café or restaurant.

There are five reasons for making the reconnaissance trip:

1. **To find out the best way to get there and how long it will take. This means that, on the day of the interview, you can leave with comfortable time to arrive, confident that you won't be late. This takes a lot of stress out of the day.**
   Before your reconnaissance, decide whether to use public transport, a taxi, to get a friend to drive you

there or to drive yourself. If you drive yourself, you need to be careful to concentrate on your driving rather than thinking about the interview. When at all possible, I recommend using one of the other methods of getting to the venue unless you are very confident.

2. To know the venue for the interview. If the interview is to be held on the 14th floor of the Archibald Building, go right up to the 14th floor so that the venue is no longer unknown territory. While you may not be able to see the actual room where the interview is to be carried out, you will have seen the sort of place it is and you will be better able to envisage yourself being successful in the interview. This can make a significant difference to your confidence.

3. To establish a good rapport with the receptionist. Reconnaissance gives you the opportunity to make face-to-face contact with the receptionist. It is always important to establish a good rapport with the receptionist. If you don't know her name, telephone beforehand to confirm the address of the venue or the time of the appointment and ask for her name. On your reconnaissance trip, introduce yourself and tell her that you have come to check out where your upcoming interview will be held. If you have been speaking to her on the phone, ask, 'Are you the Susie I was speaking to on the phone yesterday?'
    It doesn't happen every time but quite often the chairperson of the interview panel will ask the receptionist which candidate she preferred. This makes sense because the organisation wants a good team player and the one that has made the best impression on the receptionist is likely to be a good team player.

Try to make sure that you are that person.

If you are having a job interview and you expect to be interviewed by a selection panel, you might want to take the opportunity to ask the receptionist if she could let you have the names of panel members. Write them down and make sure that you get the correct spelling as well as the correct pronunciation. Also, check preferred titles. You may want to use their titles during the interview and using the right one is important for your objective of getting them to like you. I recommend that you write these names down on the top of the Interview Notes form which is discussed in Chapter 12. In this way, you will have the names in front of you throughout the interview.

You may also be able to get the names of panel members from the contact person mentioned in the ad or the position description.

4. To learn the dress code for the organisation. Being suitably dressed for the interview is important. If you are wearing a three-piece suit and the person you are meeting is wearing slacks and an open-neck shirt, you may feel very uncomfortable.

There are three rules for dressing for an interview and they don't entirely coincide with each other. The first rule is to be dressed as you expect your interviewers or informants to be dressed, but be neater and cleaner. The second is to be dressed as if you were already working there and a VIP is coming to visit the workplace, and the third rule is to wear something that makes you feel good about yourself. Because those rules don't entirely agree with each other, the best way to decide what to wear is to consider all three rules and then make up your mind. If you do this, it is likely that you will be appropriately dressed.

5. To find a café for a light meal before the interview. You will be using a lot of mental and nervous energy during the interview, so it is important to have fuel in your system to produce this energy *before* the interview. The more nervous you are, the more energy you will use, so it is important to have something to eat. Don't eat too much or you might be wanting a siesta afterwards! Choose something light, with complex carbohydrates like vegetables, wholemeal bread and cereals. Avoid sweet foods high in sugar. Because sugar is so quickly digested, these foods will boost your energy for a very short period and then leave you feeling tired and listless.

   Sports psychologist Dr James Loehr found that complex carbohydrates do two things to increase your energy level: they raise your glucose level giving you steady energy for an extended period of time, and they help ensure that you have the right balance of the neurotransmitters norepinephrine (to help you feel alert) and serotonin (to relax your nerves).[1]

   By choosing a café or restaurant a little more up-market than those you might more frequently use, by having a light meal that is a little more gourmet than your usual, you will be giving yourself a bit of a treat. This will make you feel good about yourself. When using the restaurant before the interview, treat the waiting staff in the way that a successful person would — that is, with respect. They, in turn, will treat you with respect and this, again, will help feed your self-confidence.

The big day: The job interview

This section refers principally to performing well at the job interview but some strategies can also be beneficial for an information interview.

In order to reduce stress to a minimum on the day itself, decide what to wear and have it all ready the night before. Get ready and leave so that you have plenty of time to get to the restaurant for your light meal.

If you have had a drink, especially a coffee or tea which both contain caffeine, use the toilets at the café. Caffeine is a diuretic. It would probably take a bit of the shine off your performance if, in the middle of the interview, you ask to use their toilets.

Walk to the interview

Your meal will have provided the fuel you need; a burst of oxygen will help you convert that fuel into energy to sustain you through the interview. If possible, walk briskly from the café to the interview venue. The exercise will cause you to fill your lungs and so get enough oxygen into the bloodstream to sustain you for some time. Aim to arrive about ten minutes before your interview time.

Greet the receptionist

When you arrive, let the receptionist know that you are there. Greet her by name: your rapport with her is important. If you didn't manage to get the names of the interview panel during your reconnaissance, ask for them now.

If you are given the questions before the interview

Sometimes employers give interviewees the questions in written form before the interview. When this happens, you will be asked to arrive 15 to 20 minutes early so that you can prepare answers to the questions before going in to the interview.

You will probably have no more than two minutes to prepare your answer to each question. Don't try writing out an answer in full: instead, select the achievement statements that you would like to use to answer the question and jot down the keywords that will help you identify them.

Envisage success

While you wait to be called into the interview, envisage success. Don't pick up the newspaper; newspapers are filled with stories of doom and gloom and you don't want any of that sort of thing. Instead, open your compendium. You don't need to read the notes you have prepared unless you think that would be helpful. Instead, concentrate on envisaging success.

Before a concert, Spanish singer Julio Iglesias goes out onto the stage with a dead microphone in his hand and mentally rehearses every song that he is going to sing. As he does so, he looks out over the empty auditorium and envisages the audience reacting to his singing. This envisaged audience reaction then colours the way he starts his performance before the live audience.

If while waiting you mentally rehearse answers and envisage the panel members nodding and smiling at your answers, this will help give you the confidence to put on a really good performance.

Meeting the panel

When you are called in to the interview, shake hands with the person who comes to collect you and use his or her name. A firm handshake is an effective way to quickly establish a good physical rapport.

If it's a panel interview, repeat the names of each member of the panel as you are introduced to them. If it is feasible, shake hands with each one; if it's not you still need to repeat their names when you are introduced to them.

As soon as you are seated, write their initials as shown in the diagram at the top of the Interview Notes form (see Chapter 12, page 219). This will help you to easily remember and use their names during the interview.

Body language in interviews

Do not get hung up on body language. Body language is important but if you are motivated for the job and confident that you would do it well, your body language will reflect it naturally. This applies to both information and job interviews. If you spend time and effort in the interview trying to present the best body language, you are likely to lose sight of the main ball and so spoil your performance. The only thing that I will suggest on this topic is that you make sure that you are not sitting in such a way as to be directly confronting one of the interviewers. When you are facing someone directly, you are confronting them, front-to-front, and opposing them. That is not the best way to get them to like you. So, when you are invited to take a seat, if you notice that the chair is directly opposite one of the interviewers, before you sit down, turn the chair slightly so that you are not directly opposing them. You will still have good eye contact but you are showing a slightly angled profile which is more friendly. And, should you forget to turn your chair, sit in it at a slight angle — that will have the same effect.

Watch the time in an information interview

If you have asked for 20 minutes of someone's time for an information interview, make sure that you don't take up more than that.

Watch the time and when it's nearly up, thank your informant and prepare to close. Remember always to ask for a referral: 'Is there anyone else you suggest I should talk to for further information?'

It is quite possible that your informant will be valuing the interview, perhaps seeing you as a potential colleague, and he may suggest that you prolong the interview a bit. This is a good sign. However, you still need to be mindful of his time and you should keep the extra time to perhaps a further ten minutes.

Closing the interview with thanks

You want to leave on a positive note, and thanking the panel is always a plus. As the job interview draws to a close, and you have asked all your questions, thank the panel for asking you to the interview. Choose one thing that you like about the organisation and comment on it briefly. Sarah Vaughan, applying for the Health Educator Coordinator position, might say something like this: 'Thank you for the interview. I have enjoyed meeting you and I am really impressed with the work that you're doing. I was especially interested in the strategies you mentioned for encouraging exercise and an active lifestyle. I would very much like to be part of that.'

Leave it at that. You have expressed a strong interest in the position, you have demonstrated your motivation, so don't spoil it by 'begging'. Don't say, 'Please let me know as soon as possible whether or not I have got the job.' That's begging and, as we said in Chapter 1, beggars are by definition losers — and employers want winners.

For a panel interview, say goodbye to each member of the panel using their names.

In an information interview too, an effective close is beneficial. It leaves your informant with a positive impression of you. The close should be the last thing said in the interview. It comes after asking for a referral in an information interview.

Thank the receptionist

When you leave the interview room, make sure that you stop by the receptionist's desk and thank her for the help she provided. If you have just had an information interview, your informant is probably going to become part of your network and you may need to contact him by phone. Having the receptionist on side will be an advantage. And if you have just had a job interview, remember that it is quite possible the panel chairperson will ask the receptionist which candidates she preferred.

Interview evaluation

Immediately after the meeting write a brief evaluation of the interview. In this way, you will be using each interview as a learning experience, developing your interview skills with each one. You may want to return to the café to do this because it is better to do it when there are no other priorities competing for your attention.

Use an interview evaluation sheet to assess the interview (you can download a free one from www.jobwinnersguides.com).

Thank-you note

A thank-you note is important for both types of interview and I recommend that you write one as soon as you have finished the interview evaluation. A hand-written thank-you note on your letterhead will ensure that you are remembered.

The note does not have to be long; normally about 150 words would be the maximum. Sarah Vaughan might write something like this:

Sarah Vaughan

132 McIntosh Street
Queanbeyan NSW 2620
02 6291 4357 (h)
0428 135 246 (m)
sarah.vaughan7@yahoo.com.au

Wednesday, 10th June 2015
Mrs Heather Turnbull
CEO
Arthritis ACT Inc
PO Box 4017
Western Creek ACT 2611

Dear Mrs Turnbull,

Thank you very much for the interview this morning.

As I said, I am very impressed with the work that you are doing, especially in the area of arthritis prevention. I believe that the strategies you suggested for encouraging more exercise and an active lifestyle could make a significant difference. And I would love to be a part of what you are doing.

Yours sincerely,
Sarah Vaughan

WRAP-UP

■ Thorough preparation is essential if you want to be successful in interviews, whether for information or a job. Because the strategies for success are so similar for both sorts of interview, through developing the skills to perform well in information interviews, you will develop the skills and confidence to do well at the all-important job interview as well.

■ In an information interview, your preparation demonstrates your proficiency and gets people to like you and to want to give you the answers you are seeking. Prior to the information interview, research the target organisation, prepare relevant questions to ask, visit the interview venue beforehand, and psyche yourself for success so you can establish a good rapport with your informant.

■ Thorough preparation builds your self-confidence and makes it easier in a job interview to project your qualifications and your motivation for the position. In a job interview, your preparation demonstrates your motivation and convinces the employer that you will be quickly productive in the position. On the day of the job interview, mentally rehearse your answers, greet the receptionist, don't get hung-up about body language, and always finish the interview on a positive note. Immediately after the meeting write a brief evaluation of the interview.

CHAPTER 12

Questions and answers for the job interview

Preparing questions to ask at the job interview and practising answers to possible interview questions form a major part of your preparation. Both are essential to interview success. It will take quite a lot of time, so don't try to rush your preparation; it is critical to your interview success.

Preparing questions to ask

It is important to prepare three or four questions to ask at a job interview. If you don't ask questions, your interviewers will think that you have not thought very much about the job and that you are not very motivated. So, prepare these questions with care. They will not be quite the same as the questions you were asking in information interviews. These ones should be firmly based on your research and your knowledge of the organisation and of the role that you are applying for. They are for two purposes only:

1. **To confirm or correct your picture of the job and the organisation.**

2. **To find out how you can best help the organisation.**

In spite of all the research that you have done, to create your plan of the first few weeks in the job you will probably have to make some assumptions. These assumptions can provide the basis for your 'confirm or correct' questions. Marama Tuatini who is applying for the position of Artist Development Manager at Chamber Music New Zealand (CMNZ) might ask: 'One of the key expectations of this role is to foster at least two emerging ensembles through providing a performance platform and promoting regional tours for them. Would CMNZ approve the promotion of an amateur group such as the "Milford Sound" brass ensemble?' This sort of question not only shows the extent of your research but also the thought that you have put into the position and the idea that you have already started planning how you would operate in the position. It gives the panel a strong impression that you would hit the ground running and that would clearly stand in your favour.

The second type of question, to find out how best you can help them, gives you the opportunity to highlight some special skills that you would bring to the position. Katharina Hochstein has years of experience as a teacher but now, as the result of an ankle injury, she is having to change her career. As a result, she is applying for the position of Administrative Officer at Museum Victoria. At her interview, she might ask: 'I know that you run education programs. With my teaching experience, I would be very happy to help prepare teaching materials for these programs. Would this be possible in this role?'

There is a likelihood that some of your questions may cover both purposes and that is fine. Linda Heatherton, another former teacher, is applying for a position as tour guide for *The Lord of the Rings* and *The Hobbit* film sites. A possible question that she might ask could be: 'I would imagine that many of those who come on your tours are from overseas. I have a fairly good working knowledge of Mandarin. Do many Chinese people come on your tours and would my knowledge of the language be useful?'

Preparing answers to possible interview questions

There are many types of questions asked at interviews but there are just three steps to preparing answers to any of them. These steps are:

Step 1: Identify the real question behind the spoken words; what do the interviewers really want to know? Why are they asking this question? What are the criteria being assessed in this question?

Step 2: Answer the real question in the way that best shows how you match the requirements that they are asking about, the criteria being assessed.

Step 3: Back up your answer with achievement statements. Achievement statements should make up at least half of every answer — sometimes an achievement statement can very satisfactorily provide the whole answer.

This three-step process is the same whether you are trying for a private sector position or a position in the public sector or publicly funded community organisation. For these positions, the questions are usually based on the selection criteria making Step 1 a bit easier.

It is important to remember that your answers should not just be about you. The interviewers are not as interested in you as a person so much as they are interested in how you would perform in the position. So, your answers should primarily be about the job you are seeking; how well you would do it and how well you would fit into their team.

Preparing answers to private sector questions

In an interview for a private sector position, the questions you are asked need not necessarily be the same as those asked of the other candidates for the same position. This allows for more flexibility for the interview panel and it can mean that you get asked supplementary questions towards the end of the interview. This is usually a good sign.

Here are 20 frequently asked questions:

1. **Tell us about yourself.**

2. **What would your colleagues say about you?**

3. **If your previous (or current) boss were here, what would he/she say about you?**

4. **What would you say are your greatest strengths?**

5. **What would you say are your greatest weaknesses?**

6. **Why should we employ you?**

7. **What would you bring to our organisation?**

8. How long do you think it would be before you started making a significant contribution to our organisation?

9. What would you say have been your two greatest career accomplishments?

10. Why do you want to work here?

11. What are your career goals?

12. Tell us about a time when your work was criticised.

13. Tell us about a project or task you were responsible for that didn't work out.

14. Tell us about a recent problem you solved.

15. Can you tell us of a time when you had to resolve a difficult issue with a client?

16. Supposing a customer came in and complained that the article you had sold her was not satisfactory. How would you handle the situation?

17. How would you define success? And according to your definition, how successful do you think you have been so far?

18. How well do you work under pressure?

19. What frustrates you the most?

20. What do you know about our organisation?

Let's take a look at the question 'Tell us about yourself':

Step 1: What is the real meaning of this question? What do they really want to know? Almost certainly they are asking to find out how you would fit into their team.

Step 2: To answer the real question, you need to show that you are not only competent to work as a member of their team but motivated to do it well. Linda Heatherton, applying for a position taking tours around *The Lord of the Rings* and *The Hobbit* film sites, might answer the question like this: 'I love educating people, showing them things of interest and engaging them in new knowledge. I love *The Lord of the Rings* and *The Hobbit*.'

Step 3: Back up your claim with achievement statements. Linda continues: 'I have read *The Lord of the Rings* at least five times for my own pleasure and, since filming began in 1999, I have used the book as a major text for both English and Drama.' Just saying 'I love *The Lord of the Rings*' is not really convincing but 'I have read *The Lord of the Rings* at least five times for my own pleasure' is. So, make sure you remember Step 3 and that every answer is packed with achievement statements, with examples that demonstrate your skills and motivation.

ACTIVITY

Using the three-step process, prepare your answer to one of the 20 questions above:

The question

_____

_____

_____

_____

_____

_____

Step 1: Identify the real question

_____

_____

_____

Step 2: Answer the real question in the way that shows how you best match the criterion/criteria being assessed

_____

_____

_____

_____

Step 3: Back up your answer with achievement statements

_____

_____

_____

_____

Now write up your complete answer

_____

_____

_____

_____

_____

_____

_____

_____

_____

_____

Make sure that your answer is relevant to the job you are applying for; that it demonstrates how you would perform in that position.

Preparing answers to public sector questions

If you are seeking a job in the public sector or in a government-funded community organisation, the questions they will ask you will usually be based on the selection criteria. They will usually be of three types:

1. **Knowledge type: 'What would you consider the key OH&S requirements in relation to this role?'**

2. **Hypothetical type: 'What would you do if ...?'**

3. **Experience type: 'Tell us about a time when ...?'**

The hypothetical and experience questions are considered behavioural questions and these are discussed in greater detail on page 212.

One of the criteria for the position Don Bradley is applying for is 'Sound knowledge of human resource management including Equal Employment Opportunity'. A possible question of the knowledge type might be: 'How would you interpret the term Equal Employment Opportunity if you were in this position?' A possible hypothetical question might be: 'What would you do if you were in the position and recruiting for a project manager for road and infrastructure projects and there were two applicants equally qualified, one who is in a wheelchair?' The third type of question, the experience type, could be something like this: 'Tell us about a time when you had to make a difficult decision as part of a selection panel.'

ACTIVITY

Now, using the selection criteria for a position you would like, write one question of each type below:

Knowledge type

_____
_____
_____

Hypothetical type

_____
_____
_____

Experience type

_____
_____
_____
_____

Choose two questions from either the private sector list or from the public sector questions you have composed and, using the three-step process, prepare answers for those questions.

This is not easy if you haven't got a clear picture of the job you are going for. If you do not yet have a clear picture of the job that you are seeking, for practice purposes, you may find it useful to pretend that you are interviewing for your present or most recent position. However, it is essential to have a very clear picture of the job that you are applying for before attending a job interview. Do not stint on the research.

Question 1

_____

_____

_____

_____

Step 1: Identify the real question

_____

_____

_____

Step 2: Answer the real question in the way that shows how you best match the criterion/criteria being assessed

_____

_____

_____

_____

Step 3: Back up your answer with achievement statements

_____

_____

_____

_____

Now write up your complete answer

_____

_____

_____

_____

_____

_____

_____

Question 2

_____

_____

_____

_____

Step 1: Identify the real question

_____

_____

_____

_____

Step 2: Answer the real question in the way that shows how you best match the criterion/criteria being assessed

_____

_____

_____

_____

Step 3: Back up your answer with achievement statements

_____

_____

_____

_____

Now write up your complete answer

_____

_____

_____

_____

_____

_____

Once you have prepared your answers, practise them with your spouse/ partner or a trusted friend. Don't learn your answers off word-perfect. Just know what you have to say in each one. In this way, you will sound natural. One way of giving yourself a good prompt is to use the form on page 219 (a blank template is available on www.jobwinners-guides.com) to prepare your notes to take into the interview.

Behavioural-based interviews

Behavioural questions are of two kinds: the hypothetical 'what-would-you-do-if' type and the experience 'tell-us-about-a-time-when' type. Behavioural interview techniques are now common practice because, according to Katharine Hansen of Quintessential Careers, a career practice in the USA, behavioural interviews have a 55 per cent success rate in predicting future on-the-job performance compared to just 10 per cent for traditional interviewing methods.[1]

Behavioural interviews are more likely if you are being interviewed for a professional position in a large organisation or if you are being interviewed by trained interviewers. However, they are becoming more and more common and may be experienced across all levels in an ever-increasing range of industries. In other words, be prepared for behavioural questions. Behavioural interviews are also used at assessment centres, which are covered in Chapter 13.

Both types of behavioural question are easy to answer with a SAO (situation, action, outcome) achievement statement. In fact, SAOs are what the interview panel is wanting to hear. (For more on how to create SAOs and other forms of achievement statements, see Chapter 6, 'Writing achievement statements'.) Here are two typical behavioural questions:

- ■ **'What would you do if you were faced with a difficult customer?'**

- ■ **'Describe a time when you took the initiative to try to prevent trouble.'**

However, behavioural interview techniques can also ask for contrary evidence. If you are asked to 'Tell us about a time when your skill in lateral problem-solving saved the day', be prepared to answer another question along the lines of 'Tell us about a time when your lateral problem-solving skills got you into trouble' and 'What did you learn from that experience?'

Responding to a hypothetical question

Let us take a look at answering a hypothetical 'what-would-you-do-if' question. Assume for the moment that you are applying for an administrative position in a major sports club. 'What would you do if the club's Chairman has just phoned to say that he will be dropping into the club in fifteen minutes to see the Manager and you know that the Manager is out undertaking some private business?'

Use the three-step process. The real question is to judge your values, your loyalty to the club and to the Manager. Step 2, answering the real question could be something like this: 'I would say to the Chairman that the Manager is occupied at the moment and ask him to delay his arrival by 30 minutes. Then I would phone the Manager on his mobile to tell him of the Chairman's impending visit.'

As it stands, this is not a very useful answer and it wouldn't get you many ticks of approval, so this is where you bring in the SAO:

A situation like this occurred in my current job about three months ago. It was just before Christmas and my Manager had a cousin from the UK coming to stay. She worked very hard, through her lunch hour and usually until 6.30 or 7.00 in the evening. However, this one day, she took the opportunity to slip out to buy a present for her cousin. And shortly after she left, the General Manager phoned asking for her. Because I knew how much my Manager did for the organisation, I covered for her by saying that she was not available for the moment but could I ask her to ring him back as soon as she was free, probably in about 20 minutes? The result was that the General Manager was satisfied with that, my Manager was very grateful for my covering for her, and she phoned the GM immediately on her return.

The SAO shows both your loyalty to your supervisor and to the employer organisation. It implies integrity and strong teamwork.

The answer to a hypothetical question is best answered by turning your response into the sort of answer you would make to an experience question and illustrating your answer by some achievement from your past. It is not generally advisable to develop a full answer to the hypothetical situation — what you actually did in a somewhat similar situation in the past is usually much more convincing and it will provide the interviewers with the information that they are seeking.

Responding to experience questions

This means not only having SAOs for when you have been successful but also for having SAOs for when you haven't. If you are asked a question like this: 'Tell me about a time when you were able to motivate a team to achieve a particular task,' the contrary evidence question that could follow might be something like this: 'Tell me about a time when you were unable to motivate a team for a particular task. What did you learn from this experience?'

Let's look at a possible answer to the first question:

I was asked to organise our trade stall at last year's national conference. I called the team in together to brainstorm how best we could achieve this and to work out who should do what and when. We knew that the task would require quite a lot of weekend work but because all the team members felt ownership of the whole project, they volunteered willingly to work in their own time and they worked very efficiently. As a result, we were able to put up an excellent display that gained us excellent exposure and generated a lot of interest from other organisations, interest that has since been translated into increased business.

And now the contrary evidence answer.

I was also asked to organise the trade stall for the previous year's conference and I didn't manage it nearly as well. Instead of involving all team members in the planning process right from the outset, I adopted a top-down approach. Because I had never done this sort of thing before, I asked team members to undertake tasks that proved to be counter-productive, tasks that they recognised to be inadvisable. And the team members were initially unwilling to put in the weekend work to complete something that they didn't believe would work. When I realised that they knew far better than I did how best to make it work, I changed my approach. Then, through seeking the advice from team members and getting them 'on board', we did manage a creditable display — but it was nothing like as good as last year's effort because I had left it too late. However, because of the generous way the team had put in once I had changed my approach, I invited them and their families round for a barbecue after the conference and we all had a good laugh at my earlier efforts.

What did I learn from that experience? I learnt that a team works best when everyone is involved from the start. I also learnt to be willing to seek advice and ideas from subordinates, especially if they have more experience than I have in a particular area.

This SAO describes an event that was not as successful as it could have been — yet the candidate comes across in a positive light because he candidly admits his mistakes and shows how he learnt from those mistakes.

This method of seeking contrary evidence is probably more commonly used in questions seeking information about personal qualities, attitudes and values — the 'soft skills'. They could cover such factors as work ethic, loyalty, teamwork, interpersonal and communication skills, creativity, trustworthiness and integrity.

ACTIVITY

Take one of these factors, or a factor that you believe could feature in an interview for a position that you are seeking, and compile two questions, one for the successful achievement and then the one seeking contrary evidence from an incident that was not so successful. Remember that the contrary evidence question should always ask what you learnt from the experience.

Successful achievement question

_____

_____

_____

Contrary evidence question

_____

_____

_____

_____

Now, use the three-step process to make sure that you provide the information that the interviewers are looking for and then compile your complete answer using a SAO.

Success answer

_____
_____
_____
_____
_____
_____
_____

Contrary evidence answer

_____
_____
_____
_____
_____
_____

Rehearse your answers

As I said earlier, it is important to rehearse your answers with a partner or a trusted friend and to rehearse them again and again until you are really confident that you can get the right points across in every case. Also remember that it is important not to learn your answers off by heart. This could make your answers sound 'wooden' and false. If you know the points that you must get across and you know their importance, you will come across with conviction.

Taking notes into the interview

To make it easier to remember all these points in the stress of an interview, make notes and use these notes to help shape your answers. I suggest that you use an Interview Notes form like the one on the next page. Paste it onto the top sheet of the pad in your compendium. You can then sit in the interview with the compendium open and use the notes as you work out the best way to answer each question.

It would be wise to have a copy of your résumé and application in your compendium just in case you need to refer to it.

If you feel uncomfortable taking notes into an interview, ask if they mind you working from notes. If they ask why, you can say that you like to be organised and that you want to make sure that you remember everything accurately. The interviewers are more likely to be impressed with your preparation than turned off by your using notes.

Consider the fact that the interviewers will be working from notes and taking further notes throughout the interview. During the interview, you are on an equal footing with the interviewers. Certainly, if you are successful, one of the interviewers may be your boss but, at this stage, you are equal. They are using notes; there's no reason why you shouldn't use notes too.

How to use the Interview Notes form

Here is an example showing how Sarah Vaughan might use the Interview Notes form for her interview for a Health Education Coordinator position with Arthritis ACT. To make it easier to read, it is somewhat abbreviated; the number of selection criteria has been reduced and only two of the four questions which Sarah has prepared have been included. Notice that in the 'Points I want to get across' section, only keywords are recorded. These are to help identify relevant achievement statements.

Seating plan	Notes
Mrs Heather Turnbull (CEO) Dr Muriel Dunne MD Mr Andrew Postlethwaite (Finance) AP HT «(me)	
Points I want to get across at the interview Criterion 1: Community sector/education 20 yrs teaching exp, 3 yrs pharmaceutical sales Criterion 2: Develop & present training materials Written materials, slide presentations, podcasts Presentations to students, parents, drs, pharmacists Training adventure education & volunteers Nightcliff Communication & writing reports Incident reports Sales reports Interpersonal & team Ability to build relationships w/ health profs Doubled sales over 3 years as pharm rep	

The questions I want to ask at the interview	
Better Arthritis and Osteoporosis Care national initiative currently focusing on Greek and Chinese; is there a large G&C population in ACT with arthritis?	
I was unable to find specific reference to educating the healthy population avoid arthritis? Is this an area in which Arthritis ACT already has programs or could this be an initiative you would like to pursue?	*MD diet*

Notice how Sarah has used Dr Muriel Dunne's initials in the Notes column. Dr Dunne asked a question regarding diet as a method of reducing the risk of arthritis and this partially answers Sarah's question about educating the healthy population. Sarah might now phrase her question like this: 'Dr Dunne touched on this question when she mentioned diet to help prevent the onset of arthritis. My question is regarding the education of the healthy population in ways to prevent or minimise the risk of contracting arthritis. I was unable to find specific reference to programs of this sort and I wondered whether Arthritis ACT does have such programs or whether it is an initiative that it might like to consider in the future.'

Formal presentation

Some employers may ask candidates to make a formal presentation at the start of the interview. The topic is likely to be what you see as the priorities of the job and how you intend to meet those priorities — where you see the greatest challenges and how you plan to deal with them. You would be given details about this when you are told you have an interview. Researching the position thoroughly to create your action plan for your first few weeks in the job will really pay off here. Don't be afraid to confidently portray your vision strongly and enthusiastically. You may not have all the facts but the assessors will be impressed by your research as well as your motivation to tackle problems vigorously. For more information on how to make presentations, see Chapter 13.

Video and phone interviews

Sometimes prior to, or indeed instead of, a face-to-face interview, you will be offered an interview over the telephone, by video call, videoconferencing or Skype. The phone or video interview is a cost-effective option, especially when applicants live at some distance from the prospective employer. As a result, it may be used for a preliminary interview to decide which candidates to invite to a face-to-face interview. Video interviews in particular are becoming used more frequently in place of a face-to-face interview.

The phone interview, whether voice or video, is just as important as the face-to-face interview and it needs just as much preparation — research into the employer organisation, developing the questions that you want to ask and preparing answers to possible interview questions.

Like the face-to-face, a phone interview is a two-way conversation; don't let it become one-sided by meekly answering all the questions that the interviewer is asking. Instead, ask for further clarification of questions when it would help, tell stories that illustrate the skills and personal qualities that you would bring to the position and, if you think that you might have strayed off the point, ask if you are giving them the information that they want. Don't be afraid to ask them to repeat the question. If the interviewer asks you a question that requires a bit of thought, say that you would like a bit of time to think about the answer so that your silence doesn't provoke an 'Are-you-still-there?' question.

Have questions to ask just as you would for the face-to-face interview. Be prepared to ask those questions at any time that they might seem relevant. For instance, if the interviewer asks something about teamwork, after answering the question, you might follow-up by asking about the size and composition of the teams you might be working with.

As in a face-to-face interview, use a strong close to complete the phone or video interview. Then complete the interview evaluation form and write a thank-you note.

The phone interview

Preparing the environment before a phone interview is essential. Unless you are very confident of the signal strength for your mobile phone, I would suggest using a landline for the interview. If the call comes through on your mobile, ask if you could ring them back on the landline.

Use a clear desk or table in an area as free of background noise as you can make it. Have a couple of pens and a notebook, or a tablet, your résumé and/or application for the specific position and a calendar or diary in front of you. Take brief notes during the interview, notes that you can complete after the call is finished. Organise the papers on your desk carefully so that you can easily find the right one and avoid having to shuffle through a pile.

Ensure that you will not be interrupted for the duration of the interview, which could take as long as one hour although it is more likely to be about 20 minutes to half an hour. If you have call waiting on your phone, make sure that it is turned off.

Although you will not be seen in a telephone interview, dress just as carefully as you would for a face-to-face interview. This will help ensure that you have the confidence you need. Sit up straight or stand so that you project more energy into what you say.

Don't let nervousness cause you to rush your answers; speak slowly and clearly. And don't be afraid of silences. When you have completed your answer, wait for the next question. It is important not to babble just to fill in the silence.

Smile before you pick up the phone and as often as is appropriate while you are talking. Make the effort to consciously smile whenever you can and this will carry through to the interviewers by subtly changing the intonation of your voice. This is something which salespeople have been taught for years and, remember, you are the sales representative for Yourself Pty Ltd.

The phone interview call might come at any time. Don't allow yourself to be interviewed at a time that is difficult for you. If the call comes through at a bad time, be prepared to say so and to ask if you could ring them back when it is more convenient.

The video interview (video calls, video conferencing or Skype)

For a video interview, quite a lot of careful preparation of the environment is required. You are going to be seen and you want to ensure that it is only you that is seen. You don't want the interviewers to be distracted by a fussy background or movement behind you. A plain wall behind you is good. A tidy bookcase of good quality reference books projects the impression of someone who is interested in ongoing learning and that may be why it is one of the favourite backgrounds chosen by academics and politicians. A window looking out onto a busy street or playground might allow too much noise and movement behind you. Extra movement behind you means that your computer has to work harder to transmit the extra information this produces and unless your internet connection is very fast, this could cause buffering. When this happens, the image you are transmitting freezes, breaks up and shudders.

Prevent any unnecessary noise. Make sure that other people and pets are kept out of the way. Unplug the phone and turn off your mobile. Close any windows if there could be noise coming from outside.

You may face a number of video interviews during the job search, so it may be worth your while to invest in some reasonable quality equipment. A high definition webcam with zoom capability means that you can focus it tightly on your head and shoulders. This will give the interviewers the best picture of you and make it easier for them to see your interest in the position. If you have 'picture in the picture' facilities, you can use these to help you frame the picture of yourself to the best advantage. If you don't, set up a video call to a friend and ask him or her to tell you how to produce the best picture.

Place the webcam at or slightly above your eye level so that it is looking straight at you or slightly down on you. When you are slightly looking up, you are probably showing the most attractive view of your face. And if you hold your head up, your posture will be better and, as I said in Chapter 10, this has been shown to have a marked effect on confidence.

Obviously, your microphone needs to be good as well. If possible, place the microphone close to the webcam so that, as you speak into it, you are also looking straight at the webcam. This is the nearest you can get to making eye contact. Make sure that when you are answering, you are looking directly into the webcam and not at the picture on the screen.

Having the microphone a little above the desk means that any noises you make shuffling paper are further away from it. Microphones are very sensitive and pick up little noises that the human brain filters out. These little noises can be very loud and distracting at the interviewers' end.

Lighting is another consideration. Good natural lighting falling on your face is probably the best. Your computer screen will also provide some lighting. If this is not sufficient, consider a desk lamp shining down onto the surface of the desk so as to provide additional indirect lighting. Strong overhead lighting is likely to put shadows in your eye sockets and under your nose — probably not your best look!

Understand the equipment and don't be afraid of it. Test it out. Practise video interviewing with friends until you are not only satisfied with the quality of the picture and sound you transmit but are also confident in your ability to handle the technology and to solve any problems that might arise.

Dressing for a video interview requires some additional considerations. Stripes and checks are not good. As you move, they may cause buffering by overloading the system with additional and unnecessary information. Most authorities advise wearing solid colours but not white. If you are planning to wear a tie, choose a solid colour for that. Look at the clothes worn by television presenters and the people who appear on television and see what works best for them. However, be aware that the transmitting power of a television station is probably greater than that of your computer and the signal much faster.

In a video interview, you can't turn towards, and make eye contact with, individual panel members. For this reason, it is important to know their names so that if you need to address a particular person you can use the name to attract their attention.

Be as naturally enthusiastic as you can be. Your interest in the position and your belief in your ability to perform well in it will help you naturally maintain good posture and good body language throughout the interview, which will help to reinforce your self-confidence.

Because the camera is concentrated on your face and your face fills the interviewers' screen, your facial expressions are more noticeable. If you lose concentration, your face may show it, so it is essential to listen carefully to everything the interviewers are saying. Your nods of understanding and your smiles will be noticed.

After the interview

Whether you have been interviewed face-to-face, over the phone or by video, unless there is a further interview likely, you will have done all that you can achieve for this opening for the moment. Therefore, write this particular job lead off and find another to take its place. Then, if you hear that you have not been successful, you will still have two job leads on the go. If, on the other hand, you are offered the position, you can put other job leads onto the back burner. However, once a job offer is made to you there will be a whole lot more considerations that you have to make. These are discussed in Chapter 14. In the next chapter we cover how to succeed at an assessment centre.

WRAP-UP

- The most important thing you can do at the job interview is to get the interviewers to like you. They are most likely to do so if you demonstrate enthusiasm for the position and interest in the team. This will be achieved much more easily if you have well-prepared questions to ask and answers to possible interview questions.

- Use achievement statements; ideally achievement statements should comprise at least 50 per cent of every answer. Be prepared for questions seeking contrary evidence, asking you about times when things have gone wrong.

- Rehearse your answers, get your partner or close friends to ask you possible interview questions but don't learn your answers off by heart. Just remember the points you want to get across and this will be easier if you take notes into the interview.

- Telephone and video interviews are becoming increasingly common, so be ready for them. Prepare the environment where you will be taking the interview call. When you answer, let the interviewers hear the smile in your voice even if they can't see the smile on your face.

CHAPTER 13

Assessment centres

An assessment centre is not a place; it's a procedure, a combination of various activities designed to see how candidates would perform in a particular job. It is used as part of the selection process when an organisation is recruiting several people for similar positions at the same time. The employment of a new recruit is expensive; getting the wrong person is costly and has a detrimental effect on productivity. Although assessment centres are also expensive, they offer a greater likelihood of getting the right people than the traditional face-to-face interview.

For university students applying for graduate positions in government or large organisations, assessment centres are to be expected. For older workers and for job seekers who have applied for positions that they found through networking, assessment centres are less likely. However, as a mature job seeker, you might face an assessment centre if the position you are applying for is with a new, local branch of a large organisation, or with a major project starting up, or with an organisation undertaking a large-scale recruiting drive.

You may also experience some assessment-centre-type activities in an otherwise standard face-to-face interview.

The term 'assessment centre' is used because the employer organisation usually conducts these extended selection processes in a single location or centre. This may be the organisation's own offices, or a hotel or function centre. Activities may last a morning, a whole day or even two days. Candidates are being assessed throughout, including during coffee and meal breaks. How they interact with other candidates, with the recruiting organisation's officers and with the human resources professionals running the program is a major part of the program. In group exercises, it is not the successful achievement of the set task that is important; it is how each member of the group contributes to the team effort.

If you are invited to attend an assessment centre, don't consider yourself to be in competition with the other candidates there. All the candidates attending have been chosen because they have shown the potential to be good employees and the organisation may well hire all those who perform well, as good performance basically means being good team members. The successful candidates are those who collaborate, rather than compete, with the others.

What the assessors are looking for at assessment centres

The purpose of any interview or assessment centre is to check whether or not you would be a good match with the organisation, to see how you would fit into the team. So, you need to continually demonstrate your willingness and ability to support other members of the group as you work towards the team objectives. This is much more important than coming up with a brilliant solution but not involving the others.

Along with team skills, assessors are also looking at communication, interpersonal effectiveness, assertiveness and customer service. In addition, for many jobs, employers are seeking motivation and initiative, creativity and problem-solving, analysis and decision making, strategic thinking and leadership. The research that you have carried out on the position and the organisation will give you a good idea of what personal qualities they are looking for.

The assessors may be visible and may be people who have been introduced to you. But they may also be invisible and watching you on CCTV. This means that you have to demonstrate the desired attributes throughout the process, whether you can see the assessors or not. Don't let this faze you; if your research told you that you were right for the job, your natural behaviour will be what the assessors are looking for. However, this does not mean that you don't have to prepare. To be your best, you need to be confident and relaxed, and you will have the greatest likelihood of achieving this if you are well prepared.

Assessment centre activities

It is useful to be aware of the sorts of activities you might face at an assessment centre. Most activities will fall into one of the following categories:

- **group activities**
- **ice-breaker activities**

- **in-tray (or e-tray) exercise**
- **role-play**
- **case study analysis**
- **behavioural interviews (see Chapter 12)**
- **formal presentations**
- **social activities including coffee breaks and lunch.**

You may also be asked to undertake psychometric tests. These are a standardised and scientific method of measuring your verbal, numerical and technical reasoning and also your personality or behavioural style.

A one-day assessment centre might be organised to start at 10 a.m. with morning tea. During this time, make it your business to talk to other candidates and find out a bit about them. This networking is seen as evidence of your ability to work in a team and to be socially adept. In addition, you could be working in group activities with your fellow candidates for the rest of the day, and having a good rapport with them from the beginning will be a big help.

The organisation may then make a presentation to say something about itself, its vision and purpose, after which you could be asked to take some psychometric verbal, numerical and perhaps technical tests and a personality questionnaire.

These could be followed by lunch with managers and employees of the organisation. Do not slacken off — you are still being assessed! However, do be yourself, open, friendly and appearing relaxed and comfortable in the environment.

In the afternoon, you might have an in-tray exercise followed by a group task. It is quite possible that you may also have a face-to-face interview at the centre at some time.

How to prepare for an assessment centre

People can feel intimidated if they are invited to participate in an assessment centre program, possibly even more so than for the more regular form of interview. The way to overcome this nervousness is to prepare as thoroughly as you would for a panel interview.

The most important factor in assessment centre success is being relaxed, feeling fit and 'on the ball'. You should not try to be anything other than yourself. That said, proper preparation is important and, if you are well prepared, you are also likely to be much more confident and relaxed.

Preparation for the face-to-face interview as described in Chapter 12 is a must, including the research, preparing questions to ask and answers to possible interview questions. This is because the assessment centre process may include a face-to-face interview which is likely to focus on behavioural questions (see Chapter 12 for how to prepare answers to possible behavioural questions).

Reconnaissance is also strongly advised: assessment centres are big-ticket projects and can't be delayed just because one person has lost the way. However, you can probably skip the pre-interview light meal discussed in Chapter 12.

Psyching yourself is vitally important, so carefully follow the advice given in Chapter 11 and implement the strategies that you believe will be most effective.

Group activities

Group activities are designed to indicate how well candidates perform in a team setting. Assessors are not looking for someone who dominates the group. Don't fall into the trap of trying to monopolise the conversation.

If your group is asked to create a 2-metre high construction using newspaper and sticky tape and you know exactly how best to achieve that, don't insist that it be done your way. Suggest it, certainly, but as a question involving the other members of the group. 'How do you think it would work if we did it this way?' It is not so much the quality of your idea that is important; it is the way you 'sell' the idea to other members of the group.

If the activity is to analyse a problem and devise the best strategies to solve it, or to discuss a topic of current general interest, you are more likely to get brownie points for trying to involve the quieter ones in the group than for stating forcefully how the problem should be solved. It's all about how you would perform in a team.

To prepare for these group activities, practise with friends building towers out of newspaper and sticky tape, or analysing and devising strategies for solving problems. But focus on being a good member of the team rather than the 'hero of the day' and trying to solve the problem on your own. You can find practice exercises on the internet but you need to complete the task as a member of a team, not as an individual.

Ice-breaker activities

Ice-breakers are an effective way of quickly building team spirit and energising a group of people who don't know each other. Their purpose is to help you get to know the other candidates and may include such activities as asking you to introduce one of the other candidates.

The way to be successful at this sort of activity is to throw yourself wholeheartedly into it. This may involve talking to people you don't know and finding out interesting things about them. Get involved straight away and show great interest in the person who you are talking to.

In-tray (or e-tray) exercise

The in-tray exercise, or its electronic equivalent the e-tray exercise, gives you a number of documents (hard copy or electronic or a mixture of both), to sort through and action. The workload is designed to be too much for you to complete in the time allocated. The exercise measures your efficiency, your ability to analyse and prioritise your workload, your ability to identify, investigate and address key issues and your commitment to customer service. In addition, it tests your ability to read and quickly understand, to take decisive action and to delegate to others.

This is an exercise that you will be required to complete on your own. Practice questions can be freely downloaded from the internet and it is a good idea to practise as much as you can. You will find that your skills in this area will stand you in very good stead when you start in the new job because it is likely that, on your first day, you will face a similar in- or e-tray to deal with.

When faced with this task, always read through all the items before taking any action on any one of the items. It is surprising how frequently candidates respond to one item, only to find conflicting evidence in another document. Once you have read all the documents, arrange them in chronological order and highlight important or urgent items. At the same time, note which documents relate to each other or to similar situations. Then you can start to prioritise and to action and delegate.

Again, you can find in-tray exercises on the internet. Use these for practise and time yourself while doing them. You may also find it useful to have a trusted colleague watch you while you practise and suggest ways you might be able to do it better.

Role-play

If you are asked to role-play, the role will almost certainly be relevant to the position that you are applying for. Generally role-play will involve yourself and one other person who might be someone from the organisation, a professional actor or one of the other candidates. You are likely to be given a situation, one that you might face in the job you are applying for. Then you act out how you would resolve the situation.

The better your knowledge of the position and the organisation, the easier this will be. Act as if the situation were real and you were in the position. Often the hardest part in role-play is taking it seriously. Don't get caught this way; take it as if the situation were real and your responsibility.

Case study analysis

For a case study analysis, you would be given fictional information and three or four proposals. Your task would be to analyse the information and then choose the best proposal to meet the situation. The choice you make is not important: what is important is the way you process the information and how logically and forcefully you put the case for your choice.

You could be asked to complete a case study analysis on your own or it could be made a group exercise. If the latter, the essential is to work as part of the team and to encourage others to contribute. If you can help the group process the information logically and then present the choice in a logical and persuasive manner, you will be well regarded.

You may be asked to make a formal presentation of the proposal you have chosen.

Formal presentations

If you are required to make a formal presentation, you may be given a list of topics to choose from. These could include instructions to make or do something, or a political or social argument or a humorous subject. Or, of course, you could be required to present the findings of your case study analysis.

You are likely to be given five minutes for the presentation and 30 minutes to prepare. You will be assessed on your ability to present in a logical and engaging way and, if it is a group exercise, on your participation in the team.

Plan your presentation to have three parts: the introduction, the body of your argument and a conclusion. The introduction and conclusion should each constitute between 10 per cent and 15 per cent of the whole presentation.

Grab the assessors' interest with your first line, make it really strong and compelling, and then develop the theme so that you hold their attention all the way through. Likewise, end with a strong conclusion clearly showing your understanding of the topic.

Keep visual aids to a minimum; preferably don't use them at all. They can certainly be useful when you are trying to get a group to understand complex concepts but, in this instance, visual aids deflect the assessors' attention from you, and that's not what you want.

Psychometric tests and personality questionnaires

Psychometric tests are a standardised and scientific method of measuring your abstract, verbal, numerical and technical reasoning skills and some also assess your personality or behavioural style. The tests are held under very strict conditions and timed to the second. Typically the earlier questions will be easier than the later ones. However, all questions are worth the same points. They are often multiple-choice questionnaires requiring quick answers. Tests are designed so that very few candidates can complete the test in the allotted time. Therefore, if you can't answer a question quickly, guess the answer and move on to the next one. Some people get bogged down and waste up to one-third of the allotted time trying to figure out the answer to one difficult question.

The most important preparation for psychometric testing, as it is for the whole assessment centre experience, is being bright, fit and 'on the ball'. A late night beforehand is not recommended. It is also important to know exactly what the organisation is looking for, the selection criteria and, hopefully, you will have gained a good understanding of this through your research.

Taking practice psychometric tests, however, will definitely help you give a better performance. There are a number of internet sites offering free psychometric tests and it would be foolish not to try them if there is a possibility that you may face this sort of test.

Psychometric personality questionnaires are different to the aptitude tests we have been discussing. Basically there are no right or wrong answers. Answer as truthfully as you can. Do not allow yourself to be tempted to put in the answer that you think the assessors would like most. You believe that you are right for the job; therefore, truthful answers will give the assessors the picture of someone who is right for the job.

Remember that no one is perfect. If your results come out looking too good to be true, the assessors will pick this up. In fact, personality questionnaires usually have a built-in lie-detector process.

Having said that, taking a few online practice questionnaires will give you more confidence and is well worth doing.

WRAP-UP

- Assessment centres may not affect as many mature-age job seekers as they would younger ones but you can't guarantee that you won't have to face one during your job search.

- An assessment centre is not a place; it's a procedure, a combination of various activities designed to see how candidates would perform in a particular job. It is used as part of the selection process when an organisation is recruiting several people for similar positions at the same time.

- Whether or not this happens, preparing for an assessment centre will help in the event that an assessment-centre type of activity is included in the interview process. In an assessment centre, continually demonstrate your willingness and ability to support other members of the group. Remember, assessors are looking for people with interpersonal effectiveness, assertiveness and good communication skills. Motivation and initiative, creativity and problem-solving, analysis and decision-making, strategic thinking and leadership are many of the qualities employers are looking for.

CHAPTER 14

Succeeding in the new job

Congratulations! You have been offered the job you want. Now you need to accept the offer in a businesslike way. How you communicate your acceptance of a job offer is an early indication to an employer of how you will perform in the job. It gives an impression of how you will fit into their team and so, like every other part of the job search process, it's important to get it right.

Remember the three things that every employer is looking for in every applicant for every position: the *skills* to do the job, the *motivation* to do it well and the ability to fit well into their *team* (SMT). Let your letter of acceptance clearly show your enthusiasm for the position and for the organisation. You might write something like this:

> Thank you for offering me the position of [...]. I am very pleased to accept.

I am looking forward to meeting the team again and to working with them to tackle the immediate challenges you have mentioned.

My current position requires me to give four weeks' notice and I would like to start in the new role on [date]. Please let me know if this would be convenient for you.

Yours sincerely,

This letter, as with all other letters relevant to your job search and career transition, should be on your 'letterhead', that is to say good quality white bond A4 paper with the masthead of your résumé at the top.

Whether to accept the first job offer

In times of uncertainty, or if you have been job searching for a long time, it's tempting to take the first job that is offered to you. However, this may not always be the wisest course of action. Stop to consider whether the job is really what you want. Before accepting the offer, make sure that the job is right for you and that you are keen to work towards the organisation's objectives and will therefore develop the attitude to succeed in the job.

If you have been offered a job with Organisation A but you are confident that you have a good chance of being offered a position with Organisation B, which would better suit your personal situation, you will need to make a decision. To help you make the right decision, you will need some additional information from Organisation B regarding the status of your application. You might telephone the contact person and say, 'I have been offered a position at [Organisation A] but I believe that I would be able to make a greater contribution as [position] with you. Are you able to let me know the status of my application to help me decide whether or not to accept their offer?' Tell them the timeframe that you have been given or that you have negotiated. If your application is at the top of the shortlist and they really want you, they will do their utmost to get back to you with a decision before your timeframe expires. If this is impossible, they might tell you 'off the record' that you are highly regarded for the position but that they won't be able to give you the formal result until after your deadline. This will leave you in the uncomfortable position of having to decide whether or not to take the risk.

Employers do not want to mess you about. They want good people and they will do what they can to help you. However, big organisations can be less flexible than small businesses or individual people. If you are in this situation, you may still want to consider inviting the contact person from Organisation B for a coffee with the aim of being better able to assess your chances of getting the job. That will make your decision-making easier.

Asking for time to consider an offer

When an employer makes the offer of a job, he usually wants a fairly quick response but you may want to ask for an extension of time. If you are not absolutely sure that taking the job would be the best move for your career, or if you think that you might receive another offer for a job that you would prefer, asking for an extension of time is important.

If the offer comes via letter or email, it would be wise to respond along these lines:

Thank you very much for the offer of [position]. I feel privileged to be offered the position and I am very grateful for the time and effort that you have taken in assessing my application, and the interest that you have shown in me.

You have asked me to give you an answer by [date]. I appreciate that now you will want to get on with making an appointment and that you would prefer a quick response. However, I have another option to consider and I need to decide which position would give me the better opportunity to be productive. I don't think that I will be able to properly make such an important decision within the timeframe you have set. May I therefore request an extension of the time until [new date] by which time I will have made a firm decision?

I look forward to hearing from you. In the meantime, I sincerely thank you for the offer of this position and I assure you that I am giving it serious consideration.

Yours sincerely,

Notice that in the second paragraph, the candidate phrases the request for more time in terms of benefit to the employer: '[…] which position would give me the better opportunity to be productive'. In any negotiation, it is important not only to be aware of the needs of the other party but also to show how your proposal would benefit them.

Choosing between two job offers

To choose between two job offers, you may like to use a 'mechanical' process like the one provided by this table. You identified your Satisfiers, Values, Other factors and Personal goals in Chapter 2. Use them in the activity opposite.

ACTIVITY

Position 1 _____

Determinant How well does the position match your:	Score	I-factor	Score x I-factor
Satisfiers			
Values			
Other factors			
Personal goals			
Overall satisfaction rating			

Position 2 _____

Determinant How well does the position match your:	Score	I-factor	Score x I-factor
Satisfiers			
Values			
Other factors			
Personal goals			
Overall satisfaction rating			

By using this table, you will be able to assess how good a match each position is to your specific needs: your Satisfiers, Values, Other factors and Personal goals. Two lines have been left blank for other determinants that may be important to you or if, for example, you have completed a personality type instrument and would like to include the results from that.

Rate each of the two positions against each determinant. If a position matches your Satisfiers very well, give it a Score of 5. Compare what you know about each position with your Satisfiers in the same way that you did when completing the Career Action Planning Matrix on pages 36–37.

The I-factor represents the relative importance of each determinant to you. If, for example, your Values are very important to you, the I-factor would be 5. If they don't worry you a great deal, you will probably give it an I-factor of 1 or 2.

Multiply the Score by the I-factor to give an overall rating for each determinant. Add up the ratings for each position and the one with the highest overall satisfaction rating may well be the one most likely to give you both job satisfaction and success.

However, it is important to remember that this is a mechanical process, that the scores are arbitrarily assigned and that the process may not cover all the relevant factors. It is therefore important to use your intuition. Engage your gut feeling in the decision-making process. This may also be a very worthwhile time to discuss the decision with your support network or 'Board' (see Chapter 10). How well the job matches your personal attributes will affect your attitude to the job and, as a result, your likely success in the position.

Negotiating the right conditions

If you want to accept a job offer but are hesitating because some of the conditions don't suit you, you may be able to meet your needs through negotiation. It is important to seriously consider negotiating before accepting any job offer. Not only may negotiation gain you the respect of the employer organisation, it may also help you achieve the conditions necessary to meet your needs and, therefore, create the environment in which you can be most successful. Negotiation is for a win–win situation; you need to negotiate to meet your needs. It should not be merely a grab for more money. And the best time to negotiate is after the employer makes an offer and before you accept.

Salary, however, could be an important element of the conditions you are seeking. Some years ago a client of mine who had lost his job through redundancy was offered two positions. One offer came from the local branch of a national company, a major player in the field. They offered him a very generous salary. The other offer was from a small, local firm, and they offered a lot less. Having recently relocated with his wife and teenage children, he had taken out a substantial mortgage to buy a home. The larger salary would easily allow him to maintain the mortgage repayments whereas the salary offered by the smaller company would not. However, my client saw the smaller company as offering the greater chance for advancing his career in the longterm.

I advised him to approach the smaller company and negotiate, putting his requirements in terms of benefit to the employer. He explained his situation to the company. He said that they obviously wanted someone who was going to be able to fully focus on the project that they had in mind and that he was keen to do just that. However, he believed that he would be better able to do that if he did not have to worry about how to meet his mortgage repayments. The company agreed and raised his starting salary by $10K and brought forward a performance and salary review by six months. They also offered him a company car, which would reduce his cost-of-living expenses. Although the salary package was still below that offered by the bigger company, he was able to accept because he now knew that he could meet his financial obligations.

Let's look at how best to prepare for successful negotiation.

Your needs (*not* your wish list)

First, consider your budget and how much you need to live on. How much do you need for normal everyday living? Decide on the lifestyle that you believe would be appropriate — not too extravagant but one that allows you to meet social and recreational needs. If you cannot meet these needs, you will find that you become stressed or dissatisfied and your performance will deteriorate as a result.

If you need to relocate to take the new job, would the organisation be willing to provide relocation expenses, perhaps including accommodation while you look for a suitable rental property or a home to purchase?

Other conditions that are important to consider are how well the position meets your Satisfiers and your Values. If there is significant conflict in these areas, you may well suffer stress and so underperform.

All the way through the job search, your focus has been on how you can benefit the organisation. Negotiating the right salary and conditions is no different; you are still trying to maximise the benefit you will provide to the employer. If the pay and conditions are not satisfactory, this will affect your productivity. As we saw in the story of the client with a mortgage, financial worries could distract you from putting all your effort into succeeding in the new job.

Some of these worries may be temporary such as the additional expenses of starting in the new job, for example relocation, purchasing an additional vehicle, buying a new computer or paying for a uniform, tools or training. Other worries may be longer term. It is useful to distinguish between the two. Short-term issues are usually easier to negotiate but the longer-term worries may well be of greater concern.

List the specific conditions that would affect your ability to perform at your best and show how they would impinge on your output.
Start with the short-term worries and then make a separate list of the
longer-term ones. Your list might start something like this:

Shortfall in salary and conditions	Impact on performance
$1100 net per fortnight insufficient to allow planned superannuation savings	Worry over inability to make needed superannuation savings every fortnight would make it harder to concentrate fully on the challenges of the new job

Putting your requirements in terms of benefit to the organisation

You are not begging. The organisation will get better value for money
if they provide the conditions that would best allow you to work at
peak performance. If you are grateful to an employer who has treated
you well, and the position meets your Satisfiers and Values, you will
be motivated to be as productive as possible. If you have no financial
worries, you will be better able to fully concentrate on the challenges
of the new job, of fitting into the team and, therefore, providing the
greatest return on the organisation's investment in you.

Use the 'Impact on performance' column to show how an improvement in salary and/or conditions would benefit the organisation. In
the case above, your response might be something like this:

Thank you for offering me the position. I am really looking
forward to meeting the challenges that you have outlined.

However, I do have some concerns. These challenges are going to require my undivided attention and I am a little anxious that I may be distracted by financial worries. A salary of $X0,000 may not allow me to comfortably meet the superannuation savings that I need. Is there some way we could negotiate?

Before negotiations start, make a list of your achievements that are especially relevant to the position. If the new position requires sales, talk about your past achievements in sales; if it's about customer service, talk about your customer service achievements. You need to be able to convince the organisation that you are worth the extra cost.

Alternative solutions and a fall-back position

You need to be prepared with alternative solutions and a fall-back position. Using the example above, the company may say that salaries are non-negotiable because if you get a raise, then others might also want a raise. But salary is not the only way to enable you to meet your superannuation savings. A fully serviced car would save you a lot of money, as it did for my client with the mortgage, and so make it easier to make those repayments. If you are renting, the company may be prepared to rent the house on your behalf and then deduct an amount significantly less than the rent from your salary.

Other benefits you may want to consider are external training or a role in a major project which will build your skills base, look good on your résumé and improve your attractiveness to other employers should this one fail to provide the conditions which you require. Once again, when suggesting the training option, you need to show how your attending this training will benefit the company.

It may be worthwhile finding out how the organisation has handled this sort of negotiation in the past. Perhaps you could talk to people who have joined the organisation reasonably recently. If you do this, you need to be careful not to come across as grasping or greedy. If, however, you explain how the offered conditions could impact your performance, you should get a sympathetic ear and some good advice. On the whole, employer organisations want their employees to be satisfied with pay and conditions and they want them to be motivated and loyal to the organisation. Most will therefore listen to you with respect and will want to meet your needs as far as they feel able to do so.

You need to have a fall-back position. What are the least concessions you would accept? If the organisation gives you a firm 'No' to a salary increase and refuses the other fringe benefits that you have thought of as alternative solutions, would you be prepared to accept a salary review in three months?

At what point do you say 'No' to the job? If the organisation is not prepared to budge and you, although reluctantly, accept the offer, your work will probably be affected adversely and you could be one of the 46 per cent of new employees who fail in the first eighteen months (see page 252). Therefore, it could be worthwhile deciding to decline the job offer. If you are serious in your negotiation, you need to be ready to say no to the job. To quote American novelist Ellen Glasgow: 'What happens [to you] is not as important as how you react to what happens.' Say no politely and firmly and, if they really want you, they may come back with a better offer and, if they don't, you may be better off refusing that job and getting on with finding a better one.

You are not a job beggar. You are worth employing, you have a future and you want to be successful. Therefore remain steadfast in your determination to strive for the conditions which will provide the greatest likelihood of your achieving that success.

Declining job offers

Your principal objective throughout the job search has been to get employers to like you. This is still your objective when declining job offers. Sometime in the future, you may want to work with the organisation whose offer you are now declining. So, when you decline a job offer, you need to maintain that same, open, friendly and professional approach which you have used throughout.

Your letter declining the offer needs to first thank them for the offer, to compliment the organisation in some way and to say that you have decided to accept a position with another organisation. Your letter could read something like this:

> Thank you for offering me the position of [...]. After a lot of careful consideration, I have decided not to accept your offer but to accept another position which will, I believe, allow me to use my skills to even better effect than would the position you offered me.
>
> I have been very impressed with the way your organisation is run and I would very much like the opportunity to work there in the future should a suitable opening arise.
>
> Thank you again for the time and trouble that you have taken with my application and I hope that our paths will cross in the future.
>
> Yours sincerely,

Resigning from your present job

In the same way that you would like to keep the goodwill of an employer whose offer of a position you have just declined, you want to keep the goodwill of your current employer. You never know when you might want to apply for another position with the organisation and you may well want to use people from that organisation as referees. You want them to continue to like you. You therefore need to be very diplomatic in your letter of resignation.

It does not need to be long. Three or four one-sentence paragraphs could well be sufficient.

The first paragraph states your intention to resign and your termination date. The second explains your reasons for leaving. End your letter on an upbeat note: briefly relate some of the positive experiences you have had with the organisation and an appreciation for the support and opportunities for training and career development that the organisation has provided.

Here is a typical resignation letter:

It is with some regret that I am resigning from the position of [...] with [name of organisation] with effect from [date of last day].

As you know, I have been seeking opportunities to further develop my career along the lines of [...] and I have accepted a position with another organisation which will provide me with this opportunity.

I have enjoyed the years that I have been with [name of organisation] and I would like to thank you and all the team for the friendly support and encouragement that you have given me over this time.

I wish you all a successful future and I look forward to catching up with you at some stage.

Yours sincerely,

Keeping your new job

Winning a job is great. The next thing is to keep it. Mark Murphy, an author, researcher and trainer in leadership in the US, gives these chilling statistics in *Forbes* magazine: 'When our research tracked 20,000 new hires, 46% of them failed within 18 months.'[1] You don't want to be part of that 46 per cent.

Murphy goes on to say that 89 per cent of those who failed were terminated not because of a lack of skill but for their attitude. To make sure that your attitude is right means that you need to ensure that the job is a good match for you; that the corporate culture fits your values and the way you want to work. As discussed at the beginning of the chapter, you need to enjoy the job to be successful, so don't just accept the first job that's offered to you.

Your first and most important task on joining a new organisation is to become a valued member of their team. Without a good team around you to help and support your efforts, you will achieve little and your employment is likely to be short-lived. Those who try to do it all on their own are likely to be part of the 46 per cent who fail within eighteen months.

Essential to this is remembering people's names. Write them down and jot down notes of things that you ought to know about them, their roles and responsibilities and personal details such as the names of their partners, or whether they have children living at home. Be open and friendly. Accept invitations to social events. Get to know your colleagues; show an interest in their interests and leisure pursuits, their favourite sports teams and their families. Be a friend and get them to like you.

You will find it useful to maintain your network after you have started in the new position. As I said in Chapter 1, the average tenure of a permanent full-time job is currently about four years and getting shorter. During the next few years, many of the members of your network will be making career transitions and they may need your help. Help them generously; if you are seen to give generously, you will be given generous help when and if you have to make a further transition yourself.

This part of the chapter was written before I had read Stephen Covey's *The 7 Habits of Highly Effective People* and it was based on the factors that had characterised my most successful clients. Unsurprisingly, there is a close correlation between the strategies that I recommend and Covey's 7 Habits.

Three of Covey's 7 Habits are all about teamwork and cooperation and they are well worth reading and incorporating into your life as you start this new phase in your career. Habit 4 is to 'think win–win', to seek cooperation as an essential ingredient for a successful life and to avoid competition. Covey explains that: 'Win/Win is a frame of mind and heart that constantly seeks mutual benefit.'[2] To succeed in your new position, you must strive not only for the organisation's goals but to help your colleagues achieve them. Become a valuable and respected member of the team. Help your teammates whenever you can. This includes trying to establish a good rapport with those who initially appear hostile or resentful. In *Mandela's Way*, author Richard Stengel tells us that Nelson Mandela looked first for the good in everyone, seeking out the positive and constructive of those around him. Not only did this enable him to get something from everybody, he won tacit support and a sympathetic hearing from those who had previously been vehemently against him.[3]

If, therefore, you are confronted with someone, a colleague or subordinate, who is resentful and antagonistic, be friendly and courteous and comment on the things he does well not only to his face but to others. It's very hard to sustain hostility against someone who is being friendly. In this way, you will win him over or, at the very least, neutralise his opposition.

To do this successfully requires you to develop Habit 5: 'Seek first to understand, then to be understood.'[4] Understand why certain people react in a certain way; understand the difficulties that they may have faced in the past, experiences that perhaps made them the way they are. This is not dissimilar to Mandela's looking for the good in everyone. Unsurprisingly, there is a lot of overlap between the way Covey expresses the habits of highly successful people and how Stengel expresses the habits of one highly successful man.

Covey explains that to fully understand the other person's point of view, you need to listen with the aim of fully understanding their situation, to 'walk in their shoes'. Do this and you will win friends as well as loyal teammates.

When discussing issues with your team, you may hold strong views about the way the issue should be handled. And maybe your way is the best way. However, listen to what other team members say and be content to go along with the way that the majority adopt. Mandela called this 'Leading from the back'.[5] If that way doesn't work very well, your colleagues may decide to do it your way next time and you'll have gained some credibility. But if you argue forcefully to do it your way from the start, your colleagues may resent the new person telling them how to do the job. As a result, they may do it unwillingly and perhaps badly and so make it not work. If this happens, you will not be seen in a good light and your way to tackle the issue will be seen as a failure and, perhaps, never adopted in spite of being the best in theory.

Opening your mind to other people's ideas, to new possibilities and alternatives, is the basis of Covey's Sixth Habit, synergy.[6] When the whole team works together to find a solution and then implements it, all the members are driven by the same shared determination to make it work. That is when the greatest productivity occurs, that is when the best results will be achieved.

Being a member of the team and developing more and more confidence in the team's ability to perform does not mean abdicating responsibility for your own performance. When things go wrong — and they will from time to time — never be tempted to blame others, even if their actions might have been partially to blame. Always be prepared to admit your role in the incident. In this way, you will gain the respect of your superiors and the support of your colleagues.

Begin each day with a clear picture of what you hope to achieve during the day and keep that picture in front of you as the day progresses. In this way, you will find that you achieve so very much more than if you just complete work as it comes along.

Furthermore, keep in mind what you want to achieve in the coming twelve months, the next three or five years, and what you want your life to be like at these milestones of your future. The way you envisage your future will provide the motivation to drive you forward.

And finally, don't settle in comfortably and think, 'Now I've got a good job, I can relax.' Instead, continue to think of yourself as self-employed, the CEO of Yourself Pty Ltd, a micro-business with a major contract with your new employer. Then, instead of easing up and nestling down into a comfortable rut, you will always be on your toes, looking for ways to provide better customer service to your current employer, your 'client' and, of course, ready to look for a new 'client' whenever the need might arise.

Appendix:

Specimen résumés

James Schofield

37 Crystal Drive, Wainuiomata 6008

04 564 7357 (h)   021 740 566 (m)

jschofield@inet.co.nz

Summary

A cabinetmaker by trade, I have nearly 20 years' experience as Foreman at Wildwood Furniture, a high-quality furniture manufacturing plant. I have participated in Occupational Safety & Health training courses, taken part in skills audits, assisted the Factory Manager with job procedures, shut-downs and maintenance, and sustained close contact with all the workers on the shop floor.

To ensure that all orders are delivered in full, on time and in spec (IFOTIS), I have been active in all management meetings, including sales budgeting and reviewing performance measures in all areas of the factory — machine shop, assembly area and spray line. I participate in stocktakes and liaise with the Purchasing Officer re inventory control.

Relevant Skills and Achievements

Interpersonal, communication and team leadership skills

Since being appointed Foreman, I have supervised the work of a team of six full-time employees. My former co-workers were quick to accept my leadership and have worked well under my direction. During this time we have improved quality control as well as increasing production.

I initiate team meetings to talk through issues as they arise. This has led to a good team spirit and a commitment to working together to achieve our team goals. It has also led to specific improvements to both products and processes.

Occupational Safety & Health (OSH)

Have just renewed my first aid qualification which I have held since I was appointed Leading Hand in 1994.

Have undertaken training in harassment and government regulations regarding reporting levels of injury.

(This section continued next page.)

Further enhanced housekeeping procedures, ensuring all tools and materials are put away, trolleys moved in an orderly manner and floors swept. This has resulted in keeping both product loss and minor injuries to an absolute minimum.

Knowledge of operations and maintenance

Made sure that I know the proper procedures for stopping, starting and operating each machine (but not including programming).

Performed fault-finding procedures on various machines to correct boring and cutting tolerance inaccuracies.

In conjunction with the operators, I have ensured scheduled maintenance is properly performed on each machine, records kept and any problems reported for immediate rectification.

Understanding of IFOTIS

During my time at Wildwood, we have created a reputation as a reliable producer of high-quality furniture. In May 2009, when Perrimans first listed the Royale bedroom suite for their catalogue sale for all stores in both North and South Islands, I worked with the Purchasing Officer to make sure that we had the inventory, and briefed machine operators so as to ensure proper flow through the shop, in preparation for expected orders. When these came, we were able to produce 62 suites within the stipulated four-week timeframe, with not one unit requiring repair or touch-up.

During the first three years of my being Foreman, the production team reduced callouts for repairs from 4% to less than 1%.

Understanding of design drawings and lateral thinking

Over the past eight years, have been involved in the design of new furniture lines from the productivity point of view so as to make sure that the job flows smoothly through the workshop. Have developed good skills in visualising products and processes.

Proposed two modifications to the Royale bedhead to simplify assembly. These modifications were adopted and resulted in reducing average assembly time by 34 minutes — a considerable saving when working on the 62 suites ordered for Perrimans.

Saw a way of modifying four of the old jigs to suit the new Impériale dining suite, resulting in considerable cost saving in the set-up phase.

Inventory control

Suggested modifications to the job cards issued for each job. These now give not only a description of each job, the number to be cut and the next location, but also record the number completed and the number, if any, to be reworked or discarded.

Continue to work in close cooperation with the Purchasing Officer to decide on stock levels, the quality of hardware etc.

In the 19 years I have been Foreman, we have been able to reduce inventory levels by almost 20% without impacting on production or quality.

Career History

Foreman
Wildwood Furniture, 1982–present

o   Joined the company on completion of my apprenticeship in 1982 and was made Leading Hand in 1994 and Foreman in 2007.

Training and Development

National Certificate in Joinery, qualifying in Cabinetry, from the Joinery Industry Training Organisation, 1982.

o   Won award for best third-year apprentice.

Currently enrolled in the NZIM Certificate in Management (part-time) through Wellington Institute of Technology.

Numerous short courses in OSH, communication and customer service.

Personal Information

Born   31 October 1961

Health   Excellent, keen walker, social rugby

Happily married   Four adult children

Referees

Chris Foster
Purchasing Officer
Wildwood Furniture

04 526 8300
fosterc@wildwood.co.nz

Craig Hamilton
General Manager
Wildwood Furniture

04 526 8300
hamiltonc@wildwood.co.nz

Ms Felicity Tolman
(a senior teacher at my children's old
school and fellow member of Rotary)
Wainuiomata High School

04 524 7539
tolmanf@wainuiomatahigh.school.nz

Key Personal Qualities

o   Very conscious of both safety and quality issues.

o   A good leader and motivator.

o   Creative problem-solver.

Janet Turner

Samford Qld, 4520
0437 468 975 (m)
janet.turner@netspace.net.au
au.linkedin.com/in/janet_turner

Career Objective

Senior Account Manager where successful experience as an Account Manager and Marketing Manager together with strong customer service commitment, excellent organisation, communication and interpersonal skills will result in satisfied clients and increased business.

Professional Achievement Record

Marketing Manager
Grand Imperial Hotel, 2009–present

- Through targeted promotion, increased conference revenue by 17% over this time. This has been achieved through:
  o Identifying higher spending corporate organisations that hold conferences.
  o Developing a targeted advertising campaign in relevant journals and publications to build awareness and the profile of the hotel in the MICE sector.
  o Building close working relationships with key professional conference organisers with clients in the higher yielding corporate sector and facilitating site inspections and familiarisation tours of the property.

Account Coordinator and then Account Manager
BCM Advertising, 2006–2009

- Maintained excellent relationship with my clients.
- Developed and managed from the start the Teledome promotion.

Marketing Officer
Brisbane City Council, 1995–2006 (part-time until 2000)

- Led the team promoting the Brisbane Festival, 2002, 2004 and 2006.

Qualifications   **Bachelor of Commerce**
University of Queensland, 1978

- Major in HR.

Personal   Born   Ely, UK   23 May 1957
Information

Australian citizen since 1985

Health: excellent, keen walker and sailor

Married 27 years; 2 adult children

Referees   Antonio Felicetti   9459 4014 (w)
Senior Business Development   afelicetti@grandimperial.com.au
Manager
Grand Imperial Hotel

Don Treadwater   0457 623 983 (w)
(conference client)   treadwaterd@qantas.com
National President
Australian Association of Aeronautical
Engineers and
Manager, Qantas Maintenance Section
Brisbane

Key Personal   • Love challenge; quick to grasp complexities; can-do attitude.
Strengths
    • Hard-working, efficient and target-driven.

    • Committed to meeting and exceeding client expectations.

Marama Tuatini

73 Rodrigo Road
Kilbirnie, Wellington 6022
04 387 2376
0 27 437 2376
maramatuatini@xtra.co.nz

Career Profile

A career centred around music with a special passion for chamber music. Since graduating 30 years ago, I have played the cello in chamber music ensembles in New Zealand, Australia and Canada. Currently librarian at Orchestra Wellington and a regular performer in the Wellington Chamber Orchestra (WCO).

In the early 1990s I studied part-time for a degree in journalism and since then I have become a by-line music correspondent for Fairfax New Zealand with credits in *The Dominion Post* and *The Press* as well as articles in several other newspapers and magazines.

Employment

Librarian
Orchestra Wellington, since 2005

- This role has involved accessing music and managing copyright issues. It has given me a wide knowledge of musical repertoire and given me the knowledge and skills to help the Wellington Chamber Orchestra library access great music.

Journalist
Sydney and Wellington, since 1992

- Music correspondent for Fairfax NZ since 1996.

Freelance cellist and teacher
Sydney and Wellington, since 1993

- Member Wellington Chamber Orchestra (unpaid).

- With three other members of the WCO, attended the Banff Centre Chamber Music Residency, Canada, June 2010.

- Taught music and dance to private students and junior classes in both Sydney and Wellington.

- Competed in the national swing dance championships 1996; we came fourth.

Education

Master of Education (Music Education)
University of British Columbia, 1985

Bachelor of Music (Classical Performance)
NICAI, University of Auckland, 1981

- Performed in, and helped write and choreograph *A Prince for the Theatre*, a student-written, student-led and student-performed opera based loosely on the London musical *Chorus Girls*. The show was a success and the season was twice extended.

Bachelor of Journalism
University of Technology, Sydney, 1996

- Studied part-time by distance education while working full-time.

Personal Information

Born Rotorua, 15 July 1957

Excellent health; non-smoker, keen walker and dancer

Married; 1 adult daughter

Referees

Bernard Halliday   04 386 4880 (w)
Music Director   hallidayb@orchestrawellington.co.nz
Orchestra Wellington

Jessica Chalmers   04 388 9753 (w)
President   chalmers.j@gordonsmith.co.nz
Wellington Chamber Orchestra

Key Personal Attributes

- Hardworking and efficient.
- Highly organised to facilitate flexibility.
- Very good interpersonal and communication skills; a good team member and a good team leader.

Matteo Buonopane

237 Albert Street
Brunswick Vic 3056
03 9387 6835 (h)
0437 468 975 (m)
buonopane.m3@gmail.com

Objective

Assistant (Duty) Manager where a commitment to excellent customer service, the ability to solve problems quickly and effectively and the interpersonal and communication skills to motivate and lead, will help ensure excellent service and highly satisfied guests.

Relevant skills and achievements

Previous hotel experience

Twenty years in the hospitality industry as Owner/Manager of a motel and of an award-winning heritage B&B.

- With my wife, built the Welcome Nugget B&B in Ballarat from a three-room establishment to a 20-room luxury accommodation enterprise.

- Over the past three years, achieved a 77% occupancy rate through providing exceptional customer service and off-season special events.

- A large percentage of our customers became regulars, staying with us whenever they were in town or just enjoying a weekend break.

Availability to work shifts and weekends

Able and willing to work shifts and weekends. With 20 years in hospitality, I am well accustomed to the 24/7 nature of the industry.

Well developed problem-solving and analytical skills

Twenty years in accommodation management have given me excellent problem-solving and analytical skills.

- The wild storm in December last year caused the roof to leak in two suites when we were fully booked. One leak was in the ensuite but the other was over a bed.

  The occupants of both rooms were regular and valued customers. For those whose suite had the leak over the bed, I immediately

Relevant skills and achievements (continued)

phoned other suitable accommodation venues, booked and paid for a room and then provided a taxi at no cost to our clients.

For those whose suite had the leak over the bathroom, I provided extra bathmats to minimise the risk of slipping and waived payment for the room.

As a result, both clients have since stayed at Welcome Nugget and both attended my farewell in April.

Previous experience in a reservation system

Used RMS at both the Mountain View Motel and the Welcome Nugget. Confident that I could learn other systems reasonably quickly.

Ability to work autonomously and as part of a team

- As joint Owner/Manager, I worked autonomously much of the time but always in collaboration with my wife and business partner. I always saw us as a team.

- As a member of the Rotary Club of Ballarat South, I have been part of the team organising our stand at the Sunday market for the past five years.

Exceptional customer service skills

Commitment to excellence in customer service has been the hallmark of my more than 30 years in customer service industries, both retail and hospitality.

- A regular customer at the Welcome Nugget wrote: 'We have really enjoyed staying at your B&B because of the outstanding customer service you and your wife always provided.'

A strong work ethic and the ability to lead

Without a strong work ethic and without the ability to lead, we would not have been able to run such a successful, award-winning B&B over the past 15 years.

Career history

Joint Owner/Manager
Welcome Nugget heritage B&B accommodation
Ballarat, 1998–2014

- Won the HMAA Excellence in Luxury Boutique Accommodation award in 2009, with honourable mentions in 2008 and 2011.

- Managed a highly motivated team of five part-time staff including reception/bookings and housekeeping.

**Career history
(continued)**

Joint Owner/Manager
Mountain View Motel
Dunkeld, 1993–1998

- Previously Owner/Manager grocery retail: convenience store, gourmet foods, fruit and vegetables.

**Personal
information**

Born Naples, Italy, 9 August 1957

Arrived in Australia in 1960, Australian citizen since 1978

Health, good, walk one hour each day

Referees

Greg Hall
(regular customer)
Manager, Western Farm Machinery,
Sunshine

9363 7200 (w)
0438 543 987 (m)
g.hall@wfm.com.au

Don Treadwater
(Immediate Past President, Rotary Club of
Ballarat South)
Chief Financial Officer
Ballarat Base Hospital

0457 623 983 (m)
treadwater@bhs.org.au

**Key personal
strengths**

- Enjoy helping people and giving excellent customer service.

- Very good lateral thinker and problem-solver.

- Conscientious, reliable and responsible.

Penny Marshall

4371 Moratui Road
Colehaven Bay SA 5876
08 7345 8967 (h)
0409 458 967 (m)
pennymarshall@ozzienet.net.au

Career Summary

More than 15 years in retail and office administration including three in management positions. Experienced in stock control, account keeping and general administration and going the extra mile to provide great customer service.

Skills & Achievements

Computer skills

- Competent in using MS Word and Excel at basic level.

- Have used MYOB for stock control and sales.

Account keeping and stocktaking

- Compiled all weekly and monthly financial reports at The Natural Warmth Shop, 2008, when the Manager was overseas. Was complimented by the Accountant for handling it so efficiently with little training.

- Responsible for all banking, Kakadu Souvenirs, Birra Birra, and the Watermill Gift Shop.

- Undertook all buying for Watermill, priced all items and maintained strict stock control.

- Worked out the payroll for 20 staff at the Watermill on a relief basis.

Interpersonal and communication skills

- Spoke to clients over the telephone all the time at The Natural Warmth Shop including initiating follow-up calls.

- Worked as part of a close and efficient team at The Natural Warmth Shop and Watermill Gift Shop.

Penny Marshall

Skills & Achievements
(continued)

Responsibility, reliability and capacity to work hard

- Acted as Manager, The Natural Warmth Shop, while the Manager recovered from illness.

- Managed both the gate and the souvenir shop at the Watermill. Took up to $6000 per day at the gate and $3000 at the souvenir shop.

Career History

Sales and Office Assistant (casual and permanent)
The Natural Warmth Shop, 2005–2011

- Resigned to care for my husband.

Manager, Assistant Manager and Sales Assistant
Watermill Gift Shop, 1999–2005

Sales Assistant
Kakadu Souvenirs, Birra Birra, 1996–1999

Personal Information

Born Wincanton, 23 August 1963

Health, excellent, non-smoker

Widow, 1 adult son

Referees

Carmen Sawyer (formerly Manager, The Natural Warmth Shop)	08 7345 6325 (h)
Anthony West Regional Manager SA/NT, The Natural Warmth Shop	08 8832 7111 (w) 0409 523 498 (m) awest@naturalwarmth.com.au

Key Personal Attributes

- Friendly and outgoing.
- Hardworking, honest and reliable.
- Conscientious, accurate and efficient.

Richard Parker

Marri Park Drive
Casuarina WA 6167
08 9439 7452 (h)
0458 776 391 (m)
richardparker65@iinet.com.au

Career Objective

To use the skills developed over 25 years' successful experience in building and a further 10 in sales and marketing of roofing products and services to the building trade with the aim of providing excellent service to inbound customers at Barnard's Building Supplies and Hardware. This will result in strengthening and growing the existing loyal customer base and thus increase sales, market share and profitability.

Professional Experience

Account Manager/Sales
Over-the-Top Roofing Centre, Geraldton, 2003–2015

- Set-up a 'supply and fit' service to the domestic building industry throughout the Mid West region. This enabled the start-up company to gain significant market penetration against two already well-established national roofing suppliers.

- Built and maintained a loyal customer base across the whole region. This has enabled me to meet all sales targets in spite of a depressed building market.

Builder/Site Supervisor
Carnegie Constructions, Geraldton, 1993–2003

- Responsible for the construction of the Garth Penderbury Centre, a $27 million hospitality development at Yalgoo. The project consisted of a three-storey hotel, 52 self-catering units, five restaurants and an information centre. The Garth Penderbury Centre now caters for about 20,000 tourists a year.

Builder
Self-employed, Perth, 1978–1993

- Worked mainly in the new housing/renovation area.

Relevant Training

Certificate IV in Business Sales
TAFE WA, 2005

Certificate IV in Building and Construction (Estimating)
OTEN (Open Training and Education Network), 1998

Building Certificate
Perth Technical College, 1978

Community Involvement

Member
Geraldton Lions Club, since 1994
- Club President, 2006
- Currently Tail Twister

Personal Information

Excellent health, non-smoker, play social golf

Happily married 38 years; 2 sons, both adult

Referees

Ben Knight   0448 136 836 (m)
General Manager   bknight@overthetop.com.au
Over-the-Top Roofing Centre

Harry Everglade   0417 123 069 (m)
(President, Geraldton Lions Club) harry@everglade.com.au
Owner/Manager
Everglade Constructions

Key Personal Strengths

- Strong communication and interpersonal skills.

- Committed to providing excellent service to customers — understanding client needs and ensuring that they are fully met.

- Well organised, efficient, reliable and hard-working — I like to get the job done to the best possible standards within the right timeframe.

Steve Burton

435 Main Road
Kurri Kurri NSW 2327
02 4978 8901 (h)
0402 963 352 (m)
steveburton@hotmail.com

Summary

Twenty years in the Royal Australian Navy, rising to Chief Petty Officer. Nearly six years in logistics, facilities and maintenance management, responsible for coordinating and supervising the work of contractors in Simonstown and Fremantle. Managed budgets that sometimes exceeded $1 million.

Career Record

Royal Australian Navy 1981–present

Facilities Manager
RAN Logistics Office, Simonstown, March 2010–February 2014

Chief Engineer
HMAS *Perth*, 2006–2010

Facilities Assistant Manager
RAN Maritime Headquarters, Fremantle, 2003–2006

Relevant Training and Education

Diploma of Engineering in Marine Systems
RAN, 2005

Have almost completed **Certificate IV in Frontline Management**
RAN, two units still to be done.

Have also partially completed **Certificate IV in Government Procurement**
RAN

- Successfully completed major unit on Contract Management

Building Management System training
(covering computerised controls for air-conditioning, lighting, lifts etc.)
Grubb Technologies, Perth, 2003

Qualified Fitter and Turner (NSW qualification)
HMAS *Nirimba*, 1984

Biographical Details

Born Albany, WA, 27 July 1963

Health, excellent, non-smoker; regular gym

Happily married 21 years; 2 children, 18 and 16

People Who Know My Work Well

Lieutenant Commander Barry Turnbull
Commanding Officer
RAN Logistics Office, Simonstown

05 9321 7104 (w)
Barry.Turnbull@defence.gov.au

Greg Caldicott
(formerly Building Manager,
RAN Maritime Headquarters, Fremantle)
Facilities Manager, Family Law Courts

02 9876 5432 (w)
caldicott.g@justice.ca.gov.au

Key Personal Qualities

- Good team member and good team leader
- Hard-working and efficient
- Determined to maintain very high standards

Steve Burton

435 Main Road
Kurri Kurri NSW 2327
4978 8901
0402 963 352
steveburton@hotmail.com

Statement addressing the selection criteria

Contract Services Manager

Position number 0123456

1. **Demonstrated experience in contract management, maintenance management and a sound understanding of warehousing, freight distribution and operations under a defence contract.**

My 20 years in the RAN in positions as Facilities Management, Marine Engineering Chief Engineer on a ship and the later position of Technical Assistant to RAN Logistics Office (RANLO) Henty Bay, PNG, have given me excellent skills in Defence contract management in relation to facilities maintenance management, Naval engineering maintenance and the defence warehousing and stores management system.

- Six years highly successful experience responsible for the contract maintenance of buildings, plant and equipment worth approximately $100 million held by the Royal Australian Navy in Fremantle and Henty Bay. Have the reputation for getting things done fast, efficiently and to a very high standard. More than 10 years experience in project management in the repair and maintenance of ships, buildings, and plant, coordinating and supervising the work of many contractors. My success in these areas is largely responsible for my rapid promotion to Chief Petty Officer within 13 years.

- 20 years of engineering training in the Navy in various maintenance disciplines leading to a Diploma in Marine Engineering.

- As the Facilities Contractor Administrator (Fremantle) I was responsible for Maritime Headquarters, a 7-storey building accommodating 350 people; Headquarters Australian Theatre, a 6-storey building providing offices for 200 people; and the transmitting stations HMAS *Pinjarra* and HMAS *Doyle*. I supervised the General Building and Fixed Plant and Equipment (GB&FM) maintenance contracts and the contractors performing planned and breakdown maintenance required for 24/7 operation of the two multi-storey office buildings. Minor contract administration included cleaning, gardening and security contractors.

- As the Facilities and Property Officer (Henty Bay) I was responsible for a single-storey office block, a large engineering workshop designed for ship repair and incorporating a warehouse facility with a floor area of approximately 500m^2, and 10 residential houses. Evaluated tenders, short-listed and selected contractors for major housing renovation projects. Through better selection processes and refining the contract details, achieved significant

Steve Burton

savings over previous projects of a similar nature. Total contract value was in excess of $60,000. These projects involved painters, carpenters, electricians and plumbers. At the conclusion of these projects, because of my stringent quality control, the bungalows were in significantly better condition than had been anticipated and the projects came in under budget. I was commended for the careful way I had managed these projects. Contract administration included cleaning, gardening, pest and security contracts.

- When HMAS *Gondwana*, a fleet tanker, visited Henty Bay in November 2002 for planned repair work, I developed the request for quotes and tender (RFQ&T) documentation in accordance with the ASDEFCON regulations and subsequently managed the repair work. Project value was in excess of $0.7 million over 21 days. My work involved very close supervision and liaison to ensure the vast amount of contractors that worked together to achieve all planned works on time and to eliminate potentially dangerous situations. For example, I ensured that no welding was being carried out while the ship was refuelling and allocated painters to other areas while pipework was being carried out.

- I proposed, planned and managed a $200,000 contract upgrade of the heating, ventilation and air conditioning (HVAC) chiller control system at Maritime Headquarters within budget and ahead of schedule. This project made a significant reduction in energy consumption and extended the life of the machinery. For this project, I was awarded the Maritime Commander's Commendation (Admiral's Commendation).

2. Well-developed communications skills, both written and spoken, including effective representational, liaison and negotiation skills.

My ability to communicate and negotiate effectively across a range of levels and cultures has been one of my major strengths and been one of the reasons for my success in facility management and ship repair in Henty Bay.

- My commanding officer wrote: 'Much of Steve's success in Henty Bay can be attributed to his excellent interpersonal skills and sense of judgement. He displayed an exceptional level of cultural sensitivity and mixed well with people of all backgrounds with whom he dealt with, regardless of whether they were military, civilian, locals or expatriates.'

- Provided technical assistance to visiting RAN ships and submarines in Henty Bay. This required extensive liaison with local repair authorities, relevant class logistics office in Australia and the command structure of the visiting unit. The Commanding Officer of HMAS *Elphinstone* wrote in a signal to Naval Headquarters: 'RAN Logistics personnel (in particular CPO Burton) provided excellent support. Contractor liaison occurred in a prompt and professional manner resulting in the rectification of 5 urgent defects, including one at priority one.'

- Commander Collins wrote in a minute to the Director of Sailors' Career Management prior to my posting to Henty Bay: 'He and his family are well suited to representational duties and would be model ambassadors for the RAN and for Australia.

Steve Burton

3. **Demonstrated knowledge of Commonwealth procurement guidelines including complex procurement procedures and financial regulations, or the ability to quickly acquire this knowledge.**

My 6 years in Facilities Management as well as my experience as Chief Engineer on a ship have given me excellent skills in implementing procurement guidelines, including complex procurement procedures, financial regulations, and monitoring quality control guidelines with auditing contractor performance.

- Evaluated tenders, short-listed and selected contractors for a major housing renovation project in Henty Bay. Through better selection processes and refining the contract details, achieved significant savings over previous projects of a similar nature.

- Inspected assets and compiled appraisals for budgetary and proactive maintenance planning purposes. Planned works and prepared budgets for approval to achieve proposed works in accordance with government procurement regulations. Typically the budgets I managed were in excess of $400,000 value, and included lease component values, planned or reactive works and utility expenditures.

- An active member on the evaluation board conducting the tendering process for the General Building and Facility Maintenance contract (GB&FM) and Fixed Plant and Equipment (FP&E) for the southern region of Fremantle's Defence Establishments. I had particular responsibility for the two multi-storey buildings at Maritime Headquarters and Headquarters Australian Theatre, and the two transmitting stations HMAS *Pinjarra* and HMAS *Doyle*.

- Maintained extensive and detailed databases of the performance of individual contractors. As a result, I was better able to provide feedback, both positive and negative, to management and to the contractors. This also resulted in contractors making greater efforts to ensure that their work was of a high standard.

- Currently studying for Certificate IV in Complex Procurement.

4. **Demonstrated ability in problem solving, research and analytical skills, setting priorities, meeting deadlines and achieving work unit goals.**

Over my 20 years in the Navy, I have become an excellent problem solver. Whether it has been engine breakdown at sea or logistic support for vessels entering harbour for resupply or repair, I have become very adept at identifying the key issues, prioritising tasks and getting the necessary work done on time and within budget.

- When HMAS *Gondwana*, a fleet tanker, visited Henty Bay in November 2002 for planned repair work, I managed the contractor-assisted maintenance period. The work package involved researching repair methods of various fitted equipment and setting priorities and deadlines for works to be completed.

- I was required numerous times to co-ordinate at very short notice emergency repair of ships in the South East Asia region including Henty Bay with great

Steve Burton

success. HMAS *Melbourne*, while en-route to Sri Lanka, requested urgent assistance to rectify several defects with the ship's fitted breathing air-compressors. I arranged a contractor from Henty Bay to provide onsite assistance and I managed the project and solved any problems from Henty Bay.

5. **Demonstrated computer literacy skills including the ability to utilise corporate information systems, such as Standard Defence Supply System (SDSS) (including MIMS Maintenance Management (MMM) and standalone databases, or the ability to quickly acquire this ability.**

Since 1997, I have been using SLIMS (a shipboard version of SDSS) on a daily basis, along with a number of other databases, for store management, usage and upkeep, and requests for stores and returns. I am competent in MS Word and I have basic knowledge and experience of MS Excel.

- As the IT/LAN manager for the RANLO Henty Bay office complex, I proposed, planned and managed the procurement of new computers, including software, LAN upgrade and the installation of high-speed broadband Internet and e-mail access.

- Performing duties as the Chief of Propulsion required the extensive use of database management for compilation and tracking of contractor-assisted maintenance requests and raising Urgent Defect signals (URDEF).

- I am very conversant with the SLIMS database for the ordering of engineering consumables and machinery spare parts. SLIMS is very similar to, and compatible with, the SDSS database and is linked to SDSS to process demands and returns and to conduct stock checks. I have received training throughout my career regarding the Defence Military Stores system and its usage including terms such as FAD, UND and priority designator in obtaining stock numbers utilising the Common Management Code or microfiche card systems.

Linda Heatherton

10 Panners Way
Queenstown 9300
03 443 5632 (h)
0 27 265 3759 (m)
lindaheatherton@xtra.co.nz

Friday, 17 April 2015

Marion Carmichael
Managing Director
Lord of the Rings Tours
37 Shotover Street
Queenstown 9300

LOTR / Hobbit Tour Guide — Expression of Interest

Dear Mrs Carmichael,

I would love to help visitors experience the filming locations for *The Lord of the Rings* and *The Hobbit*. I have a passion for the writings of JRR Tolkien and I loved the way these great books were transformed for the screen.

I will bring to the position:

- A thorough knowledge of both books which comes from using them as major texts for secondary English and Drama classes for more than 10 years.

- A commitment to providing the highest possible level of customer service.

- The ability to think on my feet and to solve problems quickly and decisively as they arise; a can-do attitude.

- The people and communication skills to engage and motivate people to participate enthusiastically in the programs that I lead.

My thorough knowledge of *The Lord of the Rings (LOTR)* comes from reading it at least five times and *The Hobbit* three times just for my own pleasure and from using *LOTR* as a major text for years 9 and 10 English and Drama since filming began in late 1999.

Customer service in the teaching profession means providing excellent teaching service to students and advice to their parents. I have an absolute commitment to both and my success in this area is demonstrated by the excellent rapport I have with both students and their parents.

The best example demonstrating my cheery, can-do attitude and effective problem-solving skills is probably the fact that I have directed the school musical for the past 7 years. This involves staying calm and positive when things go wrong, motivating the 20 or more students in the cast and stage crew, and encouraging rather than chastising them when they make mistakes.

It also requires quick thinking to resolve the frequent problems inherent in such a venture.

Through teaching, interacting with other staff members and by talking to parents, I have developed strong interpersonal and communication skills. As a teacher, I work autonomously but I am always aware that I am part of the team at Wakatipu High. The relationship that I have developed with my colleagues is testimony to my success in this area.

I have travelled a little in China and I have a very basic understanding of Mandarin.

I have researched the requirements for a P licence and I am confident that I would be quickly able to obtain one. I am a good, careful driver and a 'fit and proper person'.

My résumé gives a more detailed outline of my background and the qualities and qualifications that I would bring to the position and an insight into my bright, cheery, can-do attitude.

Yours sincerely,

Linda Heatherton

Linda Heatherton

10 Panners Way
Queenstown 9300
03 443 5632 (h)
0 27 265 3759 (m)
lindaheatherton@xtra.co.nz

Objective

LOTR/Hobbit Tour Guide where a love of the works of JRR Tolkien and of the films *The Lord of the Rings* and *The Hobbit*, together with a commitment to exceeding customer expectations, excellent interpersonal and communication skills and a cheery, can-do attitude will help ensure highly satisfied customers and increased business.

Employment History

Teacher
English and Drama, Wakatipu High School, since 1993

- Head of Drama Department, since 2005

Raising children and providing administrative support for Snow Day Ski School, 1984–1993

Teacher
English and Drama, St Joseph's School, 1981–1982

Ski Instructor
Snow Day Ski School (my husband's business), 1980–1981

Education

Bachelor of Education (Honours 1)
University of Canterbury, 1979

- Majors in English and Drama

- Won the Katherine Mansfield Memorial Award for Greatest Proficiency in Second Year English, 1977

Linda Heatherton

Community Involvement

Queenstown Film Society
Member since 1987; held positions of Treasurer and Secretary at various times

Wakatipu Walkers
Member for about the last 10 years and regularly walking with them during school holidays

The Sociable Book Club
Member since the club reformed last year

Personal Information

Born   Christchurch, 12 September 1955

Health   Excellent, non-smoker; enjoy bushwalking and skiing

Married to John since 1981; 2 children, both adults

Referees

Manuka Williams   03 441 3244 (w)
Principal, Wakatipu High School   principal@wakatipu.school.nz

Mrs Rowena Hatton   03 441 3244 (w)
Head of Music   hattonr@wakatipu.school.nz
Wakatipu High School

Key Personal Strengths

- Thorough knowledge of *The Lord of the Rings* and *The Hobbit*; read both books and seen the films of *LOTR*; would love to help others come to love them too

- Excellent communication and interpersonal skills; a careful and patient listener interested in what others are saying

- Responsible and reliable, and committed to excellent customer service

Tom Matlock

Balcomba Qld 4702
07 6274 1407 (h)
matlockt7@optusnet.com.au
http://au.linkedin.com/in/tom_matlock

Tuesday, 9 December 2014

Tony Burroughs
HR Manager
Cuthbertson Roofing
48 George Street
Rockhampton Qld 4700

Senior Safety Consultant

Dear Tony,

I have enjoyed 12 years' managing OH&S in the RAAF, and I would love to be able to provide effective OH&S policies for Cuthbertson Roofing. I notice that, although risk is inherent in the roofing industry, you have an enviable safety record. I would like to help you maintain that record.

My experience covers providing OH&S in catering, accommodation and transport. In spite of the risks in all three areas, we managed to keep lost time through injury to well below the national frequency rates.

I have developed policies, negotiated with management to change procedures to reduce risk, and run training programs for supervisors, for operative staff and for contractors. I wrote from scratch the OH&S policies and procedures for Messing Services, RAAF Glenbrook, and these now form the basis for OH&S practices for most of the other sections on the base.

My management skills have been developed when I was responsible for eleven facilities providing catering, accommodation and recreational services and through my supervision and coordination of 70 permanent civilian and Defence Force personnel and looking after the requirements of up to 2000 people at peak times.

Through lateral thinking and careful negotiation, I was able to provide alternative transport facilities. I ensured that all personnel on the base were aware of the new transport arrangements and, as a result, I was able to virtually eliminate fuel fraud and the misuse of service vehicles at RAAF Balberra. This has resulted in an annual saving of about $10,000.

My résumé provides further details of the relevant skills and experience that I would bring to the position and an understanding of my determination to do the job properly.

Yours sincerely,

Tom Matlock

Tom Matlock

Balcomba Qld 4702
07 6274 1407 (h)
matlockt7@optusnet.com.au
http://au.linkedin.com/in/tom_matlock

Summary

An innovative and effective OH&S Manager with a history of establishing and improving OH&S policies and procedures for RAAF bases in NSW and NT.

Career History

Royal Australian Air Force, 1984–present

Transport Manager
43 Squadron, Balberra, 2007–present

- Eliminated fuel fraud and misuse of squadron vehicles, an estimated cost saving of $10,000 per year.

Senior Messing Services Manager
RAAF Base, Glenbrook, NSW, 2006–2007

- Responsible for the logistics of accommodating and feeding up to 2000 personnel each week.

Contract Liaison Officer
Air Headquarters, Tindal, NT, 2004–2006

Mess Manager
RAAF Base, Tindal, NT, 2001–2004

RAAF Representative
USAF Inyokern Training Squadron,
California, USA, 2000

- Studied US workplace systems to facilitate and capitalise on change and innovation.

Tom Matlock

Education and Training

Diploma in Front Line Management
Australian Defence College, Canberra, 2004

Advanced Occupational Health & Safety Management
National Safety Council of Australia, 2003

Certificate of Attainment in Hazard Management
Australian Public Service, 2002

Personal Information

Born   Singapore, 23 March 1955

Australian citizen

Health Excellent, non-smoker, keen bushwalker

Happily married 24 years; 2 children, 21 and 18

Referees

Flying Officer Rob Porter   08 5432 6789 (w)
RAAF Base, Darwin
Robert.Porter@defence.gov.au

Squadron Leader Mick Cheltenham
32 Squadron, Glenbrook
Michael.Cheltenham@defence.gov.au

Key Personal Attributes

- Clear thinking, good problem-solver.
- Effective team leader with good communication and people skills.
- Hard-working, responsible and efficient.

David Campbell

149 Cribbes Road
Sudbury Vic 3745
03 5922 3562 (h)
0457 654 927 (m)
david.campbell33@gmail.com

3 March 2015

Dorothy Dando
Chairperson
Star Futures Youth Services Inc
PO Box 1276
Wangaratta Vic 3676

Chief Executive Officer, Star Futures Youth Services

Dear Mrs Dando,

This position would allow me to make full use of my leadership skills and business background while fulfilling my passion for helping young people.

I will bring to the position:

- Seven years' experience in residential care, three in management.
- Twenty years in banking, rising to Compliance Manager.
- The leadership and interpersonal skills to successfully build and develop an outstanding team.
- The ability to lead a team through significant change.
- The communication and persuasion skills to attract sponsorship and support.

With this letter, I enclose my résumé and statement addressing the selection criteria. These will provide further details of my relevant skills and achievements and an understanding of my determination to help young people achieve happy and productive lives.

Yours sincerely,

David Campbell

David Campbell

149 Cribbes Road
Sudbury Vic 3745
03 5922 3562 (h)
0457 654 927 (m)
david.campbell33@gmail.com

Career Objective

Chief Executive Officer where my passion for helping young people coupled with my business background and ability to build and lead happy teams will help Star Futures remain financially secure and continue to provide much needed support for Wangaratta's youth.

Professional Experience

Residential Care Worker/Supervisor and Group Manager
Widdicombe Downs Residential Care, Sudbury, since 2007 (Supervisor since 2009, Group Manager since 2011)

Widdicombe Downs has three houses in the Sudbury area, providing accommodation for up to ten young people, aged between 13 and 17. These young people have challenging and complex needs. They have often suffered great distress and significant harm growing up with violence, neglect, abuse, trauma and poverty.

Widdicombe Downs is a not-for-profit, non-government organisation overseen by a Community Board of Management.

- Through involving staff and volunteers, and where appropriate the young people themselves, in the day-to-day management of the homes, we have built a close-knit team and a harmonious environment in all three houses.

Joint Owner/Manager
Sudbury General Store, 1998–2010

This is the only grocery business within 15 km of Sudbury and the main source of groceries for local residents.

- When a major supermarket chain planned to open a store in Bright, we developed strategies with our permanent and casual staff to retain our local customer base through enhanced customer service.
- Established a service of free home delivery to make it easier for rural customers to get their groceries.

Compliance Manager
Cornwallis Bank, Wodonga, 1995–1998

Other positions in banking back to 1978

- Identified emerging and changing regulations that could affect the business and informed internal stakeholders, providing them with sound and practical advice on corporate risk and compliance issues.

David Campbell

Qualifications and Training

Bachelor of Commerce (Accounting)
Melbourne University, 1978

Diploma in Youth Work
OTEN (part-time, online) since 2012; expect to complete in June

Workplace II First Aid
St John Ambulance, last renewed March 2013

Community Involvement

Member
Sudbury Lions Club since 1999

- Member of the finance committee organising and managing budgets for the annual music hall and mountain bike championships.

Personal Information

Born   Geelong, 23 November 1956

Health   Excellent, non-smoker, regular fitness program

Happily married 32 years, 3 adult children

Referees

Faye Donaghue   03 3945 7234 (h)
Chairperson, Sudbury Board   0456 321 987 (m)
Widdicombe Downs Children's Home   donaghue@widdicombedowns.org.au

Barry Churton   03 3843 9087 (w)
(President, Sudbury Lions Club)   0424 934 774 (m)
Manager, Engineering Services   barry.churton@indigo.vic.gov.au
Indigo Shire Council

Key Personal strengths

- Passionate about the welfare of young people.
- Energetic, lateral thinker, vision driven.
- A good team leader and motivator.

David Campbell

149 Cribbes Road
Sudbury Vic 3745
03 5922 3562 (h)
0457 654 927 (m)
david.campbell33@gmail.com

Statement addressing the selection criteria

Chief Executive Officer

Star Futures Youth Services

1. **Understanding of the issues and challenges facing young people in contemporary culture, including the impact of social policy. Ability to engage with and communicate effectively with young people.**

   Almost seven years as Residential Care Worker, five as Supervisor and three as Group Manager, at Widdicombe Downs Residential Care have given me an excellent understanding of the issues and challenges facing young people in today's culture and developed my ability to engage and communicate with young people.

   - Three weeks ago, counselled a 17-year-old boy who had been suspended from school because of fighting. He had been doing well and was in line for a traineeship but his suspension could jeopardise his chances. He told me that he fought because he was being bullied by a number of students about being in residential care. Explained the situation to the school principal and arranged for details of all the work that he would miss during his suspension to be sent to the group home.

     Helped him learn the material and complete the assignments as well as assisting him to develop strategies for coping with the bullying. The principal also agreed to speak to the students who were bullying him.

     The result is that he is now back at school; he is no longer being bullied, his studies are going well, and he has every likelihood of getting the traineeship.

2. **Demonstrated leadership and motivational skills.**

   Good leadership is essential to running residential care. Not only do I lead the team of paid employees and volunteers across the three houses but I also need to lead and motivate the young people.

   - Mediated in a dispute between a staff member and a resident. This was a boy who was rostered on at short notice for kitchen duties. He had planned to play computer games with one of the other residents.

     He reacted angrily and threw crockery into the sink, breaking some plates and splashing a lot of water over the floor. I took him aside, and explained that it was not the staff member's fault that he had been rostered for helping in the

David Campbell

kitchen. When he had calmed down, he agreed and I asked him how he intended to make amends.

He said that he would clean up the kitchen area immediately and he would do the washing up after tea for the next two nights. He did this and apologised nicely to the staff member.

3. A record of success in working effectively with a Board of Management.

Work very harmoniously with the Board of Management of Widdicombe Downs Residential Care and have worked especially closely since taking on the role of Area Manager. I keep the Board informed of issues across all three houses and up-to-date with the progress that we are making.

- Three years ago, we had two houses accommodating seven young people. We knew that there was an urgent need for more residential care. I worked with the Board to do a business plan for building or purchasing a third house. To do this, I consulted Department officials and visited a number of residential care establishments in the State to get specifications and ideas. I then consulted architects to get suitable designs and cost estimates and I took these to the Board to choose a design. I researched possible sources of funding, put a proposal to the Board which was accepted and wrote a submission for a grant under the Cornwall Scheme.

  The submission was successful and, under the Board's direction, I invited tenders for construction. The Board selected a tender and then I oversaw construction including monitoring the budget. Completion was delayed by bad weather but came in on budget.

  Before completion, I worked with the Board to recruit and select staff for the house. I organised the necessary training and clearances, and the first young people were in residence within three weeks of completion.

- Work very closely with the Board each year to plan and implement fundraising activities. The Widdicombe Fair last year attracted people from as far away as Beechworth and Bright and raised $22,000.

4. A proven record at a senior level of policy development, management, strategic and business planning and evaluation within a human services/community services organisation.

Almost 15 years in management positions have helped me develop high level management skills and a capacity for effective strategic and business planning. These abilities have proved invaluable in my current role as Group Manager at Widdicombe. Over the last three years, I have overseen the construction of a third residential care unit and the resulting recruitment, training and management of additional staff and volunteers. One of the most challenging instances of policy development, however, came from deciding to accept into Widdicombe a boy who initially had very challenging behaviour.

David Campbell

- Two years ago, the Board asked if I would be willing to accept a 13-year-old with a history of being very difficult. He had been in foster care and living with relatives and it hadn't worked. He had been known to frequently abuse both adults and young people and to wantonly destroy other people's property. I took the request to a meeting of staff and volunteers and then had a meeting with the other three young people in the home. There was some apprehension but we agreed to take him and together we worked out strategies to help him settle in as quickly and easily as possible. I reported these strategies to the Board, along with our decision.

  Initially he was very difficult. He was angry with everyone and deliberately stole or destroyed the property of other young people or the home. However, we stuck to our strategies. Gradually we gained his trust and I reported our progress to the Board who gave us a lot of support.

  The big leap forward came when we discovered that he loved skateboarding. With the Board's approval, we bought him a skateboard and a staff member who is himself a skilled skateboarder takes him to the local skateboard park two or three times a week. I am now working with the Board and other staff members to see if we can help him compete in the skateboard competition in Wonthaggi next month.

5. **Highly developed communication and public relations skills.**

   My communication skills have been developed and demonstrated throughout my career. As Compliance Manager at Cornwallis Bank, I had to inform senior management, often very diplomatically, about the risks involved with the strategic directions that they were proposing.

   My public relations skills have largely been developed during my time at Widdicombe Downs. Since taking up this role, I have made several presentations to service clubs, corporate management and public forums as well as several radio interviews and one television appearance.

   The effectiveness of my public relations activities is shown by more than $100,000 in corporate sponsorship last financial year. This came as a direct result of my speaking at the Wodonga Chamber Awards dinner in 2012.

6. **Knowledge of legislation, regulations and the economic and political environments relating to the human services sector.**

   I have been very conscious of legislation, regulations and economic and political environments since taking on the role of Compliance Manager, Cornwallis Bank. In that role, I developed the habit of making sure that I was totally up-to-date with all relevant information.

   Since taking over at Widdicombe Downs, I have focused on the regulatory, political and economic environment that relates to human services.

David Campbell

7. **Evidence of successful involvement in change management processes.**

The changes that have had the most impact on Widdicombe have been the addition of the third house and the admission of a boy with very challenging behaviour. Both required careful planning, extensive discussion with all stakeholders and the development of agreed strategies to manage the change.

The fact that both changes have been successful is evidence of the level of agreement and commitment we managed to get from staff, volunteers and the young people themselves. Once we were working together towards commonly agreed goals, change management was easy. When there were difficulties, and there were plenty, all parties together worked out how to overcome those difficulties and then willingly did what was necessary. It has always been a team effort and I have always involved the team in decision-making and planning.

8. **Proven capacity in budgeting, financial monitoring and reporting to achieve organisational goals.**

My accounting degree and 20 years in banking have given me excellent financial monitoring skills which have been invaluable both in the purchase and successful operation of a general store and in the management of Widdicombe Downs, especially during its period of expansion.

- Drew up a budget of $320,000 for the last financial year and presented it to the Board for approval. Projected income included State and Federal government funding, corporate sponsorship and income from the annual Widdicombe Fair.

  In spite of a reduction in government funding, we were able to achieve a slight budget surplus through some careful cost cutting that did not impact on the quality of life of our young people and through additional support provided by the Lions Club.

9. **Understanding and commitment to continuous quality improvement and best practice in the human services field.**

To ensure best practice at Widdicombe Downs and to maximise staff morale, I have been active in encouraging staff, both paid and volunteers, to undertake professional development training. I always budget to ensure that all contingent costs are covered and, as a result, have achieved a well trained, highly motivated team.

- With the Victorian Foster Parents Association and with delegates from two other residential care facilities, ran a very successful conference in Wangaratta. Three Widdicombe Downs staff members, one salaried and two volunteers, made a presentation on helping young people cope with depression which was very well received and one of the older boys was on stage to answer questions.

  Arranged for all members of staff to attend at least one day of the three-day conference. The impact of the conference on morale at the home was fantastic.

David Campbell

10. **Information technology skills.**

   Use a computer, a tablet and a smartphone all the time. Competent using the MS Office suite for emails, word processing, spreadsheets and presentation slides. Use MYOB AccountRight Plus for all the home's accounts and stock control.

11. **Ability to lead, manage, supervise and motivate staff in achieving desired goals.**

   Have held management positions for almost 20 years. Since 2012, I have led, managed, supervised and motivated a team of twelve salaried staff and fourteen volunteers to run Widdicombe Downs three houses. During this time, we have gained five new volunteers and lost no one. Morale is high, the young people are well cared for and the home is clean and well maintained.

   Much of my success has been a result of involving staff as well as the Board in setting our priorities and planning the strategies to best achieve them. In this way, staff feel 'ownership' of the plan and are, as a result, even more determined to achieve the right outcomes.

12. **Ability to develop and set objectives, performance and development criteria, targets and establish priorities.**

   Running a successful residential care facility, as with running a successful business, requires establishing objectives and performance criteria, setting priorities and then making plans to achieve them.

   My success in this area is demonstrated by the success of Widdicombe Downs. After an inspection by officers of the Department of Human Services last year, the report read that the three houses '... are clean and comfortable. There is a feeling of peace and harmony and the young people appear happy and well cared for'.

13. **Strong, clear and concise interpersonal skills including oral and written report presentation.**

   My oral and written reports to the Board, to the Department of Human Services and to sponsoring organisations have been concise, clear and well received. My ability to give less formal reports to service clubs and other community organisations together with my ability to quickly build rapport has resulted in increased support from the community in both cash donations and in-kind assistance.

14. **Negotiation and conflict resolution skills.**

   Negotiation and conflict resolution are an important component of my role. Whether it is resolving conflict between young people or between young people and staff, it requires tact and respect of all who are involved in the conflict. A lot of negotiation is required in conflict resolution but negotiation of a slightly different sort is required when seeking corporate sponsorship. My success in this area has been demonstrated by the increase in corporate sponsorship enjoyed by the group since I became Manager in 2012.

David Campbell

15. **Understanding of and commitment to contemporary HR principles and practices.**

    Having managed staff for more than 20 years, I have a good understanding of and commitment to contemporary HR principles and practices.

    Attended two one-day HR seminars last year, one on building and developing talent and the other on developing effective HR policies and procedures.

16. **A current driver's licence**

    Manual car driver's licence since 1976. No current demerit points.

17. **Full pre-employment security check**

    Currently have full security clearance including identification, national criminal history and working with children check. Willing to undergo a new check or provide certificates as required.

Don Bradley

Bridlington, SA 5678
08 3462 1792 (h)   08 3460 8879 (w)   0434 220 187 (m)
bradleyd@wellington.sa.gov.au
au.linkedin.com/don_bradley

Tuesday, 20 January 2015

Bernie Conningham
General Manager
Broadhurst Shire Council
PO Box 567
Broadhurst, Vic, 3456

Technical Services Manager (*Western Mail*, 10/01/15)

Dear Mr Conningham,

I would love to be part of your dynamic, progressive team and I would welcome the opportunity to place a positive stamp on the municipality. I do have vision and drive and I am stimulated by challenge. Here is my application for this exciting position.

I will bring to the position:

- Twenty years' experience as a graduate civil engineer, including fourteen in local government and the past five in senior management.

- Excellent human resource management, motivation and leadership skills.

- Highly developed interpersonal and communication skills.

My résumé and statement of claims against the selection criteria will provide details of the relevant skills and achievements that I would bring to the position and an understanding of my determination to complete all projects to high standards, on time and on budget.

Yours sincerely,

Don Bradley

Don Bradley

Bridlington, SA 5678
08 3462 1792 (h)   08 3460 8879 (w)   0434 220 187 (m)
bradleyd@wellington.sa.gov.au
au.linkedin.com/don_bradley

Personal Information

Born Lae PNG, 14 July 1962

Australian citizen

Health good: non-smoker, daily walking, keen cyclist, social golf

Happily married to Erica 22 years; 2 daughters, Emily 20 and Ruth 18

Career Record

Assistant Manager, Engineering Services
Wellington Shire Council, 2008–present

- Initiated self-directed work teams. This approach has improved productivity by up to 20% particularly in outlying areas of the shire.

- Designed and implemented with the approval of the Manager, waste transfer and recycling system and infrastructure. This undertaking won the Premier's Environmental Projects Award in 2010.

Design Engineer
Wellington Shire Council, 2003–2008

Site Supervisor
Wellington Shire Council, 1996–2003

Site Engineer
Bolton Constructions, Curriedale, NSW, 1991–1996

Assistant Contract Engineer
Cambridge, Danderfield & Associates, Consulting Engineers
Pembroke, NSW, 1985–1991

Qualifications and Training

B Eng
George Bass University 1984

- Majored in Civil Engineering

Grad Cert Eng (Local Govt Eng)
QUT 1999

Cert IV CAD
TAFE Bridlington 2001

Park Management Program (1 week)
Bond University 2001

Dip Bus (Human Resources)
Productivity Training P/L 2006

Professional Memberships

MIE (Aust)

Associate Fellow AIM

Local Government Managers, Aust

Community and Sporting Activities

Bridlington Lions Club

Castle Hill Cycling Club

Referees

Colin Hammersley · 08 3460 8851 (w)
Manager, Engineering Services · 0418 353 869 (m)
Wellington Shire Council · hammers@wellington.sa.gov.au

Brendan Huxworth · 08 3461 4341 (w)
Immediate Past President · brendanh@tolpuddle.com.au
Bridlington Lions Club and
co-organiser with me of
Bridlington Wheel Cycling Carnival

Key Personal Strengths

- Highly qualified and experienced in all areas of local government technical services.
- An excellent people manager, motivator and leader.
- Always willing to go the extra mile for the benefit of the team.

Don Bradley

Bridlington, SA 5678
08 3462 1792 (h)   08 3460 8879 (w)   0434 220 187 (m)
bradleyd@wellington.sa.gov.au

Statement of claims against the selection criteria

Technical Services Manager

Significant experience in local government engineering and management at a senior level with demonstrated knowledge of technical engineering standards, procedures and practices in all council's Technical Services areas.

My 20 years as a Civil Engineer, including fourteen in local government, have given me experience across a wide range of engineering projects and local government Technical Services areas including buildings, roads, bridges, drainage, sewerage, waste and park management. During this time I have earned a reputation for cost-effective yet structurally sound design and aesthetically pleasing completion.

- Under the guidance of the Manager, Engineering Services, designed and supervised a $50,000 upgrade of the East Bridlington sewerage system, 1999–2000. The job was completed two weeks early and was on budget.

- With the Manager, Engineering Services, designed and implemented a waste transfer and recycling program covering the whole shire, 2009. This program was awarded the Premier's Environmental Projects Award the following year.

- As a member of the State Emergency Service, helped prepare plans for flooding control and evacuation for the Curriedale region, 1995. Was involved in designing and directing training exercises to ensure the coordination of police, fire brigade, Australian Defence Force units and volunteers. These plans proved very effective during the massive floods of 2002.

- Initiated and coordinated emergency temporary repairs to the Belfoster Main Road within 7 hours of receiving a report of subsidence after heavy rain. Designed and implemented immediate improvements to drainage, strengthening of the embankment and resurfacing of the road. These were completed within 15 working days.

- Site Engineer, Bolton Constructions, overseeing the construction of a new $257,000 road bridge over the Sparrowhawk River, 1995. This project manifested some interesting engineering challenges. The bridge carries heavy traffic including log trucks, milk tankers, and the newly introduced B-doubles.

  When in flood, and the river did flood during the construction, the river can have a peak flow of 450 megalitres/second and it has been known to change its course through its banks of silt and sand. The bedrock is 10 metres below the surface.

Because of these factors, any inaccuracy or deviation from the carefully drawn plans could risk failure, partial or complete, of the structure. In spite of these difficulties, the bridge was completed on time and with less than a 5% overrun on the budget.

- Land use planning: a local dairy farmer sought planning permission to set up and operate a boutique cheese factory in 2012 while I was Assistant Manager, Engineering Services. I took the farmer through the whole process, ensuring that his proposals met all local government requirements as well as State and Federal regulations. This included checking his building plans for structural soundness, food hygiene requirements, OH&S factors, water and sewerage, and transport access.

  The factory has now been built and the cheeses produced there have already won medals at agricultural shows.

- Completed one-week course in Park Management, Bond University, October 2001. Since January 2004 have overseen the maintenance of Bellevue Gardens, often considered the 'botanical gardens of the west' and an important tourist attraction.

Have developed sound financial management skills through:

- Completing a unit on Accounting and Financial Management as part of my Diploma of Business – Human Resources, 2006.

- Preparing the Engineering Services budget for the Wellington Shire Council under the guidance of the former ES Manager in 2011, prior to his going on long service leave, and then on my own while he was on leave in 2012.

- Setting the budget, managing all receipts and payments, bookkeeping and acquittal for the Bridlington Wheel Cycling Carnival each year from 2005 to present.

Sound knowledge of human resource management including Equal Employment Opportunity

Under the direction of the Manager, Engineering Services, supervise and direct up to 70 employees, full-time, part-time and casual, in roads, drainage, gardens and reserves, shire buildings and infrastructure, water supply, quarries and waste management. The employees include fourteen women and five people with disabilities ranging from missing three fingers on one hand to being wheelchair-bound. Twenty-one employees claim Aboriginal descent.

- On the advice of the Manager, ES, completed the Diploma of Business – Human Resources through Productivity Training Pty Ltd in 2006. Selected two optional units on Team Leadership and Motivating the Workforce. The knowledge and skills developed through these two units have helped me develop highly productive teams.

- In performance appraisals over the past few years, have been described as an 'excellent motivator'. Delegate authority to maximise employee initiative and involvement. Ensure all employees are given the opportunity for appropriate training and development.

- Introduced the concept of self-directed teams, 2005. This has proved particularly effective in carrying out work in the more remote areas of the shire.

  Team leaders attended a three-day leadership program run by Coulton Consultants Pty Ltd.

I work with the team leaders to set objectives, quality assurance procedures and to identify strategies for solving problems that are likely to occur on particular projects.

- Conscious of OH&S issues. Organised an in-house, one-day-per-month training program for team leaders in health and safety, 2012. This six-month program has resulted in a 22% drop in lost time through injury and an 8% reduction in workers compensation insurance premiums over the past two years.

- Drew up the position descriptions and selection criteria, wrote and placed the advertisements, received and shortlisted applicants and was a member of the interview panel for 22 different positions over the past two years. Three of the people I helped to select were of Aboriginal descent and one, a draughtsman, is in a wheelchair.

Demonstrated high level of interpersonal skills

Have always enjoyed working as a member of a team as well as being a team leader. Even when engaged on a major project away from base, I am very conscious of being part of a larger team. When supervising the construction of the bridge over the Sparrowhawk River, 120 km west of Curriedale, I was in constant contact with fellow team members back at base.

- Always enjoy good rapport with senior management, colleagues and the workforce. Was described by Brendan Huxworth, who with me organised last year's Bridlington Wheel Cycling Carnival, as someone who can 'get anyone to do anything and think they're privileged to have been asked'.

- Organise a barbecue or other social event for the workforce and their families about twice a year, often at the site of a recently completed major project. This has had the effect of building a strong sense of unity among the employees and a sense of pride in their achievements.

- As Assistant Manager, Engineering Services, I have been responsible for drafting all press releases and for arranging press conferences. Over the past five years, have built up and maintained an excellent relationship with both the *Wellington Times* and Radio 5WB.

- Elected Secretary for the Bridlington Lions Club earlier this year.

Always treat residents and visitors with courtesy and respect. The residents are our clients and our employers, and visitors comprise an important element in the residents' business and social lives.

- When a burst water main required major excavations in front of the cinema during the school holidays, I had temporary raised wooden walkways constructed so as to ensure minimum inconvenience to cinema-goers. For this, I received a very warm thank-you letter from the cinema's manager.

- Emailed daily bulletins to both the *Wellington Times* and Radio 5WB so as to keep the community fully informed. Also left a pile of the daily bulletins at the cinema.

High level of oral and written communication skills in the English language

During my years in supervisory and management roles, I have developed a very high level of oral and written communication skills. As Assistant Manager, Engineering Services, I am in constant contact with the council's officers and workforce, neighbouring councils, State and Federal government agencies, residents, local businesses, community organisations and the media. I am known for clear, concise, accurate and diplomatic communication, whether written or spoken.

- My Manager, Colin Hammersley, trained me thoroughly in the processes and procedures for providing advice, documentation and reports to councillors in sufficient time to allow proper perusal before council and committee meetings prior to his going on long service leave in 2012. As a result, the Mayor commented to Colin on his return on the accuracy, thoroughness and timeliness of the documentation I provided.

- Responsible for drafting fortnightly reports on all engineering activities for approval by the Manager and submission to council meetings.

- Presented a paper on self-directed teams to the National Conference of Local Government Managers, Australia, Perth, 2010. This paper was very well received and it was subsequently published in the *LGMA Journal*.

- Announcer and press officer for last year's Bridlington Wheel Cycling Carnival. This carnival attracted some of the best riders in the State and several from interstate. Two of my press releases were published verbatim in *The Adelaide Advertiser*.

- Assistant coach for my elder daughter Emily's netball team at Bridlington High School 2007–2013. Organised a holiday netball clinic in April 2012 and persuaded Annie Turner, Captain of the State team, to coach the girls. The clinic was attended by 43 girls and was a great success.

Computer literacy

Have used computers on a regular basis both at work and at home for the past 30 years. Very competent on both IBM and Apple Mac systems. Accomplished at using:
  - MS Word
  - MS Excel
  - Lotus 123
  - MS Outlook
  - MS Project
  - TurboCAD

- Used MS Project to plan and manage the creation of the waste transfer and recycling program covering the whole shire, 2009.

- Used MS Project to organise the Bridlington Wheel Cycling Carnival last year and MS Excel to manage the budget.

- Draft press releases using MS Word and email to the *Wellington Times* and Radio 5WB using MS Outlook.

- Manage my work schedules using MS Outlook.

- Studied for Certificate IV in CAD at Bridlington College of TAFE, 2001.

Good knowledge of the role and responsibilities of local government and of acts and regulations affecting it

My ten years in supervisory and management positions in local government have given me a very good knowledge of its roles and responsibilities as well as the acts and regulations that affect it.

This knowledge has been reinforced through my studies at QUT for the Graduate Certificate in Engineering (Local Government), 1999, and the Park Management Program at Bond University, 2001, as well as the many short courses on changes to regulations such as building specifications, OH&S, town planning etc.

Narendra Chaudhry

B Eng (Electrical)
Grad Dip Management (IT)

143 Mackworth Street
Linwood, Christchurch 8062
0 3 381 0580 (h)
0270 734 567 (m)
n_chaudhry@xtra.co.nz
nz.linkedin/com/n_chaudhry

Friday, 12 November 2014

Mrs Johanna Barns
Administration and Finance Officer
Facilities Management
Aoraki Polytechnic
Private Bag 902
32 Arthur Street
Timaru 7940

Project Manager, Electrical Operations

Dear Mrs Barns,

I am very interested in this position where I could use the skills developed over 20 years' experience in electrical engineering to ensure safe, reliable electricity supply and infrastructure at all campuses of the Aoraki Polytechnic.

I would bring to the position:

- The experience of being responsible for all electrical engineering services, including high voltage electricity generation at a plant weaving 100,000 metres of cloth each day.

- The ability to think laterally, to solve problems creatively and the determination to achieve the best possible outcomes for the polytechnic.

- The ability to respect, relate to, and work with people of different backgrounds, different races and different religions.

- Integrity and high ethical standards.

I enclose a résumé and statement addressing the selection criteria which will provide a more detailed outline of my relevant skills and achievements and a glimpse of my determination to get the job done to exacting standards, as quickly as possible and in the most cost-effective way.

Yours sincerely,

Narendra Chaudhry

Narendra Chaudhry

B Eng (Electrical)
Grad Dip Management (IT)

143 Mackworth Street
Linwood, Christchurch 8062
0 3 381 0580 (h)
0270 734 567 (m)
n_chaudhry@xtra.co.nz
nz.linkedin/com/n_chaudhry

Career Objective

Project Manager, Electrical Operations where extensive graduate electrical engineering experience in an industrial environment (including design, energy management and project management), will help ensure well-designed and implemented electrical and communication systems across all campuses of the school.

I bring more than 20 years' graduate experience in electrical design, project management, electrical generation, installation, maintenance and fault-finding in electrical distribution systems in heavy industry.

Tertiary Electrical Engineering Qualifications

Bachelor of Engineering (Electrical)
Maharashtra Sayajirao University of Baroda, India, 1985

- 65% (Credit) average

- This degree is recognised by IPENZ

Member, Institution of Professional Engineers New Zealand (IPENZ)

Postgraduate Diploma in Management (Information Technology)
Nirma Institute of Management, India, 2001

PMI Certificate
PMINZ, Christchurch, 2013

Currently completing **Graduate Certificate in Business Administration** via Distance Learning through Massey University

Career History

Electrical Engineer (18-month contract position)
Ngatamariki Geothermal Power Station, 2012–2014

Senior Executive
Bharata Spinning & Weaving Mills, Pune, India, 2006–2011

Engineering Manager (and previously Executive Engineer and Engineering Officer)
Summit Textile Mill, Mumbai, India, 1995–2006 (the other positions going back to 1985)

Narendra Chaudhry

Personal Information

Born   Palanpur, India, 1964

Indian citizen in New Zealand on Skilled Migrant Visa

Health   Good, non-smoker, regular walking and yoga

Happily married 24 years, 1 married daughter

Referees

Roger Fitzgibbon	09 571 4500 (w)
Project Engineer	025 431 8742 (m)
Mighty River Power	fitzgibbon.r@mightyriverpower.co.nz
Kapil Dev Bhandari	+91 21 6423 5182 (w)
DGM Electrical & Electronics	kapildev.bhandari@bharata.com
Bharata Spinning & Weaving Mills	
Jagdeep Chandra	+91 22 2490 1000 (w)
Executive Engineer	j.chandra@summit.co.in
Summit Textile Mills	

Key Personal Qualities

- Very good analytical, fault-finding, problem-solving and design skills in HV electrical distribution system.

- Good communicator and supervisor: extensive project management experience.

- Great team member, committed to the team effort.

Narendra Chaudhry

B Eng (Electrical)
Grad Dip Management (IT)

143 Mackworth Street
Linwood, Christchurch 8062
0 3 381 0580 (h)
0270 734 567 (m)
n_chaudhry@xtra.co.nz
nz.linkedin/com/n_chaudhry

Statement addressing the selection criteria

Project Manager, Electrical Operations

Position number: SME1137

Extensive knowledge and experience in building-related electrical services including the provision of a quality service within this industry, and

Demonstrated extensive experience in the project management of a variety of complex electrical services projects from concept phase to conclusion.

Fourteen years' professional experience in utility management across all buildings at two large manufacturing complexes in India and 18 months supervising voltage control equipment at Ngatamariki Geothermal Power Station.

- With Bharata's Chief Engineer, prepared and worked to an annual budget worth NZ$250,000 for spares and materials to be ready for preventative maintenance and breakdowns. When modifying the secondary electrical distribution system at Summit, I decided to explore the possibility of incorporating a damaged and disused HT-HV or use an 11KV cable buried deep underground. Engaged a company with route tracing and fault-finding equipment to locate both the cable and the fault which was then repaired. Employed external contractor to complete this work and by so doing, saved lengthy downtime and about $25,000 in costs.

- In another project at Summit, we installed two new 800A 11KV breakers with isolators and three 11KV changeover switches and other accessories. Prior to making the order through our SAP system, I obtained several quotes and prepared a comparison report in terms of cost, technical aspects and compliance to the Indian Standards code. Having decided on a supplier, I followed up to ensure that we would get the materials on time and organised teams of contractors to be ready to install the equipment as soon as it arrived. I checked the equipment as it arrived, including documentation, and made regular inspections during the installation so as to be able to present reports to senior management throughout the project. As a result, the breakers were properly installed on time and within budget.

- At Summit, there were some breakers that were almost 50 years old and providing virtually no protection. It was obvious that they needed to be replaced but I needed to

Nahendra Chaudhry

convince suppliers that we required modern breakers that would, nevertheless, fit into our existing system with minimal modification. Because of my clear explanation of our requirements, I was able to obtain breakers that met our specifications. As a result, downtime was minimal and there was no production loss.

At the Ngatamariki Geothermal Power Station project, I was one of a team of four electrical engineers supervising the installation and testing of SVC reactive voltage control equipment.

Achieved PMI Certification through PMINZ, Christchurch, last year.

Strong work ethic, self-driven to meet/exceed objectives

My professional experience demonstrates my strong work ethic and my self-driven commitment to meeting and exceeding objectives. My success as an engineer has been largely the result of my determination to play my part in helping the organisation achieve its corporate goals.

- For example, at Bharata Spinning & Weaving Mills, I was responsible for the maintenance of all electrical plant and equipment at the spinning mill. I was overseeing the routine maintenance of the humidity control plant when we discovered that one bearing was badly worn and this had damaged the shaft sufficiently to call for its replacement.

  Humidity control is essential to maintaining the quality of the yarn being produced. Routine maintenance would normally take about four hours and humidity would be unlikely to vary sufficiently in that time to affect quality. However, to obtain a replacement shaft could take days and this would seriously impact on production.

  Thinking laterally, I considered the possibility of refurbishing the damaged shaft. I spoke first with the welders to determine the possibility of replacing the metal that had been worn away and second with the fitters to assess their ability to work the shaft on a lathe sufficiently to meet the specifications required. As both welders and fitters told me that this was possible, we repaired the shaft, replaced the bearings and had the humidity control plant running again within fourteen hours, thus reducing the impact on production to a minimum. I remained on site and supervised the whole process until it was completed and working properly. For this I received warm thanks from the President, Operations, who told me that if it hadn't been for my tenacity and commitment, the company could have suffered serious loss of production.

Demonstrated verbal and written communication skills

My communication skills, both written and spoken, have been highly developed through my work at both Bharata and Summit Textile mills. In both companies I wrote regular reports for management; I liaised continually with operations staff, with electrical engineers and trades

Nahendra Chaudhry

people and with management; and I negotiated with, and supervised the work of, outside contractors.

At both companies I wrote monthly reports for the President, Operations, and Managing Director concerning the state of electrical plant and equipment as well as the consumption of grid electricity, diesel fuel, gas and water required for our own electricity generation. These reports were always well received.

- As part of an in-house professional development program at Summit, I wrote the report for our company's participation in the Six Sigma project. I presented the report in front of senior representatives from Motorola and our own senior TQM team. For this, my leader received the Black Belt award and I was given the Green Belt.

Demonstrated ability to present complex ideas, concepts and points of view in a clear, concise and logical manner

My ability to present complex ideas, concepts and points of view in a clear, concise and logical manner has been highly developed during the eleven years I was Engineering Manager at Summit where I was responsible for electrical engineering services within the textile mills and within the office blocks both on site and in distant locations because it was my responsibility to engage the contractors required to carry out the work and to ensure that the work was carried out satisfactorily and to strict Indian standards.

Liaison was essential because all electrical engineering projects were undertaken in collaboration with the Chief Engineer and/or the General Manager. I also needed to work out the best dates for implementation with the President of Operations so as to minimise disruption to production.

All work had to be approved by various government authorities and this, too, required good liaison. I prepared contracts for both minor and major electrical engineering projects, ensuring that all instructions were clear and all materials and equipment ordered were properly defined so that contractors and suppliers knew exactly what was required.

- At Bharata, I coordinated the work of contracting companies and five suppliers when managing the project to install the two 800A 11KV breakers. And while production was stopped for this project, we took the opportunity to undertake routine maintenance on our manufacturing plant, compressors, submersible pumps, humidification plant, effluent treatment equipment and all the other equipment required for the textile mill. This meant that I also coordinated the work of three engineers, 16 electricians and 15 other tradespersons, all working in shifts around the clock.

Be reliable, responsible, dedicated, committed and fulfilling obligations

Being reliable, responsible, dedicated, committed and fulfilling obligations has been an essential part of my success. These qualities have been demonstrated in the ways I have worked to improve efficiency and cut costs.

Nahendra Chaudhry

As an Engineering Officer at the Summit Mill, I worked in shifts. It sometimes occurred that a machine would breakdown shortly before my shift ended. Machinery breakdown affected production badly, so I made it my business to never leave until the machine was repaired and working properly again.

- At one time, there was a problem in the centralised waste collection, the system that clears waste away from the production machines so that they can continue to work efficiently. It was 11.00 p.m., an hour before the end of my shift, when the problem showed itself. I identified the cause as the bearings of the drum of the waste separator. I realised that it was necessary to replace the bearings as quickly as possible but that the job would take several hours. I also realised that it was important that the engineer who came on shift after me was free to attend to all the other machinery. With these realisations, I started to do the job as quickly and efficiently as possible. I had the bearings changed and the machine operating again by 5.00 a.m. and, I left for home only after I had checked that everything was working properly.

Jenny Barnes
143 Melaleuca Street
East Calderwell, Vic, 3304
03 9764 1802

Thursday, 23 June 2015

William Shoalhaven
State Manager
Kidsafe Australia
PO Box 187
Castleton, Vic, 3300

Executive Officer (*Southern Chronicle* 18/06/15)

Dear Mr Shoalhaven,

Having devoted 30 years of my life to the safe and empowering upbringing of children, I would very much like the opportunity to be actively involved in the excellent work done by Kidsafe.

If successful, I will bring to the position:

- ❖ Fifteen years' experience in the management of a not-for-profit soccer club.
- ❖ The ability to initiate, plan and accomplish effective promotional and fundraising events.
- ❖ Highly developed organisational, interpersonal and communication skills.
- ❖ A passion for the safety and wellbeing of children.

I have enclosed both a résumé and a statement addressing the selection criteria to provide more details of my skills and achievements in this area.

I look forward to hearing from you.

Yours sincerely,

Jenny Barnes (Mrs)

Jenny Barnes

143 Melaleuca Street
East Calderwell, Vic, 3304
03 9764 1802

Summary

Thirty years' experience working with children as a teacher, parent and enthusiastic committee member and coach of a children's soccer club. Currently Secretary/Treasurer responsible for a turnover of $12,500. Involved in sponsorship and fundraising as well as organising rosters, venues, umpires, coaches etc.

Career History

Teacher
Calderwell East Primary School, 1983–1989

❖ Taught grades 3, 4 and 5.

❖ Planned and implemented the 'Adopt a Grandparent' program, 1986.

Committee member, currently Secretary/Treasurer (voluntary)
Waterloo Soccer Club, 1998–present

❖ Part of the sub-committee that planned the Girls' Soccer promotion, 2003. This resulted in the formation of the first two girls' soccer teams in the club.

❖ Lobbied Belltrees Council to change the layout of Waterloo Park to allow the creation of an extra soccer pitch for junior players.

❖ Organised the itinerary, travel arrangements, accommodation and matches for the Under-19 team's tour of southern NSW, September 2005.

312

Qualifications and Training

B Sc
Monash University, 1979–1981

Dip Ed
Melbourne University, 1982

Level 1 soccer coach
Soccer Victoria, 2001

QuickBooks course
Calderwell College of TAFE, 2000

Senior First Aid
St John Ambulance every three years since 1998; current certificate valid
until 2016

Personal Details

Born   Bermondsey, WA, 13 July 1960

Health   Very good, regular fitness program

Happily married 14 years; five wonderful children (mine, his and ours) 23,
20, 16, 13 and 11

Referees

Ms Suzen Philips   03 9774 1154 (h)
President, Waterloo Soccer Club

Mr Tony Palmer   03 9760 5412 (w)
Physical Education Teacher
Calderwell High School

Key Personal Attributes

❖ Passionate about promoting the safety and development of children.

❖ Excellent organisational skills.

❖ Good people skills, hard-working and efficient.

Jenny Barnes

143 Melaleuca Street
East Calderwell, Vic, 3304
03 9764 1802

Statement addressing the selection criteria

Executive Officer

Promotion

❖ With other members of a small sub-committee planned and implemented a highly successful Girls' Soccer promotion, 2003. Spoke to sports and other interested teachers at both primary and secondary schools, addressed P&F meetings and prepared a leaflet for students and parents.

The result of this promotion was the formation of the first two girls' soccer teams in the Waterloo Club and one at the Kookaburras Club.

❖ With the President, composed a letter to the editor in response to a letter from a mother complaining that her son should not have to play against girls. This letter generated a lot of support for girls' soccer.

❖ Lobbied the Belltrees Council to repair the playing surface at Waterloo Park after subsidence caused safety concerns, 2005.

❖ Was the teacher responsible for planning and implementing the 'Adopt a Grandparent' program at East Calderwell Primary School, 1986. This resulted in markedly increasing the school's sense of integration with the community and generated some very favourable publicity.

Management

❖ Fifteen years' experience as a member of the committee of management of the Waterloo Soccer Club. Currently Secretary/Treasurer responsible for an annual turnover of approximately $12,500, for preparing all accounts for the auditor and for complying with the rules and regulations set down by the State Soccer Association.

❖ Organised the club's FA Cup barbecue dinner, hiring a room at the bowling club, a large-screen TV and organising a monster raffle, including seeking donations from local businesses to use as prizes. The night raised $3200 to help send two players to a coaching camp in Melbourne.

❖ As a primary school teacher, prioritised the learning program to maintain the interest of all students and to maximise their achievement toward the objectives set out in the curriculum. Had to continually re-prioritise to suit changing situations.

Jenny Barnes

Interpersonal and Communication Skills

❖ Was chosen to represent the club at the State Soccer Association conference in Bairnsdale last October. Gave a full report of junior soccer in the southern region and explained the strategies we are using to promote the sport to young people.

❖ Liaise regularly with Sport and Recreation on such topics as changes to the minimum playing age for competitive sport, the safety code for Hepatitis B etc.

Sponsorship

❖ Have written many letters to local businesses seeking sponsorship for the club. These letters have resulted in free trophies and greatly reduced prices on strip and coaching aids. Keep local business sponsors regularly informed about the club and place their ads in our newsletter.

❖ Prepared a submission to Belltrees Council to seek rearrangement of the layout of Waterloo Park to allow an additional soccer pitch for junior players, 2003. Spoke at length to a meeting of the council and answered several questions. Council agreed to our request and the extra pitch was created in time for the following season.

Child Safety Issues

❖ Quickly acquired knowledge of the registration rules and requirements of soccer when I took over the position of Secretary/Treasurer. Was able to answer parents' questions on registration issues and other matters, mostly over the telephone but also in writing.

❖ Was one of the instigators of lobbying the Belltrees Council to rectify subsidence at Waterloo Park because of concern for the safety of players and spectators.

❖ As one of the club's coaches, am continuously aware of the potential for injury faced by players. Insist on proper warm-up before training or playing. Qualified in first aid so as to be able to provide immediate assistance should any injury occur.

❖ Always on the look-out for unknown adults watching matches or training and especially unusual or suspicious behaviour. Also for children leaving the grounds without permission. Ensure all children are properly collected by parents or other responsible adults after matches and training. Personally deliver to their homes any who are not picked up.

Katharina Hochstein

17 Waitchie Street, Wedderburn, Vic, 3518
03 5494 7316 (h)   0449 387 946 (m)
katharinahochstein@gmail.com

Thursday, 14 July 2015

Dean Williams
Human Resources Department
Museum Victoria
PO Box 666
Melbourne VIC 3001

Administrative Officer

Dear Mr Williams,

I would love this position where I could make full use of my administrative and organisational skills to support one of my favourite organisations.

I will bring to the position:

- Excellent administrative and organisational skills.
- The communication and interpersonal skills developed over 35 years of teaching.
- A passion for helping others gain a better understanding of our world.
- Reliability, responsibility and dependability.

I have enclosed my résumé and statement addressing the selection criteria. These will provide a more detailed outline of the knowledge, skills and personal attributes that I will bring to the position and an insight into my motivation for encouraging lifelong learning.

The only reason that I am leaving teaching, a profession which I have loved, is that a recent injury to my ankle now prohibits the significant walking and standing required.

Yours sincerely,

Katharina Hochstein

Katharina Hochstein

17 Waitchie Street, Wedderburn, Vic, 3518
03 5494 7316 (h)   0449 387 946 (m)
katharinahochstein@gmail.com

Goal

Administrative Officer, Museum Victoria, where efficiency, organisation and determination together with excellent interpersonal and communication skills will help ensure high quality and timely administration support to the Manager and staff of the Facility Management group.

Career Record

Teacher, science and maths, and Head of Science Department
Wedderburn College since 1981
- Promoted Head of Department, 2003

Secretary (honorary)
Korong Historical Society since 2008
- Member since 1988

Qualifications

B Sc
University of Melbourne, 1976
- Majored in plant science and zoology

Advanced Diploma of Teaching
Monash University, 1977

Registered as a teacher with the Victorian Teacher Registration Board

Katharina Hochstein

Personal Information

Born   Bremerhaven, Germany, 17 September 1955

Nationality   Australian citizen since 1976

Health   Excellent except for an ankle injury that restricts the amount of walking or standing that I can do

Referees

John Flemington   5494 9400 (w)
Principal   john.flemington2@vic.edu.au
Wedderburn College

Felicity Ballerton   5494 2753 (h)
Chairperson   0449 234 987 (m)
Korong Historical Society   ballerton.f@yahoo7.com

Key Personal Qualities

o   Highly organised and efficient

o   Reliable, responsible and dependable

o   Open and friendly, a good team member and enjoy helping others

Katharina Hochstein

17 Waitchie Street, Wedderburn, Vic, 3518
03 5494 7316 (h)   0449 387 946 (m)
katharinahochstein@gmail.com

Statement addressing the selection criteria

Administrative Officer

Position number MV/9065

1. **Demonstrated administrative experience, including taking minutes and the ability to understand and apply established office systems and basic finance procedures.**

   My skills in this area have been highly developed through more than 10 years as Head of the Science Department at Wedderburn College.

   - Kept detailed records of student progress against individual learning plans, developed course outlines, wrote student reports and managed the Department's budget.

   - With a colleague, developed a spreadsheet and database system for recording all the Department's records.

   - Have taken the minutes for the monthly meetings of the Korong Historical Society since being elected Secretary in 1998.

2. **Good communication and interpersonal skills with the ability to relate well with all staff, as well as government and industry figures.**

   As a teacher, I am communicating all the time with students, colleagues, parents and Department of Education officials.

   - Prepared and presented a paper on the geology of the goldfields to the Korong Historical Society, 2011.

   - Earlier this year, a parent complimented me on the way that I had explained how osmosis worked to her son in my grade 8 science class.

   - Read, write and speak German fluently.

Katharina Hochstein

3. **Competent keyboard skills and proven experience in the use of Microsoft Word, Outlook, Excel and PowerPoint.**

Through my work as a teacher, I am using computers all the time. I use MS Word to write reports and to prepare teaching resources; Excel to produce graphs and to keep records including stock control and budgeting; Outlook for emails, task list and managing my schedule; and PowerPoint for presentations.

4. **Ability to undertake basic research and prepare reports and presentations.**

I am continually researching by physical experiment or by using the internet, journal articles and reference books and, for the Historical Society, through interviewing people.

- Interviewed 34 people who had migrated from Europe after WWII or who were the children of those who had done so and who had settled in the Wedderburn district. Wrote up the stories of several of these migrants for the *Bendigo Weekly* newspaper, which published them between March and May last year.

- Prepare presentations for classes all the time and regularly for meetings of the Parents and Friends Association.

5. **High level of initiative, attention to detail and accuracy, as well as the ability to work independently and to effectively prioritise tasks in an environment of tight deadlines and rapid change.**

Running the Science Department in the college where rapid change, resulting from student behaviour or teacher absence, requires me to be able to think quickly, use my initiative and take affirmative action on an almost daily basis.

- Earlier this term, when two of my team of five reported sick, I had less than 30 minutes to prepare lesson plans and teaching resources for eight classes across three year groups. At the end of the day, the teachers who had taken those classes complimented me on the quality of preparation and the resources that I had provided.

6. **Demonstrated knowledge, or an understanding, of records management systems which may include TRIM.**

With a colleague whose computer skills are better than mine, I designed a system for managing student records, teaching resources, stock control and budgeting information that we need to run the Department properly.

Katharina Hochstein

This has given me a good understanding of computerised records management if not of any specific records management programs.

7. **The successful applicant is required to undergo a National Police Records Check and be assessed as suitable (new employees are required to meet this cost).**

   Am currently registered as a teacher with the Victorian Teacher Registration Board and willing to seek a National Police Records Check.

Sarah Vaughan

132 McIntosh Street
Queanbeyan NSW 2620
02 6291 4357 (h)
0428 135 246 (m)
sarah.vaughan7@yahoo.com.au

Wednesday, 15 April 2015

Heather Turnbull
CEO
Arthritis ACT Inc
PO Box 4017
Western Creek ACT 2611

Health Promotion Coordinator (*Canberra Times*, 10/04/15)

Dear Ms Turnbull,

It is with great pleasure that I apply for this position. I would gain immense satisfaction from being able to use my teaching and presentation skills to improve the quality of life for a lot of people like my father.

I will bring to the position:
- The skills gained over 20 years of successful science teaching.
- Knowledge of the health/medical industry gained over three years as a pharmaceutical sales representative.
- Excellent communication and interpersonal skills.
- Energy and determination to make a difference.

I have addressed the selection criteria in a separate document. This and the résumé will give you a more detailed outline of the knowledge and skills I will bring to the job and an idea of my motivation and drive.

Yours sincerely,

Sarah Vaughan

Sarah Vaughan

132 McIntosh Street
Queanbeyan NSW 2620
02 6291 4357 (h)
0428 135 246 (m)
sarah.vaughan7@yahoo.com.au

Objective

Health Promotion Coordinator where 15 years of teaching secondary science and three years as a pharmaceutical sales rep will help me fulfil a strong desire to be active and effective in improving the quality of life of people suffering from arthritis, osteoporosis and other musculoskeletal diseases.

Career record

Teacher, science and maths
Seymour College, Seymour, Vic, 2005–2014

- Taught human biology to senior classes, 2010–2014.
- Got students engaged and motivated resulting in high end-of-year marks.

Pharmaceutical sales representative
Omicron Pharmaceuticals (Aust) Pty Ltd, Townsville, 2002–2005

- My territory included Ingham, Charters Towers and Mackay. Established a strong working rapport with pharmacies throughout the territory and was meeting sales targets within three months. In my final year, I exceeded my original sales target by 85%, almost doubling total sales.
- Quickly learnt the benefits/characteristics of the pharmaceuticals that I was marketing and was able to be an effective sales rep within two weeks.

Teacher, science, maths and computer studies
Nightcliff High School, Darwin, 1996–2002

Family responsibilities
1986–1995

Teacher, science and maths
Singleton High School, 1982–1985

Tertiary qualifications

Bachelor of Science
University of New England, 1980

Diploma of Education
Armidale College of Advanced Education, 1981

Sarah Vaughan

Personal information

Born   Muswellbrook, 14 January 1960

Health   Excellent, non-smoker; social sports, netball and tennis, and regular jogging

Own reliable transport

Referees

Barbara Marekanos   03 5771 1300 (w)
Principal, Seymour College   barbara.marekanos@edumail.vic.gov.au

Alan Barton   03 5771 1300 (w)
Head of Science, Seymour College   alan.barton@edumail.vic.gov.au

Personal strengths

- Quick and efficient; like to get stuck in and achieve results.
- A good teacher and trainer.
- Very good interpersonal and communication skills.

Sarah Vaughan

132 McIntosh Street
Queanbeyan NSW 2620
02 6291 4357 (h)
0428 135 246 (m)
sarah.vaughan7@yahoo.com.au

Statement addressing the selection critieria

Health Promotion Coordinator

Experience in the community sector, education, training and/or health-related area

My teaching and training skills have been developed over 15 years of secondary science teaching and my persuasive skills were further developed over three years as a pharmaceutical sales representative. I have been able to get my students engaged in the subject and wanting to learn. As a result, my classes achieved very good results.

- Taught human biology at pre-tertiary level to Year 11 and Year 12 students at Seymour College for the past three years. Last year 17 of the 25 students in my class achieved greater than 67% in their end-of-year results.

Ability to develop training materials, surveys and evaluations

For all courses and for all classes, I had to produce training materials that were attractive, clear and easy to understand. These were sometimes slide presentations, sometimes edited compilations of podcasts, sometimes large visual representations and sometimes tactile, working models. The attractiveness of training resources is important to keeping students engaged.

Evaluations are an essential part of the education system. They covered not only the progress made by individual students but also the effectiveness of my teaching. I did not carry out formal surveys but I did ask students from time to time how they found a particular lesson or series of lessons.

Helped students design surveys for Year 11 Psychology in 2010.

Ability to write and present reports

Writing and presenting reports and other information sessions has been very much an essential part of my professional career. I wrote and presented sales reports to manangement when working as a pharmaceutical sales rep in north Queensland and I am confident that I will be able to write and present reports on the effectiveness of my performance in the role of Health Promotion Coordinator to the Board and management of Arthritis ACT.

Experience in giving presentations to members of the community and health professionals

Gave presentations to general practitioners, pharmacists and other health professionals as a pharmaceutical sales rep. The effectiveness of these presentations can be assessed by the fact that I almost doubled sales over the three years I was in that position.

Made presentations to parents, the Parents and Friends Association and colleagues on aspects of the science curriculum at Seymour College. These presentations were well received.

Ability to build relationships with health professionals and government and non-government organisations

My ability to build and maintain good professional relationships with health professionals has been demonstrated by my success as a pharmaceutical sales rep in Queensland. I have the ability to build and maintain similar professional relationships with government and non-government organisations.

Capacity to work with and train volunteers to deliver health promotion programs

My ability to train and work with volunteers has been developed through my taking part in and leading adventure education programs at Nightcliff High School. I instruct the volunteer parents in program procedures and the accident response plan.

Over the seven years I was at the school, I went on five three-day adventure education programs, two of them as leader. These programs involved rock climbing, abseiling and canoeing.

On one program, a student was slightly injured, suffering a sprained ankle. With a parent helper, I implemented the accident response plan; the student was given first aid and evacuated safely. The plan worked smoothly and the parent helper felt confident throughout the action because of the prior training that I had given him.

Ability to manage multiple tasks and competing priorities

With a husband in the Army who is often required to travel, I have raised three children and handled a full teaching load. As a result, I have developed the skills to manage multiple tasks and competing priorities.

Desirable

Tertiary qualification in either education or a health-related area

Bachelor of Science, University of New England, 1980

Diploma in Education, Armidale College of Advanced Education, 1981

First aid qualification or willing to obtain

I obtained a first aid qualification when teaching in Darwin but allowed it to lapse when I was working in Queensland. I am very willing to redo the training and regain those skills.

Own transport required to attend various locations

Own and drive a Toyota Prius. Clean driving record.

Knowledge of the health/medical industry

My knowledge of the health/medical industry is more or less restricted to what I learnt as a pharmaceutical sales rep. However, I have taught human biology at senior level and I am a quick learner. With these skills and experience, I am confident that I will gain sufficient working knowledge to quickly become effective in the role.

Useful resources

Careers websites

Here are some of the more popular online job boards and careers websites. There are hundreds of them, many more than those listed here. The jobs you are looking for could be on any but certainly not all of them. So, look at several and find the ones that seem to carry advertisements for the sort of positions that you are seeking. But don't restrict yourself to just one site or you may be missing opportunities that would suit you. And be aware that some jobs may be listed solely on the employer organisation's own website.

Australia

Seek: www.seek.com.au
CareerOne: www.careerone.com.au
MyCareer: www.mycareer.com.au
JobSearch.gov.au: www.jobsearch.gov.au
Jobserve: www.jobserve.com/au
Bluecollar: www.bluecollar.com.au
Gumtree: www.gumtree.com.au/s-jobs
Applydirect: www.applydirect.com.au
Jobseeker: www.jobseeker.com.au

New Zealand

MyJobSpace: www.myjobspace.co.nz
Seek: www.seek.co.nz
Trade Me Jobs: www.trademe.co.nz/jobs
Work and Income job search database: http://job-bank.workandincome.govt.nz/find-a-job/search.aspx
Workpool: www.workpool.co.nz/

United Kingdom

Monster: www.monster.co.uk

Executives on the Web: www.executivesontheweb.com

Jobserve: www.jobserve.com/gb/en/job-search

eFinancialCareers: www.efinancialcareers.co.uk

fish4jobs: www.fish4jobs.co.uk

GAAPweb: www.gaapweb.com

CityJobs: www.cityjobs.com

USA

CareerBuilder: www.careerbuilder.com

Indeed: www.indeed.com/l-united-states-jobs.html

Monster: www.monster.com

Simply Hired: www.simplyhired.com/k-united-states-jobs.html

US Jobs: www.us.jobs

Canada

Kijiji: www.kijiji.ca

Job Bank: www.jobbank.gc.ca

Headhunters Directory: www.headhuntersdirectory.com/canada.htm

Craigs List: http://geo.craigslist.org/iso/ca

Monster: www.monster.ca

Total Jobs Canada: www.totaljobs.com/JobSeeking/Canada

Workopolis: www.workopolis.com/EN/Common/HomePage.aspx

Careers advisers

The following websites are those of professional associations of careers advisers and government careers services. Advisers belonging to these associations have professionally accepted qualifications and follow a strict code of ethics.

Career Development Association of Australia (CDAA): www.cdaa.org.au. To find a careers adviser, click on the 'Need career services?' tab and follow the prompts.

Career Development Association of New Zealand (CDANZ): www.cdanz. org.nz. To find a careers adviser, enter your nearest centre in the search button.

Careers New Zealand is a free government service providing careers advice and information: www.careers.govt.nz.

National Careers Service, UK: https://nationalcareersservice.direct.gov.uk. To contact a careers adviser for email or telephone assistance, or to arrange a face-to-face meeting, on the 'Contact an Adviser' page, select 'Aged 19 years old or over'.

Careers England: www.careersengland.org.uk. Select the 'About Careers England' tab and on the pull-down menu that appears, click on 'Our Members'. Email addresses for members are given, however you need to click on the 'Yes' referring to their profiles to find their location.

Association of Career Professionals International: www.acpinternational. org. Select the 'Career Help' tag and complete the online questionnaire and you will receive an email response.

National Career Development Association (NCDA) (USA): www.ncda.org. The 'Find a Counselor' tab lets you search for counsellors by state.

Books

Angel, Debra, and Harney, Elisabeth, *No One is Unemployable: Creative solutions for overcoming barriers to employment*, WorkNet Publications, Hacienda Heights, CA, 1997.

Bolles, Richard N, *What Color is Your Parachute? A practical manual for job-hunters and career-changers*, Ten Speed Press, Berkeley, CA, 2014.

Bridges, William, *Creating You and Co: Be the boss of your own career*, Nicholas Brealey, London, 1997.

Bridges, William, *JobShift: How to prosper in a workplace without jobs*, Nicholas Brealey, London, 1995.

Bright, Jim, and Earl, Joanne, *Résumés that Get Shortlisted: Proven strategies to get the job you want*, Business Publishing, Warriewood, NSW, 2000.

Covey, Stephen, *The 7 Habits of Highly Effective People: Restoring the character ethic*, Free Press, New York, 2004.

Eggert, Max, *The Perfect Interview: All you need to get it right first time*, Arrow Business Books, London, 1992.

Farr, J. Michael, *The Very Quick Job Search: Get a good job in less time*, JIST Works, Indianapolis, IN, 1991.

Figler, Howard, *The Complete Job-Search Handbook: All the skills you need to get any job and have a good time doing it*, Henry Holt, New York, 1988.

Fraser, Rebecca, *How to Write a Winning Résumé: A proven method*, Vivid Publishing, Freemantle, 2012.

French, Rupert, *The Job Winners Guide to Résumés*, Maygog, Hobart, 2007.

Innes, James, *The CV Book: Your definitive guide to writing the perfect CV*, Prentice Hall, London, 2009.

Lathrop, Richard, *Who's Hiring Who? How to find that job fast!*, Ten Speed Press, Berkeley, CA, 1989.

McLaughlin, Peter, Loehr, James, and Simons, Robin, *Mentally Tough: The power to do your best*, Pacific Mountain Private Industry Council, Olympia, WA, 1990.

Medley, H. Anthony, *Sweaty Palms: The neglected art of being interviewed*, Ten Speed Press, Berkeley, CA, 1992.

Mills, Corinne, *You're Hired! CV: How to write a brilliant CV*, Trotman Publishing, Richmond, UK, 2009.

Porot, Daniel, *The PIE Method for Career Success*, JIST Works, Indianapolis, IN, 1996.

Stengel, Richard, *Mandela's Way: Lessons on life, love and courage*, Crown Publishing, New York, 2010.

Stevens, Paul, *Win That Job!* The Centre for Worklife Counselling, Sydney, 1991.

Tieger, Paul, and Barron-Tieger, Barbara, *Do What You Are: Discover the perfect career for you through the secrets of personality type*, Scribe Publications, Melbourne, 2001.

Endnotes

Chapter 1: The Right Approach

1. www.forbes.com/sites/susanadams/2012/09/24/older-workers-theres-hope-study-finds-employers-like-you-better-than-millennials, accessed 20/12/2013.

2. www.dailymail.co.uk/news/article-2548458/How-older-staff-boost-office-Employees-feel-colleagues-aged-55-act-good-role-models.html#ixzz2sNq71PiQ, accessed 05/02/2014.

3. www.bls.gov/news.release/tenure.nr0.htm, accessed 22/08/2013.

4. www.justice.qld.gov.au/__data/assets/pdf_file/0003/12279/ir-olderworkers-booklet.pdf, page 9, accessed 25/7/2014.

5. www.linkedin.com/today/post/article/20130422020049-8451-the-tech-industry-s-darkest-secret-it-s-all-about-age, accessed 20/12/2013.

6. Ng, TWH & Feldman, DC (2013). 'Age and innovation-related behavior: The joint moderating effects of supervisor undermining and proactive personality', *Journal of Organizational Behavior*, 34, 583–606. PDF of full article available at http://onlinelibrary.wiley.com/doi/10.1348/096317910X494197/abstract.

7. www.linkedin.com/today/post/article/20130923230007-204068115-how-i-hire-focus-on-personality, accessed 01/02/14.

8. http://sydney.edu.au/careers/finding_jobs/job_search_strategies/index.shtml, accessed 20/12/2013.

Chapter 2: Choosing the right career path

1. I came across the concept of job satisfiers in Paul Tiegers' excellent book, *Do What You Are: Discover the perfect career for you through the secrets of personality type*, Scribe Publications, Melbourne, 2001. In this book, the authors list the ten most important satisfiers for each of the sixteen Jungian personality types. If you have taken the Myers Briggs or MBTI, or any other Jungian personality type questionnaire, I would encourage you to read the satisfiers for your type in this book.

Chapter 3: Your résumé

1. Lathrop, Richard, *Who's Hiring Who? How to find that job fast!*, Ten Speed Press, Berkeley, CA, 1989, p 93.

Chapter 4: Writing the challenging bits in your résumé

1. Lathrop, Richard, *Who's Hiring Who? How to find that job fast!*, Ten Speed Press, Berkeley, CA, 1989, pp 93–94.

Chapter 7: Documents to support your application

1. Career Masters eNewsletter, 29 June 2006.

Chapter 8: Using social media

1. www.katieroberts.com.au/career-advice-blog/how-to-find-a-job-on-linkedin, accessed 24/7/14.

Chapter 9: Networking and research

1. www.cfel.jbs.cam.ac.uk/blog/?p=749, accessed 24/7/14.
2. Quoted in Petrilli, Lisa, 'The Introvert's Guide to Leadership'/ at www.lisapetrilli.com/2011/03/17/introverts-guide-leadership, accessed 24/7/14.
3. Silverman, Linda, PhD, 'A developmental model for counseling the gifted' in Silverman, L (Ed), *Counseling the gifted and talented*, 1993, The Institute for the Study of Advanced Development, Denver, CO.

Chapter 10: Building and maintaining a positive self-image

1. www.betterhealth.vic.gov.au/bhcv2/bhcarticles.nsf/pages/Sporting_performance_and_food?open, 24/7/14.
2. Brinol, P, Petty, RE and Wagner, B, 'Body posture effects on self-evaluation: A self-validation approach', *European Journal of Social Psychology*, first published online Feb 2009.
3. Riskind, J, and Gotay, C, 'Physical posture: Could it have regulatory or feedback effects on motivation and emotion?', *Motivation and Emotion*, 6(3), Sep 1982.

4. Lyubomirsky, S, King, L, Diener, E, 'The benefits of frequent positive affect: does happiness lead to success?', *Psychological Bulletin*, 131, 2005.

5. Delamothe, T, 'Happiness', *British Medical Journal*, 2005, 331.

6. Young, S, 'How to increase serotonin in the human brain without drugs', *Review of Psychiatry and Neuroscience*, 2007, 32(6).

7. www.sunwarrior.com/news/15-health-benefits-of-smiling, accessed 01/05/2014.

8. www.letslaugh.com.au/the-benefits-laughter-0, accessed 30/04/2014.

Chapter 11: Performing well in information and job interviews

1. McLaughlin, P, Loehr, J, and Simons, R, *Mentally Tough: The power to do your best*, Pacific Mountain Private Industry Council, Olympia, USA, 1990, p 97.

Chapter 12: Questions and answers for the job interview

1. www.quintcareers.com/behavioral_interviewing.html, accessed 24/7/14.

Chapter 14: Succeeding in the new job

1. www.forbes.com/sites/danschawbel/2012/01/23/89-of-new-hires-fail-because-of-their-attitude/, accessed 01/01/2014.

2. Covey, Stephen, *The 7 Habits of Highly Effective People: Restoring the character ethic*, Free Press, New York, 2004, p 207.

3. Stengel, Richard, *Mandela's Way: Lessons on life, love and courage*, Crown Publishing, New York, 2010, pp 117–129.

4. Covey, Stephen, *The 7 Habits of Highly Effective People: Restoring the character ethic*, Free Press, New York, 2004, p 236.

5. Stengel, Richard, *Mandela's Way: Lessons on life, love and courage*, Crown Publishing, New York, 2010, pp 80–81.

6. Covey, Stephen, *The 7 Habits of Highly Effective People: Restoring the character ethic*, Free Press, New York, 2004, p 264.

Acknowledgments

It's not possible to write a book like this and to make it as useful as possible without help and advice. By directly discussing issues with my job seeker clients, who put my ideas into practice, I was able to develop this book. And I have learnt so much about how best to overcome the hurdles faced by older job seekers from talking with other career development professionals around the world through professional associations and LinkedIn discussion groups. I particularly would like to acknowledge Rebecca Fraser's help with the chapter on the use of social media in the job search.

Developing the specimen résumés and applications for this book was the first major task. Most of the résumés and other application documents are fictitious. In order to ensure that they were realistic, I created applications for real positions and I would like to thank the employers who so willingly sent me the position descriptions and who then commented on the applications. I would also like to thank the clients who so willingly gave their approval to my 'fictionalising', allowing me to alter the real applications that I had prepared on their behalf.

Turning my ideas into a book has also been a team effort. I need to thank Monica Berton who has so carefully smoothed out the 'bumps' in my text, Anouska Jones and the team at Exisle who have so efficiently managed the production, and Gareth St John Thomas who asked me to write the book in the first place.

Finally, I would like to acknowledge my wife, Anne, who not only supported and encouraged me through the process but also carefully read through and edited the first four drafts so that the final typescript did say what I wanted it to say.

Index